FROM THE DUGOUTS TO THE TRENCHES

From the Dugouts to the Trenches

Baseball during the Great War

JIM LEEKE

University of Nebraska Press

LINCOLN & LONDON

Library of Congress Cataloging-in-Publication Data
Names: Leeke, Jim, 1949– author.
Title: From the dugouts to the trenches: baseball during
the great war / Jim Leeke.
Description: Lincoln: University of Nebraska Press,
2017. | Includes bibliographical references and index.
Identifiers: LCCN 2016053349 (print)
LCCN 2017005366 (ebook)
ISBN 9780803290723 (hardback: alk. paper)
ISBN 9781496201614 (epub)
ISBN 9781496201621 (mobi)
ISBN 9781496201638 (pdf)
Subjects: LCSH: Baseball—United States—Histo-
ry—20th century. | Baseball players as soldiers—
United States. | World War, 1914–1918—Influence. |
BISAC: SPORTS & RECREATION / Baseball / History. |
HISTORY / Military / World War I.
Classification: LCC GV863.A1 L35 2017 (print) | LCC
GV863.A1 (ebook) | DDC 796.357097309041—dc23
LC record available at https://lccn.loc.gov/2016053349

Set in Janson Text LT Pro by Rachel Gould.

In memory of
Harry and Vada Beebe
and Leonard Koppett

dug´out´: A shelter dug out of a hillside; specif., a cave, the side of a trench, etc., often roofed with logs and sod, for storage, protection, etc. Baseball. A low shelter containing a players' bench and facing upon the diamond.

—*Webster's Collegiate Dictionary*, 1942

CONTENTS

ILLUSTRATIONS

INTRODUCTION

America wasn't prepared for war in the late winter and early spring of 1917, but it certainly was ready for baseball. The Boston Red Sox were the reigning world champions, the best of sixteen Major League clubs scattered through the Northeast and out to the Midwest as far as the left bank of the Mississippi River. Below the big leagues, twenty-two Minor League clubs were set to play ball in parks across the country, from the biggest in Class AA to the smallest in Class D. Together, these many leagues comprised Organized Baseball—the national pastime, the summer game, employment for thousands, entertainment for millions, a hardscrabble business of sharp elbows, big egos, promise, failure, and reward. What would happen if war came?

Capt. T. L. Huston, co-owner of the New York Yankees, thought he knew. "Perhaps before any teams go to their training camps we will have a chance to see whether the players are as loyal to their country as to their [players] fraternity," Huston said.[1]

Harry Frazee, who owned the Boston Red Sox, thought he knew, too. "People want to get away from the war topics, and almost any kind of diversion to take their minds from the situation is welcome," Frazee said. "What can fit this need better than baseball?"[2]

Both men were right, if not at the same time. America entered the war that April and nothing much changed right away, as Frazee expected. Flags flew, rhetoric soared, and the baseball season began as usual in the Major and Minor Leagues. Then as America armed and readied for battle, Organized Baseball increasingly felt the strain of the vast European war, as Huston expected. So much changed that within eighteen months the Major Leagues were scarcely recognizable. Every Minor League but one had shut down, and the World Series was a shambles. How and why did this occur? What happened to the ballplayers? Does it all still matter, a hundred years on?

In quieter times, the first two questions might have been answered a quarter century or so after the events, when ballplayers and historians naturally looked back on their lives and times. But by then, America was fighting the Second World War, and no definitive history of baseball during the previous war was written. Any history produced today has a different, less personal perspective. Details come not from participants' living memory but largely from newspaper microfilm and digital archives, from old front pages and sports sections, and from many hundreds of columns and game stories and dispatches from France. The endeavor to find these pieces is itself entertaining and enlightening. Along the way, answers to the third question begin to emerge. Let's begin with spring training.

FROM THE DUGOUTS TO THE TRENCHES

1

Sergeants

In March 1917, with his country on the verge of entering the war in Europe, Sgt. Smith Gibson unexpectedly became one of the most famous soldiers in the U.S. Army. Gibson ran the recruiting office in Macon, Georgia, the spring-training home of the American League New York Yankees. Macon was only about 125 miles from Gibson's hometown of Opelika, to the west across the muddy Chattahoochee River in Alabama. During seventeen years in uniform, the sergeant had never received orders quite like those that had just arrived. He was to become the Yankees' new military drill instructor—among the first, so far as anyone knew, ever in the history of Organized Baseball. Soon all eight teams in the American League, plus two in the National, would have drillmasters, too.

A country boy who knew little about big cities, Sergeant Gibson could thank a prominent New Yorker for his new job in baseball. Capt. T. L. "Til" Huston, the Yankees' co-owner, was energetically pushing what newspapers up north called his pet scheme for military preparedness in baseball. In late February Huston and the sergeant had sat down for a chat in Macon. Gibson had said he was willing to drill the Yankees, if and when Huston could get him permission from the War Department. The magnate had promptly fired off a telegram to Maj. Halstead Dorey, a baseball fan serving on the staff of Maj. Gen. Leonard Wood at Governors Island in New York. Dorey had been the guest of honor at a dinner Huston had given for baseball writers and officials at the Hotel Belmont in New York City on Washington's Birthday. The major had then traveled down to Washington, DC, and "unraveled between seventeen to one hundred miles of government red tape" to support Huston's plan.[1]

Although lengthy, the red tape was only a minor hindrance. Regulations prohibited the army from assigning drill sergeants to outside organizations, but nothing prevented a commanding officer from granting furloughs of six weeks to three months to any sergeants whom the league needed. Likewise, the War Department couldn't issue arms to civilian groups, but clubs could buy condemned rifles for drilling. Major Dorey also puckishly warned the Yankees' co-owner about an ailment he called "rifle arm," which a few sportswriters apparently took seriously. This post-drill stiffness, Dorey said, was likely to appeal to tired pitchers looking for an alibi to avoid work. "I would rather have them suffering from rifle arm than from slacker's knee," Huston retorted.[2] On February 27 Huston wired Dorey from Macon:

> Sergeant Gibson on recruiting duty here says he has an efficient force which will readily permit him to give two hours or so each day to drilling our baseball club, and he is anxious to do the work for us. If you can have him made available to drill us it will quickly start the movement here and will make it easier for other clubs to get started. Your prompt action will be appreciated. Kindly answer [at] my expense.[3]

Wires flew for several days between Macon, Governors Island, and American League headquarters in Chicago. "How about Nationals?" Dorey wired to Georgia, meaning the National League under former Pennsylvania governor John Tener. "The National League has not taken up military training," Huston replied. "Gov. Tener, its president, is a high class patriotic gentleman and is very strongly in favor of the movement. Am wiring him on the subject."[4]

Huston kept up his campaign, and the army soon realized the tremendous recruiting benefits of cooperating with Major League Baseball. Dorey wired him March 4 that recruiting sergeants in Macon, Augusta, and Jacksonville had been assigned to the Yankees,

Senators, and Athletics, training in those respective cities. Every American League club soon had its own drill sergeant, although it took a couple of days for the army's Department of the South, headquartered at San Antonio, to assign men from Dallas to the St. Louis Browns at Palestine, Texas, and the Detroit Tigers at Waxahachie. The army declined American League president Ban Johnson's offer to have the league pay the sergeants' traveling expenses. Instead, the league would reimburse them for their services.

As opening day of training camp neared, Huston wondered how his Yankees would react:

> Captain Huston has been somewhat apprehensive as to the ball players' view of the military plan, and he was greatly gratified to find that every one of the 18 men in camp are enthusiastically in favor of it. He was still more gratified by the news that Macon will add 50 sons of Georgia in addition to the company. In addition to that the City Council of Macon has agreed to provide suitable drill grounds.[5]

The Yankees held their first drill on March 6. "Despite numerous disappointments . . . Huston persisted in his efforts to obtain a regular army officer to drill his ball team, and now his work is crowned with success," *New York Sun* sportswriter Frederick G. Lieb wrote from Macon, under a headline that called the club "Huston's Regiment."[6] The *New York Herald* reported the same day, "Preparedness, so far as the baseball players of the New York American League Club can contribute to it, began this morning."[7]

Sergeant Gibson's tiny regiment comprised thirty-two ballplayers, Huston, manager "Wild Bill" Donovan, business manager Harry Sparrow, a coach, a scout, a groundskeeper, eight newspapermen, and J. McKay, a Macon businessman. Fortunately, Captain Huston wasn't the only former soldier in Gibson's command. Two of the writers had served during the Philippine Insurrection (1899–1902), and outfielder Tim Hendryx, catcher Les Nunamaker, and McKay all had been in the National Guard. Gibson appointed the six old hands as his corporals. A newspaperman who didn't drill with them was promptly labeled a slacker and threatened with a court-martial.

Gibson started his troops with the basics: how to stand, right and left dress, right and left face, and right about face. He gave them a little speech, saying he hoped to make the Yankees the best-drilled team in the American League, then set them to marching. "The squad was formed in two lines and then counted off into fours," the *New York World* reported. "This arithmetical progression safely attended to, the squad marched across the field in columns of four until Harry Sparrow hollered for mercy. Harry's feet were tiring under his 250 pounds of flesh." Huston, in contrast, was "as enthusiastic as a little boy playing with his first toy. The owner of the Yankees praised the boys for their fine showing and is looking forward to a good team of soldiers as well as a good team of ball players."[8]

The New York scribes later gathered around the sergeant for his take on the proceedings. Gibson told them he was pleased by what he had seen that morning. Most of the Yankees were green, but they had followed his instructions well, and he thought they would make "corking good soldiers." The noncommissioned officer added, "Capt. Huston should be complimented for his good work in this movement."[9]

Capt. Tillinghast L'Hommedieu Huston had bought the Yankees in January 1915 with partner Jacob Ruppert, a brewery baron, sportsman, and former congressman. Both men had military experience. An army engineer during the 1898 war with Spain, Huston had stayed in Cuba afterward to make his fortune in construction. Yankees historians Steve Steinberg and Lyle Spatz describe him as "informal, familiar, rumpled, self-made."[10] Ruppert was his exact opposite, a fastidious and formal man who had taken over the family business. He was also a former colonel in the New York National Guard. Naturally he and Huston took an interest in military matters and in the war that had raged in Europe for more than two years. Huston even declared that he was "willing to pull out the old army uniform again if Uncle Sam should need his services."[11] What might have seemed an idle boast by an out-of-shape, middle-aged baseball magnate was both sincere and prescient.

Huston first floated his grand plan for drilling ballplayers in February 1917—not for his Yankees alone but for all Major Leaguers. He received the immediate backing of Byron Bancroft "Ban" Johnson, the American League founder and president, which seems surprising. Steinberg and Spatz write that Huston and Johnson had "a mutual hostility that went back many years, though its source remains unclear."[12] The league president had supported Huston and Ruppert in purchasing the Yankees, but the owners would clash repeatedly with him for years afterward. Nonetheless, in the momentous early spring of 1917, Huston and Johnson cooperated on the baseball preparedness movement. Some in the National League poked fun at the American League players as "Ban's and Till's 'tin soldiers.'"[13]

"We have no way of knowing what may eventuate in the United States during the next few months," Huston said, "and it would be a source of great satisfaction to the ball players and their followers to know that they were prepared to lay aside the spiked shoe and the glove and take up the rifle if their country needed them."[14]

The movement generated a good deal of ink on the nation's sports pages, especially in New York City. Huston "is working on a scheme whereby he hopes to make the influence of organized baseball deeply felt as a power to patriotism and action in case Uncle Sam comes to grips with the Central Powers," columnist W. J. "Bill" Macbeth wrote in the *New York Tribune*. Huston wouldn't release details, but "has been working with his colleagues for some weeks now."[15]

Johnson sounded rather martial, too. In another article in the same edition of the *Tribune*, the American League's powerful leader said that if the country entered the war, his circuit not only would release any players who wanted to enlist but also would look after their families while they were gone. "I approve of the suggestion made by Captain Huston, of the New York club, in regard to military training for ball players," Johnson added. "Captain Huston would have certain hours set aside during training season for military drill. It would set a good example for others in military preparedness."[16]

Huston had aggressively pushed the plan during the winter of 1916–17 as America edged steadily closer to war with Imperial Germany. He offered details in a letter to Johnson, reprinted in numerous newspapers February 10. Huston outlined three main points:

First, make a military school of spring-training camps. The Yankees themselves, Huston wrote, planned an hour of drill in the mornings and another hour in the afternoons, not to interfere with regular baseball work. Success depended on obtaining the services of "a good regular army sergeant to drill the company."

Second, continue the drills during the regular season for two hours in the mornings and a shorter period in the afternoons. By combining the players and officials of the home and visiting teams (about 60 men) with 140 or so local fans, a city would have enough men for two companies. "Do this on all of our eight [American League] parks," Huston recommended, "and also offer our parks for military drill purposes."

Third, open a training camp in the fall, immediately after the World Series. Huston suggested locating it in the South and opening it to all professional ballplayers, umpires, sportswriters, and anyone else connected with baseball.

"Of course, the whole scheme must have the support of the regular army, and we must have expert instruction, and the players must realize that the movement is a great one and must be approached not with levity but in a seriousness and unalloyed patriotism," Huston wrote to Johnson.[17] The Yankees co-owner had already contacted Leonard Wood, the army commander in the East, and Gen. William Black, chief of engineers, and believed he could get War Department backing.

New York World sportswriter Bozeman Bulger wrote that many Major Leaguers were looking forward to the military drills while snow still covered the Northeast. He added that several American League managers expected to field well-drilled teams in time for the 1917 season opener. Bulger also offered the view of an unnamed army officer: "It will be a wonderful help if professional baseball can have 400 men in shape for service in case they are needed. If the minor leagues should fall in line we could almost count upon another regiment." New York Giants manager John McGraw also weighed in. "If the drill exercise was too long or too severe it might be a little hard on the older players, but if all the clubs do it there will be no advantage, or disadvantage, to any one during the season," McGraw said. "You must remember that the players will have to do their hard work of practice on the diamond in addition to having military instruction. That, though, could be worked out satisfactorily later on."[18]

American League club owners expressed no reservations at all. President Frazee of the Boston club later said that the system "might with profit be followed by the great employers of this country— the great railway and transportation corporations, steel works, wholesale houses, automobile manufactories and the like."[19] The AL owners immediately backed Johnson, publicly endorsed the Huston plan, and empowered their president "to consult with Major General Leonard Wood concerning the detailed working out of this project."[20]

The rival National League, however, stayed silent. Everyone, in fact, was fairly quiet until the end of February, when Huston dispatched his telegram to Governors Island requesting the services of Sergeant Gibson. Then things happened quickly.

Out in Illinois, in the snowy Middle West, Sgt. Walter Smiley attracted the same phenomenal interest as Sergeant Gibson. Smiley's suitors were Charles Comiskey and his Chicago White Sox.

Like Gibson, Smiley was an army recruiter. He worked from Chicago, looking for able-bodied men to fill out the service's meager ranks. His job wasn't easy. A year earlier, he had recruited in several towns in southern Wisconsin and come back largely disappointed. Only six of twenty-four young men in Racine passed the army's preliminary examination. A local newspaper said Smiley found the army's strict regulations a hindrance to recruitment.

"He said that out of 3,500 applications at the Chicago office during the Mexican scare only 200 men were accepted," the paper reported. "From ten to fifteen men a week, he said, were turned down, because of inability to read and write and speak the English

7

language. These were men, too, who had been born and raised in Chicago." Even worse was Smiley's astonishment at "how many men are walking the streets with diseases of one kind or another which would keep them out of the army, and who do not know there is anything the matter with them."[21] Now, in the spring of 1917, Sergeant Smiley was preparing to take charge of a team of Major League ballplayers, among the healthiest young fellows in the country.

Smiley's name first appeared in the Chicago newspapers on the same day that the New York papers had noted Sergeant Gibson. Smiley "will probably go on the spring training trip with the White Sox to teach them military drill," *Day Book* reported. "Smiley was formerly a star player in the Manila army league and should be popular with the athletes, even though he forces them to work."[22]

Either the army had assigned him or the White Sox had selected him—perhaps both—precisely because Smiley was a good army ballplayer. He had hit .372 in Manila and won a medal as his team's most valuable player. Later he had captained an army nine in Japan and China. Now twenty-three, the Philadelphia native had first enlisted in 1911. A photo showing him wearing U.S. Army baseball flannels would soon appear in papers across America. Unlike Gibson, already on duty near the Yankees' spring-training camp, Smiley was working up north in Chicago.

White Sox owner Charles Comiskey understood public relations and quickly latched onto the athletic sergeant. "Commie" was also a longtime friend and compatriot of Ban Johnson—although their relationship, too, would soon grow troubled. Johnson no doubt kept Comiskey apprised of Huston's scheme. "Sergt. Smiley's services were offered Comiskey by Adjt. Gen. McCain, and Comiskey immediately accepted," the *Chicago Tribune* reported March 2. "The sergeant will be on board in full uniform when the Sox special pulls out for Mineral Wells [Texas] Sunday night."[23]

Johnson made it clear that he hoped to secure other army ballplayers like Smiley from the War Department. "The army by assigning drill officers who know the game of baseball will in turn be benefited, and they can then teach the regulars the scientific end of the game when they return to the ranks," Johnson said. "The ball players, on the other hand, will more readily adapt themselves to military discipline under an officer who not only knows the arts of war but is acquainted with sport itself."[24] The army got the message.

The big-city sportswriters parochially disagreed on whether the Yankees or the White Sox were the first to adopt Huston's military-training program. It was likely a tie, New York and Chicago simultaneously welcoming their sergeants. Like Fred Lieb in Macon, *Chicago Tribune* sportswriter I. E. Sanborn in Mineral Wells had fun reporting on Smiley and his baseball soldiers.

"Privates Clarence Rowland, Edward Collins, James Scott, Ray Schalk, and Albert Russell were promoted to the rank of corporal this morning by Sergt. Walter Smiley, U. S. A., in command of the White Sox company, B. B. N. G. (base ball National Guard)," Sanborn wrote. After the team drilled together in company formation, each corporal took charge of a squad. "The new 'noncoms' started out bravely and got by in great shape until the order to 'assemble' was given, then some difficulty was experienced by the corporals in getting their squads back into their original places in line. Scott came closest to it by the about face methods, but found he had the rear in front, that's all."[25]

Still, like the Yankees, the White Sox responded well to the instruction. "It was hard for the boys to keep from telling each other how their feet failed to track and how everybody else was out of line," second baseman Eddie Collins wrote in the *Chicago Tribune*. "It took the sergeant a couple of days to suppress this wordy mutiny, but once it has been accomplished the drill went like clockwork. Not that we are letter perfect, but there was that spirit present where every one tried to excel."[26] Smiley had earlier said, "Ballplayers learn military drill faster than any recruits I ever handled."[27]

Two weeks into spring training, Smiley received a letter from Capt. Franklin Kenney, who commanded recruiting in the army's Central Department. Kenney suggested that the sergeant add hand grenades to his drills. White Sox manager Clarence "Pants" Rowland agreed and said the sooner the better. "In order to make it realistic some of the players want to dig a trench and hurl the grenades at silhouette targets. Baseballs will be used for grenades."[28]

Army drill instructors reported to seven of the eight American League clubs while spring training was still in progress; the Red Sox would greet theirs later, a week into the regular season. With Gibson in New York and Smiley in Chicago, the rest of the army lineup looked like this: Sgt. A. B. Hoffman, Boston; Sgt. D. W. Dennis, Cleveland; Sgt. H. G. Thorne, Detroit; Sgt. W. E. Smart, Philadelphia; Sgt. Winfred B. Wisener, St. Louis; and Cpl. (soon to be Sgt.) John Dean, Washington.

Two National League teams also joined the Huston movement. Brooklyn owner Charles Ebbets found Sgt. Maj. Jess Trontgla while the Dodgers were training at Hot Springs, Arkansas. Once the season began, the Boston Braves would secure the services of Sgt. Perry S. Schofield. The movement also filtered down to the Minor Leagues. The Milwaukee and Indianapolis clubs in the Class AA American Association soon landed drillmasters, as did several clubs in lower leagues, although a few of these men were national guardsmen or retired soldiers. Captain Kenney again had charge of the regular army sergeants. He assigned the Milwaukee team a man with nine years' service, Sgt. Jack Waidley, who had played on all-army ball teams in Honolulu and Chicago. Kenney sent him to Wichita Falls, Texas, with instructions to teach the Brewers first aid, cooking, and how to make up a pack, pitch a tent, and take care of their bodies, especially their feet.

Fans cheered the military drills during spring training, and Sergeant Smiley believed they saw a difference in the players. "Civilians have also remarked to me on the martial bearing of the men," he wrote in *Sporting News*. "Whether this is actually noticeable to the average person or whether it is imagination I do not know, but it is nonetheless true that the men do carry themselves different from what they did at the start."[29] Huston noticed the same effect in Macon, writing to sportswriter Bulger, "In a week, it seems, the greenest and most awkward of our recruits have been cured of a slouchiness, which, as you know, has been one of the banes of the baseball manager's existence when trying to put together a club."[30]

Smiley thought his White Sox charges also displayed a military attentiveness in carrying out baseball orders on the diamond. "I do not know how long this will last or if it will ever be noticed in the heat of battle during the regular season," the sergeant wrote, "but it is certainly noticeable at the present time."[31] Second baseman Eddie Collins likewise saw a change in the Sox. "They early came to recognize that the military drill was serious business and that it might come in good stead sooner than expected. Then, again, I think that the drilling has had an influence for good on the public in general," he wrote. "The seriousness of the situation has been brought home to thousands who have seen us drill and we have been greeted with enthusiasm everywhere."[32]

The army drill sergeants were a sportswriter's dream, but some ballplayers were unhappy about having to drill under them. The National League never officially endorsed the Huston scheme, and six of its eight teams never participated. Every American League club was on board, but many of the players weren't enthusiastic, especially among the Tigers.

"Several Detroit players have claimed that the drills have caused severe strain upon muscles not brought into play on the baseball diamond and that the work has hindered more than it has helped their playing," read a widely published wire report from Waxahachie. "The local players have been drilling with bats instead of guns and it is understood this has been unpopular with them."[33]

Detroit manager Hugh Jennings believed in compulsory military training for the country overall, but said ballplayers should drill only if they wanted to. Tigers trainer Harry Tuthill, however, publicly supported the Huston plan. "The players do not get enough of the exercises to tire their muscles," said Tuthill, formerly an athletic trainer for the U.S. Military Academy. "The setting up exercises are excellent. It is my hope that we have them every spring."[34]

The Cleveland Indians were no fonder of the drills than the Tigers, although Tris Speaker was said to favor them. Word of clubhouse grumbling reached the league office, prompting Ban Johnson to fire off a sharply worded telegram to Cleveland manager Lee Fohl. "From reports there is a lack of interest shown by you and your players in military drill. This must not continue." Outraged, Fohl promptly wired back: "No truth in report. Some one is a liar, and that goes."[35] The Tigers and Indians drilled along with everyone else.

Lastly there was a strange Red Sox–Dodgers dust-up. Brooklyn wasn't even a member of the American League, but Boston's outspoken owner nonetheless criticized the club for a late start at drilling—if only to deflect criticism from his own reluctant players. "Sure, we are going to drill," Harry Frazee told writers March 21. "We start today and would have done so sooner, only we had to wait for an army officer to take us in hand. What are they doing over in the Brooklyn camp?"

Dodgers owner Ebbets retorted that his club had asked for a drill instructor weeks earlier, but the local army commander hadn't been able to provide one until Sergeant Major Trontgla stepped forward while on furlough. The Brooklyn players had then balked, Ebbets explained, at receiving only verbal instructions.

"If Mr. Ebbets wants us to drill every morning at Ebbets Field [in Brooklyn], we are willing," manager Wilbert Robinson insisted. "Uncle Robbie" then returned fire at Boston. "I don't think the Red Sox are keen on the drill. Why, [player-manager] Jack Barry told me they weren't going to take it up. They've got to show me."[36]

The Dodgers, in fact, had voted overwhelmingly against the Huston plan. They thought drills got in the way of preparing for baseball, believed that the army training had "proved a fizzle in other camps," and claimed that Trontgla had told them "the time was all too short for them to familiarize themselves with even the rudiments of field manoeuvres."[37] Perhaps to soften public perception, the players did tender a vote of thanks to Trontgla "for his offer to drill the Dodgers."[38]

Brooklyn Eagle sportswriter Thomas Rice couldn't believe "the players on the Brooklyn team are so utterly stupid that they cannot see that they are working for their own benefit by offering to show their willingness to prepare themselves to do their bit for their country"—or to see that aroused fans would drive them out of the game if they didn't. "It is reasonable to suppose that the Brooklyn and other ball players will not be utterly blind to their own selfish interests," Rice wrote, "regardless of the opinion some of them might entertain about the bitter hardship imposed by ordering them to do an hour or so of useful athletic exercises for their country every day."[39]

Still, the Brooklyn club wasn't a member of the American League, and so not officially committed to the drill scheme in the first place. No other National League club except Boston expressed any real interest, either. "What's the use of military training for ball players?" asked business manager Frank Bancroft of the Cincinnati Reds. "If it took them as long to enlist as it does to sign their contracts the war would be all over before they could start for the front."[40]

Grumbling continued periodically in both circuits during the regular season, but pressured by Johnson and facing little sympathy from fans or the press, no American League team ever publicly abandoned the drills. Likely influenced by Huston, the Yankees voted unanimously in Macon to *continue* their drills—a fact that Ban Johnson immediately shared with reporters.

To maintain momentum for the scheme, the league president also announced a $500 prize (equivalent to nearly $10,000 today) for the league's best-drilled team, plus $100 in gold for that team's drill sergeant. A competition was slated in July—which would later be pushed to August—with a board of army officers to review the players' performance and make the award. Captain Huston matched the $500 prize, and the president of the Illinois-Indiana-Iowa (Three-I) Minor League pledged another $100.

Comiskey, never a wallflower, chipped in another $200 for his players plus a $100 bonus for Sergeant Smiley if the White Sox marched off with top honors. No matter who won, the prize money would be "distributed as the players decide," a Boston paper reported, "but it is probable that the fund will be used to purchase a pennant emblematic of the honor."[41]

As they trained in their southern camps, American Leaguers routinely saw their drills reported along with the usual baseball items and scores. Panoramic photos of ballplayers performing company drills—with baseball bats across their broad shoulders instead of model 1903 Springfield rifles—appeared on sports pages across the country. A *Sporting Life* editorial later noted that the scribes had a good deal of sport early on, writing about the players and their drills.

> But, as a matter of fact the players in Captain Huston's awkward squad, under the direction of a regular sergeant, took to the scheme at once with such seriousness and determination to learn that the newspaper humorists hitting the trail with the ball club were somewhat abashed and seriously impressed, and it is fair to presume that as are the Yankees so will be the other teams in the American League.[42]

The New York writers especially sat up when Col. E. V. Smith watched a Yankees drill in late March. The officer in charge of the army's southern division, Smith offered high praise for the Yankees:

> You men have no idea of the wonderful showing you have made, compared to most recruits. And you can have no idea of the great good you are doing and will do later on. You have picked up drill in a most amazing fashion, which is but further proof that the average ball player is among the most intelligent of our citizens. This can only remain a big league country if it gets ready in a big league way. Otherwise it is back to the bushes for a nation, just as it will be for the individual who hasn't trained when the show-down comes.[43]

No club could buy better publicity. By the time the eight American League teams headed north to begin the regular season, Huston's scheme had become both a serious-minded boost to military preparedness and a wildly successful public relations ploy by owners and magnates. The army and the league mutually benefited, as Tom Rice noted in the *Eagle*.

> Will the New York Club lose money by paying Sergeant Gibson's expenses on the road in these troublous times? It most distinctly will not. Make a bet on that. The drilling by the Yankees is going to prove one of the best and most legitimate advertising schemes in the history of baseball. The same goes for the Chicago White Sox, who have been as industrious as the Yankees in their drilling. You could not imagine Charley Comiskey, the greatest advertiser the sport ever knew, missing a chance like that.[44]

Cornelius McGillicuddy, the magisterial owner and manager of the Philadelphia Athletics, universally known to fans as Connie Mack, knew a bit about Major League baseball, too. Mack wanted the Huston preparedness scheme to benefit fans as well as players, and he made sure to say so publicly. "We have entertained the American people and now we will do all in our power to protect them," Mack said the first week of April. "I realize that our small band of athletes could do nothing if they were to take their places on the firing line, where numbers count more than anything else, but I believe we can set an example for others to follow." Mack said that Shibe Park would serve as both a baseball park and a drill ground during the season, and he invited Philadelphians to join his Mackmen there. "Every morning the men who wish to train for military service are invited to come out to the park, where they will be drilled by Sergeant Smart and the ball players themselves." Mack's stance was "another reason why he is so popular in our city," the *Philadelphia Public Ledger* applauded. "He sees a chance to use his men for something else besides playing ball, and without waiting to be asked he turned his equipment over to the public. Connie is the first big league magnate to take this stand." [45]

The Athletics' leader had the exquisite timing of an old baseball man. The United States declared war on imperial Germany just two days after his comments appeared in the newspaper. President Woodrow Wilson and Vice President Thomas Marshall signed the resolution of Congress at 1:11 p.m. on Friday, April 6, 1917. The baseball season opened the following week, amid cold weather and general gloom, the first Major League campaign ever to begin with the country at war. Captain Huston's Yankees were at home against Harry Frazee's Red Sox.

"Holding aloft a banner 'Death to Autocracy,' Uncle Sam to-day is prepared to bow to the only monarch to whom he ever swore fealty, a monarch typifying the very spirit of the nation, old King Baseball," Fred Lieb wrote. "Even with the stern business of preparing for war uppermost the nation is unable to forgo interest in its leading outdoor diversion."[46] Play ball!

2

Selective Service

The Yankees opened the season at home at 3:15 p.m. on Wednesday, April 11. Their home park during the pre–Yankee Stadium years was the Polo Grounds, which they leased from the New York National League club. The Giants were on the road, but their opener would be postponed due to snow covering Braves Field in Boston.

"At an early hour this morning—sunrise, to be exact—the old Polo Grounds flared up into a great horseshoe of red, white, and blue," Bozeman Bulger wrote in the *World*. "Every flag pole in the stadium—and there are hundreds of them—floats Old Glory and even the uprights inside the stand are festooned in patriotic bunting."[1]

Despite the cold weather in New York, fifteen thousand fans, including General Wood, turned out to see the home opener, which was Jack Barry's first as the Red Sox's player-manager. His squad didn't yet have a drill instructor, so the Yankees took the field alone before the game to demonstrate the military skills they had learned during spring training.

Major Dorey led the formation onto the field, flanked by Captain Huston and Colonel Ruppert, both in overcoats and civilian suits. The team marched behind them in four columns, wearing spikes, pinstripes, and their blue caps with the white Yankees logo, with baseball bats over their shoulders in place of rifles. Sergeant

Gibson strode to their left, calling the cadence. Everyone kept in step, although a few players had to look down at their feet. Again, Bulger recorded the scene:

> New Yorkers are skeptical by nature, and all along they had this thing of ball players drilling a joke. But after the first gasp of wonder their mouths hung open in amazement as the Yankee team went through movement after movement with the precision of a machine. At the completion of every formation the gang would rise and cheer. Even Gen. Wood arose on one occasion and clapped his hands in approval when the Yank platoon executed "on right into line" as accurately as could veterans of the regular army.[2]

The team halted in company formation and presented bats as a band played "The Star-Spangled Banner." Unfortunately for their fans, the game they played afterward was much sloppier than their military maneuvers. "The Yanks were beaten to a genial pulp, but even a 10 to 3 trimming could not offset the fine impression Sergeant Gibson and his troop made before the game," wrote columnist Grantland Rice.[3]

Other American League squads also demonstrated their military skills on opening day. At Shibe Park in Philadelphia, the Athletics marched from home plate to a tower topped by a flagpole in deep centerfield, where they raised an American flag to the strains of "The Star-Spangled Banner." "There was no suggestion of comedy when Sergeant Smart, the army officer in charge of their training, lined them up for the flag-raising exercises. They went about the ceremony with earnestness and enthusiasm," the *Philadelphia Public Ledger* reported. "'Old Glory' was raised over a ball field with more dignity than ever before, and when the young men who play ball for Connie Mack marched back to the home plate they had done more for the game of baseball than if they had won a hundred victories."[4] Unfortunately for the Mackmen, Washington's Walter Johnson then hurled a three-hit, complete-game shutout, winning 3–0.

Minor League clubs likewise displayed their patriotic fervor. In the American Association, the Indianapolis Indians won at home

over the Toledo Mud Hens, 6–5. "Preceding the game civic organizations and local clubs joined the contending clubs in a patriotic
parade, and at Washington park Governor Goodrich and Mayor
Bell hoisted the Stars and Stripes while the standing audience sang
'The Star-Spangled Banner.' The Indians demonstrated the military drill learned while in training camp."[5]

The Chicago White Sox opened on the road before returning to the South Side for their first home game on April 19. Captain Kenney and Maj. Gen. Thomas H. Barry attended and saw
Sergeant Smiley drill his charges before a crowd of twenty-five
thousand. The White Sox now wore regulation army khaki and
shouldered Springfield rifles, all delivered the day before. "For an
instant there was a pause of surprise, then as the rooters recognized their idols they realized the transformation that had taken
place since they last saw them," I. E. Sanborn wrote. "There was
a roar that fairly drowned the band, which was trying to furnish a
quickstep for the Sox to march by."[6]

A representative of the Chicago Board of Trade presented manager Rowland with a regimental flag, delivering a speech that echoed
the Civil War. It was as if the Sox were planning to march straight
from the park to a troop train following the game. The large crowd
rose and removed their hats as bands played "God Save the King"
to honor the country's new ally. Charles Comiskey's team then
lost a rainy, mud-splashed contest to the St. Louis Browns, 6–2.

"It will be an interesting thing to watch as the season goes on,"
Sergeant Smiley wrote in *Sporting News*, "but I do not hesitate to
state that the men will find in the long run that they will be better off with the drill than without it.[7]

The same day, as part of New York City's huge "Wake Up, America!" campaign, the Yankees and Senators drilled together at the
Polo Grounds, "forming for the first time a full company of baseball soldiers," Bozeman Bulger wrote. The visitors then headed
south to Washington for their home opener on April 20. There
the Griffmen marched for 6,730 fans. Three hundred soldiers from
nearby Fort Myer also showed how regulars drilled (and got into
the game for free), and Assistant Secretary of the Navy Franklin

D. Roosevelt helped Senators manager Clark Griffith raise the American flag in center field.

While all very heady, baseball's red-white-and-blue displays actually accomplished very little. A few owners had begun to take more productive measures. Dodgers owner Charles Ebbets had opened a military recruiting station in his business offices, following the lead of Charles Comiskey and Charles Weeghman, "the Chicago magnates, in whose ball parks recruiting stations have been established."[8] Comiskey also would contribute 10 percent of his club's gross receipts throughout the season to the American Red Cross. Unmatched by any other big-league magnate, the owner's offer contradicts his later reputation as an awful miser when it came to clubhouse expenses and ballplayer salaries.[9] By season's end, Comiskey's contribution to the Red Cross would total $17,000.

Clark Griffith went a step further, offering a novel scheme of his own to benefit American troops at home and overseas. He announced it two days after the Senators' home opener:

> Now comes the Old Fox forward with the first effort in behalf of the United States soldiers, who will no doubt be encamped many months before they are shipped across the big pond for action.
>
> The Old Fox figures that one form of recreation which will be indulged in by the men while encamped will be the great and grand national pastime, and in an effort to meet the requirement that this new move will no doubt demand, Griff has started a campaign to gather in funds in order to supply the soldiers with the baseball paraphernalia.[10]

Griffith had hit upon the idea during the spring while traveling with his Senators (who were interchangeably called the Nationals during that era). "We would often pass a little group of soldiers guarding bridges," he recalled later. "As a rule there were several of them playing catch to pass the time away. Then the boys were called to the camps. My original intention was to supply only the boys in America, but as the thing developed and as the scheme received such hearty approval and support I decided to include the boys who went 'over there.'" The U.S. Navy, in contrast to the swiftly growing U.S. Army, was well organized, and many warships had their own recreation funds. "The sailor boys realized this and made very few requests for outfits." [11]

The manager took a simple, direct approach with his first appeal. He wrote to prominent sportswriters, asking each to send him twenty-five cents in care of a local bank. "Of course you realize that if you fail to comply you break the chain and put an obstacle in the way of the success of the project," Griffith added. "Just a quarter from you and a little time and trouble and we will be able to supply the thousands of red-blooded young soldiers the material for wholesome and pleasant recreation whenever their duties permit it."[12]

The letter was widely reprinted in the nation's newspapers, often in its entirety. Donations poured in, including a quarter from President Wilson. Dealers sold Griffith baseball equipment at cost, nearly doubling his buying power. The Washington manager didn't yet fully realize the scope of what he was proposing. His scheme quickly evolved into the Clark Griffith Bat and Ball Fund, among the most popular and successful charitable enterprises of the war.

How long could Organized Baseball now continue? The question was on everyone's mind—magnates, players, fans, and sportswriters. Both leagues rushed to reassure everyone. Ban Johnson spoke for the American League on front pages and sports sections across America:

> If war demands, the American League will close its gates, and I am
> sure all of us will do whatever we can for our country. But war should
> not interrupt our schedule. Every club will have a drill sergeant from
> the regular army with it all season and military training will be prac-
> tically compulsory. Thus the players will advance in army drill just as
> well as if they were in active service, and they will be ready for the
> call whenever it comes. [13]

Governor John Tener was briefer but equally upbeat for the National League. "Unless great loss of life is suffered through impending hostilities, I confidently believe base ball and other sports will have as many participants and patrons in the summer as heretofore," his statement said in part. "All clubs in the National league seem to have improved their playing strength and have capable managers."[14]

Johnson and Tener spoke only for the Major Leagues. From a business standpoint, both circuits looked stable going into the 1917 season. They had survived the challenge of the upstart, short-lived Federal League in 1914 and 1915 with every franchise intact. All sixteen clubs, in fact, would continue in their current cities until the Braves moved to Milwaukee in 1953. In the Minor Leagues, however, the situation was always far less stable.

Twenty-two Minor Leagues across the country were preparing to play in 1917. In descending order, the five classes were AA, A, B, C, and D. (Organized Baseball didn't include the independent, outlaw, or Cuban leagues or the many African American clubs of the era.) While generally reflective of the relative talent levels among the players, these Minor League classifications were determined strictly by numbers—specifically, by the combined population of the cities forming each league. Three Class AA leagues topped the pyramid in 1917, each with at least 1.75 million prospective fans. At the base of the pyramid were the Class D leagues, each with a total population of fewer than two hundred thousand people.

Minor League baseball was no enterprise for the fainthearted. In the best of times, the leagues were hardscrabble, chaotic, and a good way to lose your shirt—and perhaps your hat and overcoat in the bargain. That any investor hoped to break even, let alone make a profit, in the lower levels of Organized Baseball spoke to the enduring power of the national pastime and the clamor of fans for fast nines in their own communities. Business leaders often funded small-town ball clubs simply to provide recreation for their workers, provided the losses didn't prove excessive.[15] In the wartime spring of 1917, one key factor had changed: America's entry into the world war made business in the Minor Leagues vastly more precarious. The lower they were on baseball's pyramid, the greater the owners' anxiety.

The Class AA American Association decided to adopt Captain Huston's preparedness plan in this first wartime season. "I was opposed to military training for ballplayers at first," said President Thomas J. Hickey, "but now that war has been declared I will prepare the players for possible army service and stimulate recruiting."[16] The league gave no hint that it might curtail operations because of the war. To the contrary, clubs planned to open their parks to the public for drilling whenever they were on the road.

Late in April, influenced by the activities of Sergeant Smiley at Mineral Wells, Texas League president Walter Morris urged military training for every club in his Class B circuit, although not purely for patriotic reasons. "He feels sure that followers of baseball will be included in those conscripted, but if these ball players can demonstrate that they know how to drill they will not be called upon before the close of the 1917 season at any rate."[17]

Prominent, unnamed figures connected with the Class B Illinois-Indiana-Iowa League were less optimistic about completing its season. They commented that despite the war, the Three-I would proceed "according to present plans, but if the interest and attendance developed do not justify, then the club owners will suspend activities until the trouble is settled."[18]

The various Minor Leagues opened their seasons from mid-April through early May. Failures came quickly. Before the weather had warmed, three leagues died in the span of a week. The Class C Virginia League, whose Norfolk club had shared an army drill instructor with the International League's Buffalo team during spring training, suddenly disbanded May 16. "Want of interest due to the war is given as the reason for the disbandonment."[19] The Interstate League, a troubled Class D circuit that had operated in New York and Pennsylvania, disbanded two days later before its season even began. A newspaper had noted earlier that "a projected trolley league seems to excite more interest than the Interstate League and . . . expenses would be lighter in every way and the sport would be just about as good."[20] Lastly, the Class D Georgia-Alabama League folded May 23, its president citing "war conditions, cold weather and the fact that the league could not find a successor to the Tri-Cities club which turned in its franchise 10 days ago."[21] American soldiers had yet to set foot on a French battlefield, but Minor Leagues were falling like machine-gunned *poilus*.

One former Major Leaguer was already fighting in the war. He was Billy O'Hara, a Canadian who had played for several years in the Minors across North America before catching on with John McGraw's New York Giants in 1909. The next year he had gone to Toronto—at the time a member of the Class A Eastern League, later in the Class AA International—where he was an outfielder. By the time America joined the war, O'Hara was a thirty-five-year-old lieutenant in the Canadian Army.

> While playing the outfield for Toronto in June 1915, I used to stand out there and watch the airplanes whizzing over our heads. The training grounds of the Royal Flying corps were situated close to the ball park and pretty soon I got to thinking that I would like to ride in one of those things and steal bases on the Germans; so I hopped into a khaki suit and kissed my old glove good-bye.[22]

O'Hara wanted to become an aviator, "but not having the patience to undergo a long period of training, he had himself transferred to the infantry."[23] The ex-ballplayer saw considerable combat with Canada's Twenty-Fourth Battalion and in October 1916 was recommended for the Military Cross, "in recognition of his bravery and skill in hurling bombs for the British army on the Somme battlefront. . . . According to word from Toronto, the practice he had in baseball has stood him in good stead while leading a bombing squad."[24]

O'Hara was then wounded when a German shell collapsed his trench, burying him for an hour and nearly killing him. After time in a British hospital, he returned to Canada on convalescent leave, which was extended. The Yankees had wanted to bring him to spring training in Georgia to boost Captain Huston's preparedness movement. (He didn't make it, but later visited New York and took in a Giants game.) O'Hara gave sportswriter J. B. Sheridan a long, harrowing account of fighting in France.

How small the great games of baseball I have played seem beside my days in the trenches. Life and the world seem mighty small and no-account when you have seen your best friends die about you every day. I remember the time when we sympathized with a pal that got spiked in a baseball game. Day after day I have seen good pals shot through the head drop dead at my feet.

When you have looked into the bowels of hell and seen your dearest friends engulfed therein, you have endured about all that there is to endure. What may happen to you thereafter amounts to very little.[25]

Two other former Major Leaguers enlisted in the U.S. Army in the early weeks of America's participation in the war, both to considerable acclaim. The names Edward Grant and Harry McCormick would be linked in print and in fans' minds throughout the rest of the war and beyond. Coincidentally, like O'Hara, they had both played for John McGraw's Giants.

Grant and McCormick had been teammates on the New York club in 1913, and each had appeared briefly in the five-game World Series loss to Connie Mack's Athletics. Playing mostly at third base, Grant had been a utility man with the Giants, his fourth team in the Majors. McCormick had played for three Major League clubs, twice for the Giants. Many fans considered him the best pinch-hitter in the Majors, a skill he had learned playing cricket as a boy. Both men were college educated—Grant at Harvard Law School, McCormick at Bucknell—which was fairly unusual among ballplayers, although less so on McGraw's teams. McCormick also had played beside Billy O'Hara on the 1909 Giants.

Grant was a New York lawyer in 1917, two seasons out of baseball, and soon to turn thirty-four. McCormick, thirty-six, had managed for two seasons at Chattanooga in the Class A Southern Association before becoming a steel salesman. Both men applied for army training at Plattsburg (spelled without today's concluding *h*) in upstate New York. The program there had evolved from the Plattsburg Movement, a training and preparedness program for business and professional men, originally supported by Theodore Roosevelt, General Wood, and other influential Americans.

Major Dorey, then an army captain, had served as commandant of the first Plattsburg camp in 1915. Twelve hundred men had undergone training at their own expense that summer. "Nearly every tent contains either a millionaire, a captain of industry, or some man whose name is in the 'Who's Who,'" a newspaper had observed.[26]

The first of a flurry of articles about "Moose" McCormick and Eddie Grant entering the army appeared on American sports pages during the first week of May 1917. The former roommates likely enlisted together and arrived in Plattsburg at the same time. "As both possess considerable vigor and brawn, and are in their right mind, their chances for being taken to the camp are favorable, and in due course, if they go, they will try for their commissions as officers," baseball fans read across the country. "McCormick has been at Plattsburg as a private, so the course there won't be entirely new to him."[27]

The first active Major Leaguer to enlist in the army was Henry Gowdy of the Boston Braves. The lanky catcher was already immensely popular after hitting .545 for the "Miracle Braves" in the 1914 World Series. The simple act of signing his army enlistment papers instantly transformed Gowdy into Major League Baseball's greatest war hero. Grantland Rice noted the event with a poem a few days later:

Tris is up at the top again:
  Ty is out for another bid;
Alex's speed has the winning slant
  And "Big Babe" Ruth is the all-star kid;
Hand 'em the old hip-hip, and such;
  Stand 'em up in a leading row;
But don't forget, as the cheers emerge,
  That Old Lank Hank was the first to go.[28]

Newspaperman Westbrook Pegler always remembered Gowdy as a tall, gawky kid with freckles "the size of cornflakes."[29] On the sandlots of his hometown, Columbus, Ohio, friends had dubbed him Red. When he broke in as a first baseman with Lancaster in the Ohio State League, the team already had a player nicknamed Red, so Henry became Hank instead. He later switched positions to stay in the big leagues and was now an experienced backstop at age twenty-seven.

Gowdy was an outstanding friend and teammate. Southpaw Herb Pennock would credit him with teaching him how to pitch in Boston, despite the fact that Pennock played for the cross-town Red Sox. In February 1917 Gowdy received a lucrative offer to start a baseball school in Panama, which he turned down to stay with the Braves. But war had come since then, and the catcher had talked things over with army friends at home. He and teammates Johnny Evers and Walter "Rabbit" Maranville all thought they would enlist, but Gowdy was the first to do so.

"There isn't any sense in dodging a plain fact," he said. "I am a single man without dependents. I hate to go, because I am no hero in the making. But it's up to me to do my stunt, as it will be for a lot of other fellows in my position. You can't duck duty. You're a fool if you do. So I'm going to be all ready."[30]

The Braves arrived in Cincinnati at the end of May for a series with manager Christy Mathewson's Reds. When storms and wet grounds caused a postponement on June 1, Gowdy caught a train home to Columbus. The catcher ignored a telegram from manager George Stallings imploring him not to do anything until they had talked, and he enlisted in the Ohio National Guard the next morning, a Saturday. The state troops had only recently returned home from extended duty on the Mexican border.

"Before 8 o'clock Gowdy presented himself to Brig. Gen. John C. Speaks and was enlisted personally by him," the *Columbus Citizen* reported. "This in itself was a distinction as General Speaks has enrolled no other recruit." After passing his physical exam, Gowdy returned to the adjutant general's office to be sworn in by a captain. Guard officials were jubilant over signing such a blue-ribbon recruit. "When he left for Cincinnati Gowdy carried with him an injunction to see if he couldn't enlist some more members of the Boston club."[31]

By the time he caught a southbound train at 10:45 that morning, the Braves' catcher was officially Pvt. Henry Gowdy, Headquarters Company, Second Brigade, Ohio National Guard. He expected to become an orderly. The army didn't need him until July 15, when the Guard was expected to mobilize, so he rejoined his team for the long ride back to Boston. "Gowdy's action gave the baseball players something to think about on an otherwise eventless day," the *Boston Globe* reported. "His step apparently crystallized sentiment among players heretofore unable to reach a decision about offering their services, and it is believed that others will enlist before registration day."[32]

Despite that optimistic and somewhat naïve view, no other big leaguer soon followed Gowdy's example. Everyone required to do so, however, did dutifully register for the Selective Service draft three days later.

June 5 was Registration Day across America, when every male in the country who had passed his twenty-first birthday but not yet reached his thirty-first had to appear before government registrars. After giving personal information, including name, address, date of birth, citizenship status, employment, dependents, marital status, and race, each man received a small blue card to show that he had registered.

The draft lottery would be held later, on July 20, in room 226 of the Senate Office Building in Washington. It would begin at 9:49 a.m., when Secretary of War Newton Baker drew the first black capsule from a glass bowl, and end at 2:18 the following morning. Blindfolded men would draw 10,500 capsules, one by one, each containing a number. The lottery drawing depended not on a registered man's birthday alone but also on where his name stood on long lists assembled and posted at his local draft board. The government expected to draft between 900,000 and 1.5 million of the nearly 10 million men who had registered. According to the provost marshal general, exemptions probably would reduce the number to 625,000 men actually sworn in for service during the first round.

Army Brig. Gen. Enoch H. Crowder was the nation's provost marshal general. He and his assistants were largely responsible for drafting the Selective Service Act passed by Congress in May.

Crowder's name was already familiar to the American public. His decisions and rulings would become immensely important in determining the course of Organized Baseball during the war.

Major League clubs took pains to see that their players appeared on Registration Day. Charles Ebbets's Brooklyn team was on the road, so every eligible Dodger had registered early, May 26, with a deputy clerk at Ebbets Field. All but three players on manager Clark Griffith's squad had already registered, too, at a Washington federal building May 31. Pitcher Maurice "Molly" Craft would register later in Virginia, while shortstop George McBride and outfielder Jesse "Zeb" Milan weren't required to register because they were thirty-six and thirty-one years old, respectively. Milan's status was a surprise to his club, which hadn't realized his true age.

The Major Leagues observed Registration Day along with their fans. At Weeghman Park in Chicago, three companies of sailors and marines from the Great Lakes Naval Station marched before a National League contest between the Cubs and Phillies. The marines showed their disdain for the soggy conditions in the Windy City by marching back to the L station afterward, singing "How Dry I Am." In Washington the Senators welcomed hundreds of aging Confederate veterans as guests of honor at the game with manager Fielder Jones's St. Louis Browns. The teams performed together before the contest under their respective drill sergeants. The eighteen-piece Fife and Bugle Corps of Augusta supplied martial music and kept playing during the game. "It proved too much for Umpire Billy Evans, however, in the sixth inning. The band played while the contest was on, and Evans ordered Griff to stop the music."[33]

In Philadelphia Connie Mack's Athletics opened the turnstiles at Shibe Park for service members and veterans. "Nothing further than a uniform of Uncle Sam, whether the wearer be a private or an officer, will be required to secure admittance. The invitation also includes the National Guard and Civil War veterans."[34] The visiting White Sox put on an impressive display for the home team. "When they appeared for the ten minutes' drilling preceding the game each had a flag bound to the end of the bat which is used instead of a gun. Sergt. Smiley later gave the Sox some marine maneuvers, running over the diamond and dropping to their stomachs like sharpshooters. The boys finished by marching to the home plate, where they sang 'The Star-Spangled Banner,' while the crowd stood with bared heads."[35]

Fans in ballparks across the country heard the same patriotic tune that day. It wouldn't officially become the national anthem until 1931, but "The Star-Spangled Banner" was increasingly popular and had been played in parks several times since the United States had entered the war, as it had been on numerous occasions in earlier seasons. At Boston's Fenway Park, the local Ninth Regiment band played the tune when the Red Sox came to bat in the seventh inning.

Captain Huston missed his Yankees' doubleheader with the Tigers in New York before thirty thousand fans. On May 18 he had taken an entrance exam for the Army Corps of Engineers, coincidentally in Detroit. Although portly and almost fifty years old, Huston had valuable military and construction experience and possessed useful industry contacts. The army had welcomed him back at his old rank with open arms. Huston had then returned to Manhattan to wrap up his affairs and turn over the ball club to his partner, Colonel Ruppert. He had planned to return to his regiment in Detroit on June 4, the day before Registration Day, immediately after the first game in the Yankees-Tigers series. The magnate had even risen from his seat during the ninth inning, with his team trailing 5–3, when his Yankees began a rally.

> As the military magnate executed right face and started for the exit Home Run Baker connected for a clean single. Corporal Tim Hendryx drove a two-bagger to centre and placed Baker on third. Captain Huston halted abruptly and resumed his seat. He had a hunch that something of great military value was about to come off.
>
> Roger Peckinpaugh singled along the third base line and Baker scored. Nunamaker lifted a long fly to Cobb and Hendryx scored. This tied the count and Captain Huston, despite the fact that the bugles, the fifes and the drums and various other martial instruments were calling him, settled more closely into his seat.[36]

The Yanks pulled off a dramatic 6–5 victory. Huston beamed until something terrible occurred to him. "I've missed my train and I'll be court-martialed," he moaned. The captain was last seen racing from the Polo Grounds for Grand Central Station. Thus he wasn't on hand for the Registration Day doubleheader, when "Rear Admiral Jennings, of the Detroit Horse Marines, and Brigadier William Donovan, of the Tybee Light Infantry, will give exhibition drills with their troops."[37]

The 1917 Major League season got off to an uncertain start, plagued by bad weather and worries over what the war would mean to the sport. The owners in May had energetically resisted a proposed federal war tax on their gross receipts. "Baseball is not the lucrative business supposed," National League president John Tener had declared. "More is lost than is made in the different clubs."[38] Magnates were satisfied instead with a 10 percent entertainment tax on tickets, first collected in June. "For instance, a fan who wants a reserved seat in the upper tier at the Polo Grounds must pay $1.10."[39] Admission to the lower tier rose from seventy-five to eighty-three cents, the bleachers from fifty to fifty-five cents, and there was a five cent tax on free tickets. It didn't seem such a bad deal to the fans or owners.

Business conditions were much tougher in the Minor Leagues, however. In the low Minors, especially, things worsened almost daily. Down in the North Carolina League, the Raleigh and Asheville franchises had dropped from the circuit two weeks earlier. Only the Greensboro club had enough cash to keep playing. When Winston-Salem went under, league directors met June 6 to wind down the league, twenty-four hours after Registration Day. "Lack of attendance on account of war conditions was noticeable throughout the league and for several days it has been a question of just a few more games."[40]

The Central Texas League collapsed the same day, although there hadn't been much hope for the four-club circuit in the first place. "The Temple-Corsicana club has been without a home for a week and some of the other clubs are not drawing sufficiently to warrant continuing the season," a Texas newspaper reported. "The Ennis club is reported to have disbanded today and the other two teams, Mexia and Marlin, are expected to follow suit or play independent ball."[41]

President Ed Barrow of the big Class AA International League tried to sound optimistic that other smaller circuits could keep playing. "Judging from conditions in our own circuit, it is my opinion that the minor leagues will pull through the present season without any trouble," he said. "I know it is hard for some of the small leagues, but they should go through if it is at all possible. We'll finish our season if it takes every dollar we have. We've gone through a lot of trouble. I guess we can stand a little more."[42]

The International League was hardly untroubled itself, however. The circuit was still recovering from the financial upheaval caused by the Federal League two and three years earlier. Its Toronto and Montreal franchises played in Canada, which had been at war for almost three years. The season's terrible early weather had affected attendance everywhere. While expressing confidence that his league would survive the current campaign, Barrow declared that no one could predict what might come in 1918. "Next year our ball players may be taken," he said. "It may be advisable to close our parks for a couple of seasons. In fact, some clubs would save money by doing that. We'll just have to wait for next season to see."[43]

In mid-June the head of the Class B Illinois-Indiana-Iowa League urged every league playing below Class A, including his own, to suspend operations after July 4. Such a step would have left only the five Class AA and A leagues still active, but Three-I president A. R. Tearney thought the war and the horrible weather made suspension advisable. "From the canvass I made," he said, "I do not think there is a small minor league in the country, with the possible exception of one or two, that will be able to survive the season."[44]

No circuit, not even Tearney's, publicly endorsed his suggestion to fold the lower Minors after the Fourth of July, but the summer holiday would nonetheless be a pivotal moment. Tearney also wired the National Association of Professional Baseball Leagues in New York for guidance. (The Major Leagues operated within the National Agreement of Professional Base Ball Associations, which had been revised several times since 1884, most recently in 1911. The Minor Leagues operated within their National Association, which had briefly been an independent organization before it also signed the National Agreement in 1903.) What happened to player and territorial rights, Tearney asked the National Association, if the Minor Leagues abandoned their schedules? Would rights be protected, or was everything up for grabs? League owners badly needed to know the answers.

Magnates in higher Minor Leagues than Tearney's also acted to offset deteriorating conditions. The Class A Western League bisected its schedule on June 29, with the first half set to end on July 22. The winners of the two campaigns would then play a seven-game championship after the regular season, which was lengthened by thirteen days. The move was akin to the modern Major Leagues adding wild-card teams to the playoff system, to boost fan interest late in the year and in the postseason. The Western also would move two struggling franchises to more profitable cities. President E. W. Dickerson rightly believed these multiple changes would strengthen his circuit. "The Western league juggled its schedule and split the season in half," a Seattle paper wrote afterward, "and in this way managed to arouse enough interest to weather the storm."[45]

On July 2 President Tearney received the decision he had requested from the National Association. The governing board ruled that the Minor Leagues' territorial and player rights would be fully protected if they couldn't complete their seasons. Any circuit wanting to suspend its schedule had to specify a closing date, however, and players thrown out of their jobs could sign on wherever possible for the rest of the season.

> The salaries of all players in the league suspending must be paid in full and such players must report to the club holding their contracts next spring. Territorial rights cannot be infringed upon, and even should the league suspend its schedule it retains all rights, and the circuit, geographically, must be considered as remaining intact.[46]

The ruling satisfied the Three-I president and arrived just in time for several other Minor Leagues. The little four-team Class D Northern League in North Dakota, Minnesota, and Manitoba had reorganized during the spring. It now suspended play July 3, the day after the ruling. "Lack of patronage has made the paths of some of the clubs rather difficult."[47] The Class D Dixie League completed its play on the holiday itself. "There has been a hard strain on the various small towns in the league, and it was decided to abandon the schedule and conclude the season July 4th."[48] Moultrie was declared the pennant winner.

The Utica club of the Class B New York State League collapsed after its holiday games. Three days later, the circuit dropped its Harrisburg (Pennsylvania) franchise. The New York State League also reduced rosters from fourteen players to twelve, cut team salaries, and reorganized schedules. In addition, like the Western, the circuit split its season in two and planned a championship series afterward. Somewhat bitterly, the head of the dropped Harrisburg franchise predicted that the league would pull through, but without posting a profit. "He is also of the belief that had the league president and magnates put the same efforts to take care of Harrisburg as they are doing to keep the league going there would be baseball in Harrisburg and an eight-club circuit, with all towns drawing paying crowds."[49]

Several members of the Utica team told of being denounced as "foul blackbirds" for refusing to play until they had been paid by the failing club. "One of us still is owed $25 from his May salary," their signed statement read. "None of us has been paid for June, with the exception of 50¢ a day, which we have drawn in order to eat, and other small amounts as we have been able. We mean to say that none of us has been given a full pay check for the month of June. The greater part of the check due June 15 is owed us, and all of the check due July 1."[50] The sad tale didn't surprise anyone familiar with Minor Leagues, especially in 1917.

In the Midwest, Tearney's Three-I League finally surrendered July 8. It was more of the same old story: "The clubs, in the eight weeks of playing, lost approximately $25,000. War conditions are blamed for the league's failure."[51]

The bad news kept coming. Only a week passed before another Class B league went under.

> The Northwestern league has been laid to rest in Seattle, not to be revived until after peace has been declared in Europe. . . . When the final game was played here Sunday afternoon, and the old Northwestern league gulped and went down like she had been submarined, it was a sad sight, indeed.[52]

The demise of the Northwestern League should have been particularly alarming for the Major Leagues, although few people in Organized Baseball took much note at the time. With circuits collapsing all across the country, Minor Leaguers abruptly thrown out of work in the Pacific Northwest began looking around for civilian jobs. The best nearby sources were the region's shipyards, which were increasingly busy with war work and desperate for workers—and, not incidentally, for good ballplayers for company teams. The Seattle Shipbuilders' League passed a resolution to let a player enter its games immediately. Previously a man had to be employed for a month before he could play.

The sudden change "makes several former Northwestern leaguers eligible for a doubleheader in Seattle this afternoon," a Tacoma newspaper reported in late July, naming thirteen men from the defunct circuit already playing for four shipyard teams. "Altho baseball is dead in Tacoma, Seattle fans will see during the remainder of the season a brand of ball practically as good as anything furnished by the Northwestern league the past season."[53]

One final suspension followed when the Class B Central Association shut down on August 7. The Central had struggled gamely along with just six clubs after the Clinton and LaCrosse franchises had withdrawn around Independence Day. "Then Cedar Rapids, a club thought to be one of the strongest in the beat, suddenly decided to give up its franchise. Clear Lake took over their franchise. The final blow came when Fort Dodge blew up."[54]

John B. Foster, editor of *Spalding's Official Base Ball Guide*, later wrote that several Minor Leagues had shut down for the strangest imaginable reason—prosperity. "It was not their prosperity, it is true, but it was the general prosperity of the United States at large." With millions of young men bound for the armed forces, factories and farms hummed to keep up with booming wartime demand. "There was no time to go to Base Ball; and yet there was more money to spend on Base Ball, if there had been the time, than the United States ever saw."[55]

Cumulatively, the numbers in the Minor Leagues were awful. Ten circuits with fifty-eight clubs had stopped play. Two leagues had reorganized and lost members. The Class B Texas League would yet drop two clubs to keep playing. Every league in Class AA was limping badly—the American Association had slashed expenses after the early bad weather; attendance was down in the Pacific Coast League; and seven of the eight clubs in the International were losing money.

The final domino had fallen, but that wouldn't be clear for some time. Only five of the initial twenty-two Minor Leagues would complete the 1917 season intact.

3

Buildup

Hank Gowdy was in the army now. The amiable Boston catcher left the Braves on June 27, earlier than either he or manager George Stallings had anticipated. Ironically Gowdy left because he was hurt—he had wrenched his leg in practice before a doubleheader in Brooklyn the previous day. Knowing he would be of little use to the ball club for some time, he decided to go home to Columbus and join his National Guard company. Teammates threw him a farewell party in the Ebbets Field clubhouse after they swept both games from the Dodgers.

"Now remember this. Don't forget the old pepper," veteran second baseman Johnny Evers advised. "I wish I was younger and didn't have this neuritis and a crabbed disposition, and I would be along."

"I bet it will be softer than working for Stallings," Gowdy joked. "It will seem like a vacation, almost."[1]

The *Pittsburgh Press* noted the catcher's departure with a poem:

So long, old boy; good-bye, good luck,
    A cheer to speed you on your way;
We glory in your Yankee pluck,
    Your willing spirit for the fray.[2]

To replace Gowdy, Boston brought up Arthur Rico, a young catcher from the Springfield Green Sox in the Eastern League.

Although the Braves briefly nursed hopes that their World Series hero might yet return to them for a while, Gowdy was gone now for the duration. He no longer worked for a general in Ohio, having transferred into the headquarters company of the Fourth Ohio Infantry. Closer to full strength than other Buckeye regiments, the Fourth had a distinguished history, a good reputation among regular army officers, and "outstanding scores for marksmanship."[3] Gowdy received a promotion, from private to color sergeant, a big jump in rank and prestige.

"When he first enlisted he was on Gen. Speaks' staff," the *Globe* informed fans in Boston, "but friends prevailed on him to get a transfer to the regiment. He says he likes the army as well as the National game. He now is promoting a game for the benefit of his company."[4] The popular catcher and his buddy, Color Sgt. George Foerster, "cared for the colors of the regiment during most of its service, and became regimental institutions."[5]

Entering federal service August 13, the Fourth Ohio became the army's 166th Infantry. While other Ohio regiments went south to Camp Sheridan, Alabama, to form the Thirty-Seventh Division, the 166th went north to Camp Perry, on the shore of Lake Erie. There it prepared to join the Forty-Second Division, an amalgam of units from twenty-six states and Washington, DC. The army created the Forty-Second in part to lessen competition between states to send their troops first into combat. Dubbed the Rainbow Division, it would become perhaps the most celebrated American division of the war. It was surely no coincidence that Ohio's most celebrated enlistee would wear the Forty-Second's colorful rainbow patch on his shoulder.

Without Gowdy, the Braves found military inspiration elsewhere. Aside from Brooklyn's brief military instruction at spring training, Boston was the only National League club to support Captain Huston's drill scheme. Percy Haughton, team president and co-owner and a former Harvard football coach, had long supported the preparedness movement. He had even taken his Crimson gridiron team into camp at Plattsburg, New York, in 1915. "We never really knew at Harvard what discipline was until after some of us had been at Plattsburg," Haughton said later.[6]

Braves manager Stallings had secured the services of Sgt. Perry S. Schofield as drill instructor once the regular season began. It was a good choice. "Sergt Schofield is the world's record holder with a military rifle at 500 yards. He made his record shooting at a bullseye 20 inches in diameter and scored 116 successive hits, and had not darkness intervened, he might have bettered this great performance."[7] Unfortunately, as with the American League teams, the Braves weren't firing at anything at all, not even paper targets.

The Boston Red Sox, too, finally greeted their drill instructor. Owner Harry Frazee had dragged his feet until Ban Johnson issued an ultimatum, threatening to secure a noncom for him. Sgt. A. B. Hoffman then joined the team in Chicago in mid-May. Hoffman had pitched for and managed the army's all-star baseball team in 1914–15 and had actually tried out for the Red Sox in 1908. "He was some ball player, too. He was considered the best all-around player in the army and came very near joining the champions at that time."[8] Sergeant Hoffman's first glimpse of Boston came when he accompanied the Red Sox home from their road trip. "He urges the fans to be a little patient, and says that it is unreasonable for them to expect the champions to go through the maneuvers with the same smoothness as the other teams who have been drilling since early Spring."[9]

Hoffman spoke well of the Red Sox's military abilities throughout the season. Infielder Hal Janvrin, at least, showed an affinity for drill. "When Sergt. Hoffman is not on the job Janny, who used to be a company leader at English High School, takes the Red Sox regiment under his wing."[10] Many of Janvrin's teammates, however, were very reluctant soldiers. Brooklyn manager Wilbert Robinson had been right about them at spring training. During an August series in St. Louis, for example, the Boston players ran out on Hoffman when he was slightly late for a training session. "The drill master's failure to appear on the minute had given them just the chance they wanted," said the *Globe*. The paper concluded that the sergeant's restive troops had as much chance of capturing Ban Johnson's $500 drill prize "as Speaker has to overtake Ty Cobb for the batting honors."[11]

Given the team's resistance to army discipline, it seemed strange, indeed, when field leader Jack Barry enrolled in the naval reserve July 28. Barry had broken into the Majors in 1908 with the Athletics. Until Connie Mack broke them up in 1915, Barry dazzled fans with his play in Philadelphia's celebrated "$100,000 infield" with Eddie Collins, Stuffy McInnis, and Frank "Home Run" Baker. Now, in his first year as Boston's player-manager, Barry suddenly joined the colors. John Lane, Boston's club secretary, signed up with him. "Until yesterday Manager Barry said he had no idea of taking this step, and Sec Lane has been planning to enter the Reserve Officers Training Camp at Plattsburg," the *Globe* reported in some bewilderment.[12]

Perhaps theirs was a simple preference for having a solid deck under their feet rather than a trench's duckboards. Maybe they chaffed under the uncertainty. Barry's Selective Service number was near the top, which would have made a man anxious about his future. Still, no ballplayer had yet been drafted into active military service. Barry was thirty years old, college educated (Holy Cross), and married, and he might have wrangled a draft exemption, but never sought one. The Boston skipper offered a simple explanation for enlisting. "I have only one country," he said. "I have been drafted, and I consider it my duty to do all I can for my country. I'm no slacker. If I can be of any use, I'll gladly quit baseball."[13]

Thanks to his early enrollment, Barry would begin active service at a higher rank, yeoman first class, than most recruits who walked into a navy recruiting office later. Unlike Gowdy in the army, however, he wasn't expected to report for duty at the Boston Navy Yard until after the season ended—when, as it turned out, he would have plenty of company.

News of Barry's enlistment coincided with an equally surprising statement from Ban Johnson. The American League president urged professional ballplayers not to claim exemptions when called in the draft, even if September call-ups meant shortening the Major

League season or eliminating the World Series. Johnson spoke to sportswriters and reporters in New York:

> America is preparing to send two million men to France, and the baseball world must help. Ever since last March army sergeants have been drilling the American league players. Today they are well versed in military tactics. They have studied the war game with the same energy with which they have learned to play baseball.
>
> If the government calls the new conscription army to the colors in September the American league will be prepared to wind up the championship race immediately and turn over two hundred well drilled players to the army.[14]

Johnson's statement struck the wrong note with fans and commentators. "A twisting of words made it appear Johnson was of his own accord trying to wreck the progress of the current races in the two big leagues," the *Chicago Tribune* wrote later.[15] The league president's comment about an early shutdown was "regarded by those in the know as so much bunk," a Syracuse newspaper declared. "Ban was perfectly well aware that if the government felt impelled to stop baseball it would be stopped, with or without his consent."[16]

In contrast to the disinterest shown by the National League, the American League's military drills at the start of the season had proved popular and perhaps even useful. "It was a master stroke on Johnson's part, and the chances are he will keep his league together until the last minute," said the *Philadelphia Public Ledger*. "Then, why the talk of postponing the world's series?"[17] National League president Tener thought that President Wilson probably wanted to see the series played, but added, "Should he wish the games stopped, however, he will find us ready and willing to respond to any service in which he believes our men can better serve the country's interest."[18]

The White House quickly cleared any doubts about the 1917 World Series. W. S. Forman, sporting editor of the *Chicago Herald*, wrote directly to the president, asking whether he planned to shorten the season or scrap the series. Wilson answered through his private secretary: "The President asks me to acknowledge the receipt of your letter of July 28, and to say that he sees no necessity at all for stopping or curtailing the baseball schedules."[19] About the same time, also on Wilson's behalf, Secretary of War Newton Baker asked a gathering of college representatives in Washington to preserve collegiate athletics throughout the war.

Charles Comiskey was glad to hear Wilson's pronouncement. He now took a swipe at Johnson, saying that only the president of the United States, not of the American League, had the authority to cancel a World Series. "Baseball is a large and expensive institution," the White Sox owner added. "It hurts the game to have an advance man swinging around the circuit, howling calamity."[20]

Brooklyn owner Charles Ebbets expressed other worries about the effects that military service might have on drafted players. The years between ages twenty-one to thirty-one were often the entirety of a ballplayer's career. Subtracting two years for the army or navy "means vastly more than it does out of the life of a man in any ordinary pursuit which is followed from youth to old age," Ebbets said. "It represents one-fifth of his total earning period if he is good enough to last 10 years in the majors or big minors." Just as worrying to Ebbets was that a player seldom was able to return to Major League Baseball after so much time away. The Brooklyn magnate used Dodger pitcher Leon Cadore as an example: "Thus a player like Cadore, who has a number which indicates he will be called early, and who is just starting on a career at a big salary in the major leagues, may, after his two or three years in the army find himself incapacitated for fast baseball, and be compelled to start at the bottom of the ladder in some other occupation." Ebbets suggested that every Major League club play a special Sunday game to benefit the men drafted from Organized Baseball into the army or navy.[21]

The first active Major Leaguer called in the draft was Lawton Witt, Connie Mack's young shortstop. He received a notice August 2 to report to his local board in Massachusetts for a physical exam. Born Ladislaw Waldemar Wittkowski, and called "Whitey" for his very light hair, Witt had gone to the big leagues straight from boarding school in Vermont, where he played in the White

Mountain League. He had returned to the Athletics' lineup only the day before receiving his notice, after spending a month on the injured list. The A's stood seventh in the league standings at the time. "Lawton Witt is the first big league player to be called by the draft," a columnist noted. "Playing with the Athletics should be sufficient cause for rejection."[22]

Draft notices to other ballplayers followed. The Athletics were especially hard hit, with pitchers Winfield "Win" Noyes and Alexander "Rube" Schauer and third baseman Ray Bates ordered to appear before their local draft boards. "Our country always comes first," Mack said philosophically.[23] Still, no player was immediately sworn into service. Those willing to serve had months to prepare, and those determined to appeal their draft status had time as well. The country could hardly afford the delay, however.

Gen. John J. "Black Jack" Pershing, commander of the American Expeditionary Forces (AEF), had first met Gen. Henri-Philippe Pétain, commander in chief of the French army, in Paris that June. "More than ever, Pétain's sense of urgency made Pershing recognize that the war was close to being lost."[24] Despite the desperate need for American troops in France, the United States couldn't rush draftees into uniform for one appalling reason—it had nowhere to train them. Pershing recalled the situation in his memoirs:

> The actual construction of cantonments was not begun until nearly three months after we had entered the war, and even though the task of erecting them was accomplished in record time, some ninety days more had elapsed before they were ready to receive troops. Thus, it was, with some exceptions, practically six months before the training of our new army was under way. Even then several of these camps were not favorably located and training was seriously handicapped on this account during the fall and winter months.[25]

Fortunately, the situation was much different for regulars, enlistees, and national guardsmen. The government rushed these men into training and needed all experienced noncommissioned officers to instruct them. Sergeant Smiley's heady tour in the big leagues now ended. "Uncle Sam is calling in the army drill masters who have been putting the American league ball players through their paces," read a wire report. "Sergeant Walter Smiley, who handled the White Sox squad, was showered with presents by the players when he left August 20 to report for active service."[26] Thanks to the sergeant, the White Sox believed they would win the $500 drill prize.

The American League drill competition began the day after Smiley's departure, in Cleveland, where army officers reviewed the Indians and Athletics teams. Next came the Tigers and Yankees in Detroit, followed by the White Sox and Senators in Chicago, and finally the Browns and Red Sox in St. Louis. "Both the Chicago and Washington teams made a good impression in the drill, and their maneuvers were roundly applauded by the huge crowd," Washington sportswriter Denman Thompson wrote of the Chicago competition. "The Griffmen were on their mettle and, ably handled by Sergt. Dean, put up a snappy exhibition, remarkably free from even small, technical mistakes. The accuracy with which they executed squad movements and the machine-like precision with which they handled their 'guns' elicited spontaneous approbation from the thousands of uniformed men as well as the fans."[27]

In the end, lowly St. Louis rather than a flashy eastern club captured the prize, thereby demonstrating to their fans that "bad baseball does not equal bad marching."[28] The Browns were perfect in several military movements, losing only six points in drilling and one point for discipline. "The St. Louis players divided their prize money equally, each man receiving $20 and some odd pennies."[29] This equitable division, however, would later infuriate Captain Huston when he learned of it in France. "There is no excuse . . . for the miserable spirit shown by the St. Louis (American League) players who won the $500 prize for the best drilled team," he wrote. "It was suggested that they give the prize to the Red Cross. They refused and each individual pocketed the lucre."[30]

Finishing behind St. Louis, in order, were Washington, Cleveland, Chicago, Boston, Detroit, New York (no doubt disappointing Huston and Sergeant Gibson), and Philadelphia. An army lieutenant colonel praised the American League's program in his final report. "The sergeants deserve great credit for the results they have achieved in such a short time, and the ball teams are entitled to the highest commendation for the splendid manner in which they acquitted themselves."[31] Ban Johnson declared that the clubs in his circuit certainly would continue drilling in future seasons. Perhaps he even believed it.

Eddie Grant and Moose McCormick had drilled all summer in officers' training at Plattsburg. "Thru the training camp, Uncle Sam expects to secure eighteen thousand trained officers to be ready for the first army of conscription."[32] Grant served in the third New York company, McCormick in the fifth. "Eddie is up at Plattsburg, plugging away for a commission in the army," writer Dayton Stoddart reported. "Naturally we feel aggrieved that the Harvard graduate missed such a fine opportunity for publicity, but he never let go of a single chirp when he gave up law, or whatever he was practicing and started his grind."[33]

Freckled and jug-eared, a widower in 1911 after less than nine months of marriage, Grant had often looked morose in photographs from his playing days. But in a news photo from Plattsburg, he looked dashing and happy, jauntily smoking a pipe while wearing his uniform, puttees, and campaign hat. "I am going to try to be an officer," he wrote to a friend soon after reaching camp. "I don't know how much of a success I shall make of it. I had determined from the start to be in this war if it came to us, and if I am not successful as an officer I shall enlist as a private, for I believe there is no greater duty that I owe for being that which I am—an American citizen."[34]

New York newspapermen seldom reported from the upstate camp without mentioning both Grant and McCormick, usually in the same paragraph. The old Giants teammates had illustrious company at Plattsburg. Theodore Roosevelt's sons Theodore Jr. and Archibald were there, a major and lieutenant, respectively. Brother Kermit Roosevelt was present as well, in officers' training with Captain Huston's son, Arthur.

Grant and McCormick appeared in several baseball games at Plattsburg, but both had been away from the sport for some time, and neither played with much flair or drama. "Whenever they would come up to bat, everybody would say: 'Now they will bust it.' And neither one of them ever put the pill out of the infield," wrote Bozeman Bulger, now an army major.[35] Still, the pair drew a lot of favorable attention while in camp.

> It is men of this calibre and such amateur athletes as Frank Coolidge, of Yale; Dave Henry, of Brown; Sam Reid, of Princeton; Ray Snell, of Yale; F. Norris Williams, national singles tennis champion; W. E. C. Washburn, joint holder of the national doubles tennis title, and other college stars who have proved that clean living, systematic training and moderation are the greatest assets in making a good soldier.[36]

The two former Giants received their commissions August 15. McCormick received the single silver bar of a first lieutenant and was assigned to the 167th Infantry, the Alabama National Guard regiment in the Forty-Second Rainbow Division. Grant began a step higher with the twin silver bars of a captain. He was assigned to the 307th Infantry in the Seventy-Seventh Liberty Division, whose shoulder patch was a gold silhouette of the Statue of Liberty on a blue background. "The majority of officers and all enlisted men were from New York State and practically all of the enlisted men from the Metropolitan District."[37]

The two new officers reported to their respective regiments on Long Island, McCormick at Camp Mills and Grant at Camp Upton. Some days later, McCormick took in a Giants game at the Polo Grounds, where he ran into the Giants' former great pitching star, Christy Mathewson, now managing the visiting Cincinnati Reds. "McCormick and I got fanning about old times," Matty remembered later.[38]

Capt. T. L. Huston, meanwhile, was on his way to France. The Yankees' co-owner commanded Company A of the Sixteenth Engineers (Railway). Engineers shipped out first to build the infrastructure for the infantrymen who followed. "If an army of the size contemplated was to be put at the front," wrote the chaplain of a forestry regiment, "docks must be built; railroads laid; barracks, warehouses, hospitals, bakeries, refrigerator plants, and power plants provided; and trench timbers, dug-outs, and barb-wire stakes furnished."[39]

The Sixteenth Engineers sailed August 1 from New York on the *Tuscania*, a converted passenger liner. The transport grounded in a fog off Halifax, Nova Scotia, three days later, forcing ten days of repairs in the harbor. Huston's men were far luckier than troops who would embark months later, however. The *Tuscania* was torpedoed and sunk off Scotland on February 5, with the loss of 166 American soldiers and British seamen. The Sixteenth Engineers finally reached Liverpool August 23, crossed England by train, and landed at Le Havre, France, in a depressing rain four days later. Baseball fans learned of Huston's whereabouts in early September, without particulars.

> The gallant "Capt" sailed away a few weeks ago with a detachment of engineers. It was understood he had arrived safely, but nobody heard from him until one day this week, when his baseball partner, Col Ruppert, received a characteristic cablegram. It read something like this:
>
> "Have arrived somewhere in Europe. What ails those Yanks? Huston."[40]

Huston wrote to friends that he was glad to be overseas with his regiment—"a very capable body of men"—but was sorry he would miss the World Series. "We had a splendid trip over here, but can say nothing about it, except that it was chuck full of exciting events and thrilling throughout," he wrote. "We are located within easy touch of the firing line, and from indications are getting ready to start some big piece of work. . . . We occasionally see a Paris edition of a New York paper and hope to get it regularly hereafter, but the news it contains is very meagre. It does not give the baseball scores."[41]

Several past and present Major Leaguers had now either entered the armed forces or were planning to enlist. Former Indians, Browns, and Tigers catcher Jay Justin "Nig" Clarke had joined the marines in the summer. (Clark's wife had tried unsuccessfully to banish his racist nickname, a common baseball moniker at the time.) At thirty-four Clarke enlisted at Detroit "without disclosing his identity and it was some time later that the recruiting officers learned they had captured such a notable. When Nig was told that a little celebration was to be held in his honor at the Detroit ball park, he protested vigorously, but they made him go through with it."[42]

Ed Lafitte, a former starting pitcher for the Detroit Tigers and the Federal League's Brooklyn Tip-Tops, joined the army in mid-July. Now a dentist in Philadelphia, "Doc" was commissioned a first lieutenant in the Dental Reserve Corps and ordered to training at Camp Jackson, South Carolina. Dick Hoblitzell, the Red Sox first baseman, was also a dentist and expressed interest in following Lafitte into the dental corps. After initial rejection, he eventually would enter the army as a dental officer in March 1918.

Pitcher "Death Valley" Jim Scott, one of Sergeant Smiley's corporals on the White Sox squad, also hoped to earn a commission. He applied to a new officers' school at the Presidio in San Francisco. "Scott was formerly in the United States army. Asked about leaving the team in a crisis, he said his country's crisis was more vital."[43] Several St. Louis Browns players spoke of enlisting as well. Outfielders Yale Sloan and Bill Jacobson actually joined the navy, enlisting at New York during a July road trip. Like Jack Barry, neither man would be called to report until after the season. Rabbit Maranville, the Boston Braves' fine little shortstop, periodically denied reports over the summer that he, too, had enlisted in the navy; he would join Barry and several other Red Sox at the Navy Yard in November.

Most Major Leaguers, however, appeared to hope they wouldn't be forced to make a decision until after the season. But military service was clearly on their minds, especially with newspapermen and sportswriters constantly asking about it. Brooklyn outfielder Charles "Casey" Stengel, as usual, had a ready response.

> They tell me there's a lot of action on board ship, but if I would enter the navy I'd want to point and fire one of those big guns, and I must confess I don't know the first thing about it. Say, it must make a man feel great to know the shot he fired had crippled an enemy's sub. Just

like banging the old apple out of the lot with three on. But I hope they won't need us fellows until the battle out there on the diamond is over.[44]

Baseball sustained one important loss of a sort during the summer. The American steamer ss *Kansan* exploded July 10 off Belle Île in the Bay of Biscay, near the approach to Saint-Nazaire—whether from a mine or a torpedo, no one knew. (An unlucky ship, the *Kansan* had struck a mine off France and had nearly sunk in December 1916.) Hawaiian-owned and chartered by the France and Canada Steamship Company, the *Kansan* sank in six and a half minutes, killing four of the crew. Four thousand tons of steel went down with the ship. With the vessel, too, went Clark Griffith's first overseas shipment of baseball equipment. "Doubtless, the shipment comes as a godsend to the Twenty Thousand Leagues under the Sea," wrote Washington sportswriter Denman Thompson, putting the only humorous spin on bleak news.[45]

Costing more than $1,200, the lost gear had been acknowledged by General Pershing as "50 packages containing balls, bats and other baseball paraphernalia [shipped] to me here in France for the use of the troops."[46] Griffith later said that ninety sets actually had gone down with the *Kansan*. Each Bat and Ball Fund baseball set contained a catcher's mask, mitt, and protector, a first baseman's glove, three bats, twelve balls, three bases and pins, a rule book, and a dozen score cards. Although the YMCA also lost a consignment of baseball equipment worth $18,000 in the sinking, Griffith's loss captured greater attention.

> Manager Griffith is anxious to duplicate the equipment lost when the Kansan was submarined in order that the soldiers who followed Gen. Pershing to France may not be without the means to indulge in and enjoy their favorite pastime, but the cash remaining in the bat and ball fund will not permit of this being done immediately. More money will have to be forthcoming from the fans.[47]

Griffith fortunately had hedged his bets by not shipping all of his fund's baseball gear overseas on the ill-fated freighter. The manager now sent shipments domestically to Washington DC, guardsmen training in Virginia; to troops in other army installations as far away as Fort Benjamin Harrison, Indiana, and Fort Riley, Kansas; and to naval militiamen from New York. When Griffith suggested that Major League clubs might each want to plan a special Bat and Ball Fund Day in their parks, National and American League magnates readily agreed.

The first collection was August 5 in Cincinnati before a Reds-Giants game. "Griffith is hopeful that the collection will amount to several hundred dollars."[48] Chicagoans contributed almost $750 two weeks later at a White Sox–Athletics contest in Comiskey Park. An amateur game in Denver brought in $169.70. When Washington came to town August 25, nineteen thousand South Side Chicago fans turned out again to honor the visiting manager. "'Clark Griffith day' was a bigger affair than a city series game and closely approached in magnitude and enthusiasm a world series contest."[49] Soldiers passed through the stands, handing out contribution envelopes. Griffith and the two teams assembled at home plate to present seven sets of baseball equipment to soldiers and sailors about to go overseas. Similar events followed in parks across the Major Leagues as individual contributions and new requests for equipment poured in.

> The success of Manager Griffith's plan to raise funds for supplying base ball equipment to American soldiers, while very gratifying to him, has made him about the busiest man in seven states looking after the immense amount of work connected with the campaign, in addition to running his ball club. . . . Griffith daily receives letters from points all over the United States asking that balls, bats and gloves be sent to this or that organization of Uncle Sam's military service. It is manifestly impossible for him to comply with all these requests, not having access to the United States Treasury. He is doing the best he can, however.[50]

Jim Scott of the White Sox began officers' training in San Francisco on September 12. The pitcher had left Chicago on two hours' notice after his last-minute admission to the program. He reported for duty a day late, but officers at the Presidio said his desperate efforts to arrive on time "entitled him to some consideration."[51] When he joined the army, Scott possessed a season record of six wins and seven losses and an earned run average of 1.87, the lowest in his nine-year career. That same day the Chicago club stood atop the American League by fifty percentage points and ten games in the win column. "Among those mentioned in the athletic hall of fame after this war is over will be Death Valley Jim Scott who declared himself out of a chance to be in on the world series money when he quit the White Sox to join Uncle Sam's troops in training."[52]

Others deserved equal mention with Scott. Charles "Gabby" Street had been Walter Johnson's battery mate with the Washington Senators and had once famously caught a ball dropped from the top of the Washington Monument. Out of the Major Leagues since 1912, Street caught eighty-six games for the Southern Association Nashville Volunteers in 1917 at age thirty-four, "the sunny south proving beneficial in relieving him of the rheumatism which slowed him up toward the end of his service in big league company."[53]

Street was determined to get into the war once the Class A circuit ended its season September 15. "His caliber will be appreciated when it is set forth that before he could be accepted for service by the Army physicians he had to undergo an operation at considerable expense to himself."[54] The operation was minor but painful, perhaps related to his gnarled fingers, all but one of which he had broken at one time or another. By mid-November, Street was at Fort Slocum, New York, training with a regiment of engineers in the army's Gas and Flame Division. Promoted to sergeant, he would undergo further training that winter at Fort Myer, across the Potomac from Washington, before shipping overseas. The *Washington Herald* reported, "Charlie said that fourteen of his seventeen teammates of the Nashville club had joined the colors, and that the Southern league club would be practically out of commission this coming season unless the fans were willing to watch new material in its development."[55]

Chicago and New York comfortably led their pennant races as the season wound down in the Majors. The White Sox clinched the American League flag September 21. Clark Griffith, busier than ever, handed out baseball equipment at the Senators' Georgia Avenue park the next day. The recipients were drafted men from the District who were departing for training at nearby Fort Meade in Maryland. "I have given these supplies to soldiers in New York and Chicago," Griffith said, "but I have reserved Washington to the last. Today I hope to make my own boys happy."[56]

The Senators and visiting Tigers marched together to center field, where managers Griffith and Jennings helped raise the American flag. The drafted men, admitted for free to the game, "lined up a bit raggedly, but then they haven't started through the military mill yet."[57] Fans entering the park received contribution envelopes for the Bat and Ball Fund, which Boy Scouts collected later in large, papier-mâché baseballs. The grand total, much of it in quarters, was $366. Fans at the Athletics-Indians doubleheader in Philadelphia the same day more than doubled that amount, contributing more than $870.

Manager Griffith sounded pensive before the Washington game, overwhelmed by all that he had accomplished and by how much he had yet to do:

> I wish I could show to the public the letters I am getting constantly from various camps throughout the South and East. It would appear as if the whole country wanted me to provide baseball supplies. I am doing my best, too. I wish I had enough to outfit every company called to the colors, but it takes money and it takes time, and I'm limited in both. Taking care of my soldiers will be, I fear, my winter's work.[58]

The Griffmen ended their season in Boston, where on October 2 several thousand soldiers, sailors, and marines descended on Fenway Park for a final Bat and Ball Fund Day. The doubleheader drew only 1,892 paying fans, who contributed $154. "Between the games the Old Fox personally presented baseball equipment to representatives of the boys at the Navy Yard, Camp Burrage, Commonwealth Pier, Harvard Radio School, Bumkin's Island and other places."[59]

Although the Senators finished fifth in the American League, five games under .500, Griffith's reputation was never higher. "I have sent thirty thousand dollars' worth of baseball material to the training camps in this country and have just shipped one hundred complete baseball outfits to Pershing, to France," the manager wrote to Captain Huston overseas. Despite the loss of the *Kansan*, "I will have over there by spring all the baseball material the boys will need." Griffith separately sent two sets of uniforms just for Huston, with a few extra gloves and balls. "Give the Kaiser h—! Cap, and then come back and see the Yanks win the pennant in 1918."[60]

The National Commission, Major League baseball's three-man governing body in the era before commissioners, scheduled the 1917 World Series to open in Chicago on Saturday, October 6. Game 2 would follow on Sunday. The commission also arranged to have a thousand-word article cabled after every game to American troops in France. "The arrangements are such that the scores will be distributed to the Sammies as fast as cables, telephone and telegraph wires are able to operate."[61] In addition, the commission pledged 1 percent of its revenue from the series to Griffith's Bat and Ball Fund.

The White Sox took both games from the Giants in Chicago, Eddie Cicotte winning the first, 2–1, and Urban "Red" Faber the second, 7–2. Missing the World Series was tough on Death Valley Jim Scott in San Francisco.

> While his former White Sox teammates were battling with the Giants in the world's series today, Scott, a student at the officers' reserve training camp here, is at Fort Barry trying to concentrate his mind on rifle practice. Jim can't even get off long enough to watch the games on a score board.[62]

The teams then headed east for games in New York, October 10 and 11. The Forty-Second Rainbow Division was training at nearby Camp Mills, a tent city on Hampstead Plains near Mineola, Long Island. Hank Gowdy's 166th Infantry had arrived a month earlier from Camp Perry in Ohio. On the afternoon the World Series had opened in Chicago, Gowdy led his regimental ball team to a 10–3 win over the 165th Infantry (New York's old "Fighting Sixty-Ninth") in a charity game at the Polo Grounds. The color sergeant now attended Game 3 of the championship series in the same park.

Gowdy posed for photos in his khaki uniform with manager McGraw and a few of his Giants in their home whites. He was also given a gift, "making the seventh wrist watch that has been given to him since he enlisted. Hank is now said to wear wrist watches all over his person, so that anytime he wakes up he can tell what time it is without turning over, or anything."[63] The popular sergeant also circulated through the stands, helping Boy Scouts collect donation envelopes for the Bat and Ball Fund.

"It struck us that day that it was singularly appropriate for Lank Hank Gowdy to be there in that uniform; it seemed to us quite in line with his spectacular career, and it strengthened the appeal which the personality of Hank has always had for our imagination," sportswriter Damon Runyon recalled.[64] Assisting Gowdy and the scouts were Washington's Walter Johnson, Nick Altrock, John Henry, and Eddie Ainsmith, plus Rabbit Maranville and Johnny Evers from the Braves. Patriotic appeals didn't end in the grandstand or bleachers. The outfield walls were festooned with new ads urging fans to buy Liberty Bonds, the regular advertisers having given up their usual space.

The Giants won Games 3 and 4 in New York with shutouts, 2–0 and 5–0. Red Faber lost the latter game, with Giants outfielder Benny Kauff homering twice. The White Sox then won Game 5 at home in Chicago on October 13, with Eddie Collins breaking an eighth-inning tie with a single and Faber winning in relief, 8–5. Faber secured the championship for the White Sox two days later in New York with a complete game, 4–2 victory.

The World Series wasn't as lucrative as the magnates had hoped. Game 1 in Chicago was a sellout, 32,000 fans packing Comiskey Park and thousands more standing ticketless outside, but attendance at later games was disappointing, especially at the Polo Grounds.

Poor weather was partly responsible, the *Chicago Tribune* noted, but "it does seem as if there is a misunderstanding somewhere between fans and magnates."[65]

Many White Sox players used part of their winners' share of the gate receipts to buy Liberty Loan war bonds in amounts of $100 and more. Pitcher Joe Benz, who hadn't appeared in the series, spent all of his $3,666 on the bonds. American League umpires William "Billy" Evans (a future inductee into the National Baseball Hall of Fame) and Francis "Silk" O'Loughlin also invested the $1,000 they had earned for their work.

Unlike ordinary years, the season didn't quite end with the World Series. The White Sox and Giants played another game October 16 for the Rainbow Division on Long Island. Fifteen thousand soldiers took in the exhibition at the St. Paul School in Garden City. Chicago won again, 6–4.

> The extra meeting of the two contending World Series teams was arranged by the National Commission, which previously planned to have a game played at one of the great camps, either at New York or Chicago, the matter of location to be decided by the final game of the series. So Camp Mills was awarded the prize as the last game was played here. . . . Immediately after the last man was out whistles blew, bands began to play and two long khaki columns started to move in the direction of Camp Mills. No time was lost getting back from the field of sport to the business of war.[66]

In the same spirit, the Reds and Indians had played an exhibition game October 11 in southern Ohio. Thirty thousand draftee soldiers cheered them on an improvised diamond at Camp Sherman. "Such enthusiasm was shown by the boys in khaki and so persistent were the army officials in pleading that soldiers in other camps should have a like opportunity to see a major league team in action" that a group from the Cleveland team agreed to play several exhibitions for the Ohio National Guard regiments training at Camp Sheridan, Alabama.[67]

Seventeen Indians, including infielder Roy Chapman and star outfielder Tris Speaker, postponed personal plans and played without pay against soldier teams for a week in late October and early November. "Three other major league teams were asked by John B. Hebberd, in charge of recreation at the camp, but all refused." The big leaguers beat one soldier team 19–7. "Sixteen errors and thirty-one hits were made by the two clubs in the eight innings played, and practically every man on the Cleveland team took turns in pitching to the soldiers."[68] The Indians signed hundreds of baseballs and threw them to the soldiers. In true army fashion, however, they played before only ten thousand men while at Camp Sheridan, about a third of what they had expected, because many of the troops couldn't be released from training.

White Sox owner Charles Comiskey closed the 1917 big-league season with a flourish by sending pitcher Jim Scott a full player's share from the World Series.

> When Scott left the team just before the series to join the officers' training camp at Presidio, Cal., he was reluctant to go because he feared he would leave the team in bad shape. He even offered to give up this opportunity to become an officer, and enlist in the ranks as a private after the series was over, but Comiskey would not listen to it. Instead, he shook his hand and congratulated him, saying that he would not be forgotten when the spoils were divided. . . . While he was doing his bit on the coast, the players were doing their bit on the diamond, and the money was divided to include his share.[69]

On that note, the troubled 1917 season reached its conclusion. Many in both the Major and the Minor Leagues were glad to see it close.

4

Winter

Ban Johnson wanted to enlist in the army. In New York for the World Series, Johnson made his announcement at the Wolcott Hotel on October 9, surprising even his friends and associates. "As soon as the series ends, I intend to enlist as a private, and I expect to arrive in France within the next six weeks," Johnson said. "I had a talk with Gen. Carter in Chicago the other day, and told him that some time ago I had refused a major's commission in the quartermaster's department."

According to Johnson, Maj. Gen. William G. H. Carter, who headed the army's Central District, had offered to send him to Maj. Gen. Peyton C. March, who commanded the artillery. "General March is an old friend, and I want to be under him," the league president told sportswriters. "I shall enlist as a private and will be ready to handle a gun, pick, or shovel in the trenches. No, I am not joking. I mean just what I say, and in six weeks I'll be in the war."

Sportswriter Joe Vila asked whether Johnson planned to resign as head of the American League. "I will ask for leave of absence until the war is over," Johnson replied. "The American league can play ball without me, and it will be an easy matter to get some other man to run its affairs satisfactorily while I am away." Johnson insisted that he meant it.[1]

"I am through with baseball until the end of the war," he said after the World Series. "I'm going over to join Capt. Huston. I'll bet you a new hat I beat him into the trenches. The American league is well fortified against the future. Its business men can carry it safely through whatever business depression the war may involve. I am for the big German game—for America, for democracy, for France, for Belgium."[2]

Whether the army wanted him was another matter. "Johnson is 50 years of age and somewhat over weight, so it is doubtful if he will be accepted as a private," the *New York Sun* said. "He may get a place on Gen. Pershing's staff or in the Quartermaster's Corps."[3] The names of Ed Barrow, president of the International League, and Frank J. Navin, president of the Detroit Tigers, were floated as his possible successor. When Johnson visited the War Department on October 22 to offer his services, the *New York Times* obliquely noted the realities: "Mr. Johnson . . . told the officials that he would resign as President of the American League and otherwise qualify for a position. He offered to serve without compensation. He was told that the offer would be taken under consideration."[4]

By November Johnson's application was "pigeon-holed in the archives of the appointment clerk's office in the War Department," the *Washington Herald* reported, adding that "it seems that the government at Uncle Sammy's army factory could find no jobs which would fit the qualifications of the American League boss."[5] Johnson's quest to enter the army soon faded from the newspapers.

"There was not a chance for him to be accepted, and when he was offered a commission in a department of the service for which he was fitted by training and experience he refused to accept it," Governor Tener would say the following summer, when he and Johnson were again at odds. "My opinion is that if he ever goes to France it will be just as our victorious soldiers are marching down the streets of Berlin."[6]

Hank Gowdy, however, had now reached France with the Forty-Second Division. Most of the 166th Infantry, including Headquarters Company, had sailed from Hoboken on October 18 on board the troop transports *Pastores* and *Henry S. Malloy*, which had been built for the South American fruit trade. The ships crossed the dangerous Atlantic in convoy and touched at St.-Nazaire on October 31. The remainder of the regiment left the United States on the transport *Agamemnon*, formerly the German line *Kaiser Wilhelm der Grosse*, and reached Brest on November 16.

The first word the sports world received from the Rainbow Division came November 3, but not from Gowdy. "Harry McCormick, one time outfielder and pinch-hitter for the New York National League Baseball Club, has written a line to J. K. Tener, National League president, telling of his arrival in France."[7] That news came in a cablegram, as no letter could have reached New York so quickly. McCormick's division and regiment weren't identified because of wartime censorship. The former Giant would keep up a correspondence with the NL leader while serving overseas. In the spring McCormick would even ask Tener to supply baseball equipment for his company.

Sports pages noted Gowdy's arrival in France later in the month, again without saying where or with what unit. "Hank is entitled to more credit than probably is given him for enlisting early as he did, for if ever there was a home boy it was this same Hank," a Philadelphia sportswriter wrote. "During the baseball season he often got so homesick for a sight of his mother that he took a railroad jaunt of 500 miles just to spend an hour or so with her."[8]

The Sammies (as doughboys were often called) in France wouldn't learn of Gowdy's arrival until early February in the inaugural edition of the *Stars and Stripes*, a fine army newspaper published in Paris. Despite strict army censorship, the paper would print a feature on the catcher without once mentioning his last name.

> Lank used to be something of a baseball player. In fact, he's still on the rolls of a certain National League club and back in 1914 it was Lank's mighty swatting that won the world's championship for his team.
>
> Next to General Pershing himself and a few other generals, Lank is about the most popular soldier in France. When his regiment—once of the National Guard—comes swinging down the pike the sidelines are jammed with other soldiers who crane their necks to get a peek at him.
>
> Lank always carries the colors. He's now color-sergeant.[9]

Wartime censorship didn't last long in Gowdy's case. More than forty years later, columnist Westbrook Pegler remembered that the ballplayer "soon outscored all but Pershing in personal publicity. Pershing's name was the only one we could mention at will until Gowdy came along. The censors just had to make an exception of Hank and we made him famous all over again."[10]

The Rainbow settled in for additional training over the winter, learning how to fight the *Boche*. (The pejorative French slang was translated roughly as German cabbage or blockhead, but was rarely meant humorously.) As regimental historian R. M. Cheseldine writes, "The 42nd Division was too green to do any trench fighting in December 1917." The hardships included a five-day march of nearly a hundred miles across snowy France when the division changed training sites after Christmas. The men weren't yet in combat, but serving in the 166th Infantry was incomparably harder than working the count behind the plate in the National League. "Life in France that winter of 1917 was no picnic."[11]

In the United States, the flow of young men into the armed forces increased. Brooklyn pitcher Leon Cadore, mentioned by owner Ebbets as a player whose career might well be harmed by the war, left home while the World Series was still in progress. Teammates Jeff Pfeffer and Casey Stengel presented him with a gold watch from the team. Cadore caught a train for Camp Upton, in charge of dozens of fellow draftees from his district in Brooklyn. "A bag of two dozen baseballs and the promise of as many bats from President Ebbets, like Gunga Din's 'twisty piece o' rag and goat-skin water bag, wuz all the field equipment he could find' this morning after the party given to him by other men of the team last night at his home."[12] The first Dodger taken in the draft, Cadore hoped to attend the next Plattsburg camp and earn a commission.

In Boston Jack Barry reported for duty before Thanksgiving. Several ballplayers had followed his example and enrolled as yeomen in the naval reserve while the season was still in progress. "There are a few vacancies left in the Yeoman's baseball club at the Navy Yard," a *Globe* writer had quipped in August.[13] Others enlisted once the season was over. Four Red Sox reported for duty at the Boston Navy Yard on November 16.

"Jack Barry, manager and second baseman, and Chick Shorten, the utility outfielder, have been assigned to the office of Commander George G. Mitchell. The other two, Mike McNally, utility infielder, and Ernie Shore, pitcher, were assigned for duty at the office of Paymaster Goodhue."[14] Braves shortstop Walter Maranville soon joined them at the Navy Yard, after Boston mayor James Curley attended the Rabbit's rousing farewell party. Pitchers Herb Pennock and Lore "King" Bader and first baseman Del Gainer of the Red Sox came along later.

Red Sox outfielder George "Duffy" Lewis also enlisted, but he served on the West Coast as a chief yeoman. Although drafted for the army, Athletics shortstop Whitey Witt somehow managed to don navy blues as well. Red Sox outfielder Jimmy Walsh enlisted over the winter as a machinist. Arthur Rico, Gowdy's catching replacement with the Braves, signed up, too. Witt, Walsh, and Rico all served under Jack Barry at the Navy Yard. St. Louis Browns outfielder William "Baby Doll" Jacobson signed on at the navy's enormous base in Norfolk, Virginia.

The notion of ballplayers as navy yeomen didn't sit well with a few editors and columnists. *Sporting News* would become increasingly critical, but early on merely noted, "Yeomanry is not a fighting department of the navy, the work being largely clerical in navy yards and recruiting offices and it is the expectation that players who have enlisted in this branch may get furloughs next year, if war conditions permit, that will get them free to rejoin their ball teams."[15] The publication was right about the nature of the work—a yeoman's rating badge is two crossed quill pens—but Barry and the players always denied any intention of rejoining their teams before the war was over.

As the weather grew colder, baseball magnates increasingly fretted about prospects for their sport in 1918. The World Series had barely ended before rumors surfaced about combining the International League and the American Association, both Class AA circuits, and forming a new league with just four teams from each. "Such a merger is in the air, though President Barrow, of the International League, says nothing will or can be done until the annual meeting of his league in December. Several American Association magnates have been advocating such a merger for the last two years."[16] The idea soon expanded a bit further, as Fred Lieb confidently reported in the *New York Sun*:

> The creation of a third major league, through the amalgamation of the International League and the American Association, with a possibility of clubs in Chicago and Detroit, will be an accomplished fact before the winter is over.
>
> The idea is not to advertise the new league as a major league, but as a sort of semi-major league. It would have about the same strength as the late Federal League. Some of the men who will have franchises in the new league wish to start as a real major, but wiser heads see this cannot be accomplished over night.[17]

Many sportswriters believed the new circuit was inevitable. "There will be a third major league next season," one declared. "This is a practical certainty. . . . Not only will the American association and the International go out of business in 1918, but 50 per cent of the minor leagues will not toe the mark when the umpires call 'Play ball' next year."[18]

Several reports held that the proposed circuit, to be called the Union League, would be headed by Ed Barrow of the International. The clubs dropped and left in its wake reportedly would join some complicated merger of eastern and western circuits. The Class B New York State League, meanwhile, was said to be ready to close or suspend for the duration of the war. According to the *Washington Herald*, "President J. H. Farrell, with one or two of the managers, argued that, in the event of the continuation of hostilities between our country and Germany, it would be best to keep the league 'dark' in 1918."[19]

The immediate future of the minor leagues was at stake when the National Association of Professional Baseball Leagues convened for a three-day session in Louisville in mid-November. Several clubs in the American Association planned to oppose the creation of the new circuit. Other magnates thought that due to the unsettled wartime conditions, all Minor Leagues should suspend operations in 1918. In the end, the leagues remained intact. "The rival factions were brought together after the National Association of baseball leagues voted down, 11 to 2, a resolution at its convention today to redistrict the minor leagues of the country," the *Arizona Republican* reported. Barrow was unwilling to predict, however, whether the International would take the field in the spring. Other presidents were no more committal, but the National Commission promised to support the Minor Leagues in any way it could during the coming season. "The next season will be a serious one, both in the major and minor leagues," said chairman August "Garry" Herrmann, who was also the president of the Cincinnati Reds. "There will have to be retrenchment everywhere if we hope to exist. The minor leaguers need the majors and the major leagues need the minors."[20]

The phantom Union League had hardly vanished from the headlines before Ban Johnson unintentionally dropped a verbal hand grenade that exploded with terrible effect at his own feet. "Baseball cannot be maintained at its present high standard unless we can retain a fair proportion of the star players who have been developed by years of training," the American League president said the evening of November 21. "I consider eighteen men sufficient for any major league team, and if each manager were allowed to pick his quota of eighteen it would be his own fault if he fell below the major league standard." He later added, "And an unknown bench warmer might be a better soldier in the trenches than a star pitcher or a champion batsman."[21]

With these appalling comments, Johnson apparently was asking the government to exempt the Major League's top 288 ballplayers from the Selective Service draft. "That such a proposition was misunderstood seems natural in a war climate when so many men were serving in the armed forces," a biographer wrote decades later.[22] Government guidelines were still emerging, with heavy industries, agriculture, transportation, shipbuilders, and others all insisting on the importance of their manpower requirements. Johnson was immediately bombarded from all sides.

"I disagree absolutely with Ban Johnson," Clark Griffith said. "There should be no special exemption for baseball players as a class. Baseball cannot be put in a selected class. If any of my players are called in the draft I shall feel that they and the club together will be honored."[23] "Coming from Johnson, who declared he had made up his mind to serve the country in France, this announcement came as a shock to patriotic fans," said the *New York World*.[24] "Let Ban Johnson confine his remarks to his own league," added Governor Tener, the National League president. "I would not go one inch toward Washington to ask President Wilson or the Secretary of War for special favors for baseball. Should my club owners make any such request upon me I should walk out of this office and never return."[25]

Johnson's exemption remarks infuriated Yankees co-owner Colonel Ruppert. "That would be a fine suggestion for our club to indorse," Ruppert said. "My partner, Capt. Huston, is now in France, dodging German shells and helping his country to win the war. I certainly am not in favor of asking exemption for a ball player, while my partner is risking his life in the service."[26]

"That must be a pipe dream," Provost Marshal General Crowder snapped when he learned of Johnson's remarks in Washington. "There certainly is no warrant in the law for exempting baseball players from the draft, and there is nothing in the regulations to warrant making exceptional rulings for men liable to service who make baseball their livelihood. I have heard nothing officially about such a proposition coming from the baseball managers, and it is certain that exemptions for ball players can only be granted for cause, irrespective of their occupations."[27]

New York Sun sports columnist Dan Daniel got the last word by creating a fictional businessman, President Nicodemus Hassenpfeffer, who wanted eight hundred exemptions for workers in his American Pickle Works. "It seems to me that the issue is very clearly defined," the pickle magnate said. "Do the particular pickle fans of America want soldiers at the expense of their pickles, or are they ready to make the big sacrifice for the perpetuation of the American Pickle Works?"[28]

Overall, the reaction of fans, magnates, and columnists was devastatingly negative. The American League president was engulfed in the sort of modern media firestorm that was rare in 1917. "Johnson is being lambasted as few baseball officials ever have been," Fred Lieb wrote. "He has been offered the presidency of the In Bad Club and has been informed there will be no use in him declining the office. He has been elected by practically a unanimous vote."[29]

Johnson belatedly offered the explanation that he wasn't actually *requesting* exemptions for ballplayers. "I'm not asking any favors from the Government—get me right on this," he pleaded. "My suggestion that eighteen men on each of the major league teams be exempted was merely that—a suggestion." The draft law hadn't been designed to wreck any business, he added, nor did President Wilson wish it to happen. "Hence the time seems ripe for a discussion of just how the law would be administered to give baseball precisely the same safeguards that are afforded other businesses, no more and no less. . . . Exemption for eighteen men would still leave six men from each club in the American League for service and four in the National. My suggestion only represents what I believe to be the only condition under which baseball can continue."[30]

Ed Barrow vigorously backed Johnson's assertion of innocence. Barrow, Harry Frazee, and James Price, president of the International League's Newark club, had all been present in Johnson's office the evening he had spoken to the three newspapermen. According to Barrow, the American League president had simply joined in a discussion about three American League teams—Cleveland, Boston, and Philadelphia—that had lost men to the draft and about how the quality of play would decline unless players secured exemptions.

"Johnson did not say he would ask for the exemption of a single player. He referred to the players who had legitimate claims for exemption, and never for an instant intended to ask for any special favors," Barrow insisted. "His remarks were garbled and twisted around so that he has been made a target for shameful abuse."[31] Frazee, for his part, merely said later that he had been misquoted himself and that he disagreed with Johnson on the need for player exemptions.

A few others also defended Johnson. "I believe Ban Johnson's plan to exempt eighteen players from each team for army service may help to keep the game alive," said National Commission chairman Herrmann.[32] Connie Mack defended his league president even more vigorously. Mack pointed to Johnson's many accomplishments since the country had entered the war, including his support for Captain Huston's preparedness movement, Clark Griffith's Bat and Ball Fund, and the American Red Cross. "These men who are blistering Ban Johnson make me tired," Mack said. "Mr. Johnson has more patriotism in his right foot than many of them have in their hearts. Johnson has offered his services to his country in any capacity, without condition. How many of these men who are condemning Johnson have been near a recruiting office?"[33]

Captain Huston, too, offered a stout defense. It came months later in a letter from France, too late to do much good, although Johnson had never been his favorite person. "It appears to me that Ban was entertaining his New York friends, Ed Barrow and Jim Price, at a tea party and some one used the loose talk that generally characterizes such occasions," Huston wrote. "Although I differ with him radically in many things I know that there is no one more genuinely patriotic to the core in America than Ban Johnson. He is a great reader of history and from personal contact with the man I feel that his proffer of services to the Government was sincere."[34] Huston called attacks on Johnson's patriotism absurd.

Four days after his exemption remarks hit the newspapers, Johnson issued a thoughtful statement about the dark prospects for Organized Baseball in 1918. Ninety percent of big-league ballplayers met draft requirements, and the government couldn't wait for them to report for training at their convenience. "Such conditions will arise in 1918 and will result in great confusion in the great baseball family," Johnson stated. "The matter of maintaining a contest of keen interest that would appeal to the public seems impossible of accomplishment. We ask for nothing, but an interest that represents millions of dollars asks [for] wholesome advice on the subject."[35] He made no further mention of player exemptions.

The National League gave Johnson no support whatsoever. In December its owners approved a resolution urging ballplayers to enlist. After first stating that "it is our purpose to continue and foster [baseball] so long at least as the welfare of our country shall admit of its continuance," the magnates added that it was their wish "that the young and virile manhood of the profession of baseball shall offer itself unreservedly and enthusiastically to the service of the great league of allied nations in this hour of its need."[36] The resolution was widely seen as a slap at Johnson, but the rival league's owners suggested no mechanism for making it a reality within their own circuit.

Ban Johnson's reputation never fully recovered from his exemptions gaffe. Largely overlooked in the whole affair, however, was his even bleaker prediction about the Minor Leagues in the coming season. "I do not think there is a chance in the world that any minor league will go through the season," he had said, "unless there is a sudden realization among the club owners of the conditions that confront them and a greater disposition to curtail than has been shown as yet."[37]

Ed Barrow's outlook for the 1918 season wasn't much different. After heading the International League for seven years, Barrow resigned as president December 12. "I had no other alternative but to resign," he said. "I could not be expected to remain in office after a cut in salary of $5,000 [about $92,500 today]. I could hardly be expected to attempt to run a Class AA league on a Class B scale."[38] In February Harry Frazee hired Barrow as the Red Sox's new manager, replacing Jack Barry.

There was little reason for optimism. The 1917 season had been the worst for the Minor Leagues since the formation of the National Association in 1902. America's declaration of war in April "was the cruelest blow of all to the minor leagues, not one of whom escaped more or less serious damage from declining patronage due to the vast changes in social and business conditions inevitable to a state of war and to public absorption in the conflict."[39]

Several of the circuits that had suspended operations the previous summer were uncertain about resuming play in 1918. "Presidents of several minor leagues in the middle west are whole-heartedly in favor of putting baseball on the shelf for a year and possibly two.

They favor releasing all players and starting anew at the close of the war on a less expensive operating basis," stated the *Harrisburg Telegraph*.[40] Other hard-nosed discussions among the magnates included "consolidation of the Western, Central, and Three I leagues and the formation of two or three substantial organizations."[41] By Christmas, only eight of the twenty-one Minor Leagues that had played in 1917 (discounting the Interstate, which never started) said they planned to go again in 1918. Several of these eight were expected to reorganize.

The outlook was somewhat better for the Major Leagues. Attendance had fallen sharply at the start of the 1917 season, but returned nearly to normal by the end. "Under the circumstances this was a surprisingly good showing and affords convincing proof of the hold base ball, of the major league brand at least, has on the public."[42] Seven of the sixteen big-league clubs were believed profitable, the American League had earned high praise for securing army sergeants to drill its players, and no club had yet been crippled by the draft. Downplaying all the adverse news, *Spalding's Guide* wondered whether 1917 hadn't actually been a triumphant season, one that had "really demonstrated that an organized sport can live through times and trials which would have sunk unorganized sport into the oblivion of forgetfulness?"[43]

Very few fans, magnates, or writers, however, expected the same for 1918. "Facing the year which waits just over the crest, the two major leagues are up against the greatest uncertainty they have ever known," Grantland Rice wrote in his column from Camp Sevier. "Just what effect the draft will have on their talent and just what effect the first big casualty will have on public interests are things not to be figured until the actual test is made."[44] A newspaper in Cincinnati summed up the doubts about the coming season:

Of course, if the war should come to a victorious end during the winter or early spring it would undoubtedly be one of the greatest seasons ever known to the national pastime. But, if the Germans are still unbeaten next summer, the effect of the struggle will very likely be felt in the sports of the nation. Most club owners are anticipating a very bad year.[45]

5

Spring

In the third week of January 1918, Ban Johnson removed the player limit for American League clubs. Both Major Leagues had left their limits in place during the 1917 season: twenty-five per club in the American and twenty-two in the National. Johnson now believed that eliminating his league's cap would protect clubs that suddenly lost players in the Selective Service draft. "We are in the peculiar position of not knowing what will happen in the next draft," he said, "and it seemed inadvisable to keep in effect a ruling made for conditions unlike those now prevailing."[1]

Governor Tener attacked the plan and kept the National League limit in place. "Allowing any club that so desires to carry thirty-five or forty players isn't fair to the other clubs that cannot afford this extra expense," Tener said. "So the National League will try to help out the less fortunate clubs by not permitting the wealthier clubs to carry a lot of extra men."[2]

It was an unnecessary spat, a continuation of the interleague exemptions imbroglio of two months earlier. Few teams had any intention of carrying a full complement of players, let alone exceeding it. Instead, roster numbers in Johnson's American League would actually decline during the coming season. Talk of player limits before spring training, wrote one observer, was "only a whistling act to keep up courage."

Practically every club has made it known that not over twenty-five players all told will be taken south, which means that after the weeding out process few teams will consist of over eighteen men. Even the affluent Chicago National league club has stated that it will take but twenty-five men into camp. Charley Comiskey is one of the exceptions. Thirty men will be taken to Mineral Wells, according to Chicago report.[3]

Fred Lieb of the *New York Sun* believed that more players than usual would be competing for fewer spots, because the military draft hadn't yet affected Major League baseball as drastically as anticipated. "Instead of a shortage, there will be more players anxious for jobs this season than ever before," Lieb predicted. "The smashup of the minors has thrown a drove of players on the market. Should the International League fail to start . . . another 150 players will be searching for jobs."[4]

More Minor Leaguers were tossed into the market March 16, when the Class B Central League said it wouldn't take the field in 1918. President Harry W. Stahlhefer had previously pointed to the rising popularity of private automobiles and golf as contributing factors in the Minor Leagues' troubles, but his explanation for his circuit's closure now was simpler. "Failure of Springfield, Ohio, to finance a club is responsible, the prexy said."[5]

Seventy-six Major Leaguers were missing from the dugouts when the big clubs opened their camps that spring. The American League had lost forty-eight men to the armed forces, the National League twenty-eight. "Besides the major leaguers hundreds of minor and semipro players from all over the country have enlisted."[6] Sports editors printed long lists of ballplayers who had enlisted or been drafted, most of them since the World Series.

Death Valley Jim Scott was now a captain, commissioned in December. Many writers thought the army had been good for the White Sox pitcher. "The metamorphosis of Scott from an indifferent, carefree baseball player to an intrepid soldier of his country who takes his work seriously is one that has brought joy to the

Old Roman [Comiskey]."[7] The army soon assigned Scott to Fort Lewis, Washington, as an instructor teaching advanced arms to draftees. Not incidentally, he also boosted army baseball and athletic programs.

Infielder John "Dots" Miller, the St. Louis Cardinals' captain, and his wife both had joined the war effort shortly before Christmas. He enlisted in the Marines, while she joined the Red Cross as a nurse. People had speculated about Miller's baseball future after the Yankees lured St. Louis manager Miller Huggins to New York, but enlistment wasn't a path any expected. "Miller might have been manager of the Cardinals at $7,500 a year had he cared to slack."[8] Instead, he was wielding a rifle in South Carolina as the Cards headed to spring training in San Antonio. "When he established the monthly shooting record at the Parris Island rifle range on February 23, Johnny proved that he was as capable of putting steel covered rifle balls right in the centre of a bull's eye as he was in throwing the 'pill' to bases."[9]

The former redbird liked duty in the corps and resisted attempts to get him to play for a Marines baseball team in Washington. "I want to fight," Miller said. "That's why I joined this outfit. And now they want me to play ball. Can you beat such luck?"[10] An understanding general decided that Dots could stay right where he was. The ex-Cardinal would ship overseas late in the war, but wouldn't see action before the armistice. "I was soon enough to be too late," he would say ruefully.[11]

Several other Cardinals were also in the armed forces. Pitcher Marvin Goodwin, Miller's rookie teammate in 1917, had enlisted in the army around Thanksgiving. He was now learning to fly, news that *Sporting News* celebrated with a poem:

Twinkle, twinkle, little star,
Up above the world so far.
We will praise your pitching skill
If you "bean" old Kaiser Bill.[12]

Goodwin earned his commission in the Air Service after training in Texas, but like Miller he would be too late to see combat.

Retaining his reserve commission after the war, he would be killed in an army air crash in 1925.

Also learning to fly was Arthur Shafer, a former teammate of Eddie Grant and Moose McCormick. Nicknamed "Tillie," the ex-Giant third baseman was handsome, educated, wealthy, and notoriously shy. Shafer ostensibly had left baseball for a reason likely never heard before or since in the Major Leagues. "Arthur Shafer was too bashful to put up with the thousand and one perfumed notes which as a member of New York's greatest baseball team he continually received."[13] His notorious shyness didn't affect his flight or officer training in the navy, however. Stationed in San Diego, he also played a bit of navy baseball. Shafer later went on to the training station at the University of Washington and learned to fly seaplanes. He would be there still when the war ended.

The current New York Giants learned a bit about aviation, too. During spring training at Marlin, Texas, they played an exhibition game March 25 with a visiting team of army aviators. The $700 in proceeds went to the Red Cross. "A large number of officers came over from Waco to watch the game, several of them flying over," the *New York Times* reported. "During the game three of the machines did stunts above the ball ground, and one whiskered farmer concluded, 'They's so many things going on here that a country feller don't know which way to look.'"[14] The Giants visited the aviators' home field a few days later, where flying again featured in the game. Thirty or so planes soared over the diamond, performing stunts, spins, dives, and rolls. The baseball community, like the rest of the country, was fascinated by flyboys.

The list of Major League players missing from spring training went on and on. Pitcher Sherrod "Sherry" Smith of the Dodgers and catcher Joe Jenkins of the White Sox were at Camp Gordon, Georgia. "Having been originally drafted from the minor leagues to the majors, and then drafted from the majors to the Army, the battery has been drafted into the series of intercantonment games for the championship of Uncle Sam's fighting forces at home and abroad."[15] Infielder Hal Janvrin, who had aided Sergeant Hoffman in drilling the Red Sox in Boston, had enlisted in the Signal Corps and was now at nearby Camp Devens. Leon Cadore, the drafted Brooklyn pitcher, was working toward an army commission at Camp Upton. Nearly every club in the Majors had lost a handful of players and expected to lose more.

One man who *wasn't* greatly missed in training camp was Cincinnati Reds pitcher Fred Toney. The tall right-hander had won twenty-four games in 1917, second in the National League only to the Phillies' Grover Alexander. Authorities had arrested Toney two days before Christmas at his home in Tennessee on a charge of draft evasion—"the first black eye on the national pastime."[16]

Toney claimed that his wife, child, mother, stepfather, and sister were all dependent on the $5,000 salary he earned with Christy Mathewson's club. A district attorney believed otherwise. He charged that Fred hadn't lived with his employed wife for three years, "has contributed but little to her support, and, further, that his exemption claims were not supported by the facts."[17] A county tax assessor was also arrested and charged with conspiring in the fraud.

Freed on $5,000 bail, the pitcher got scant sympathy from fans or the press. One syndicated sports cartoon showed a well-dressed fan, labeled "Sporting Public," grasping Toney's pitching shoulder and declaring, "You are through!"[18] Toney likely received no great sympathy, either, from the dozens of former National and American Leaguers now in the armed forces, a number of whom were either already overseas or on their way to France.

Capt. Eddie Grant, for example, had sailed from New York on March 27 with the Seventy-Seventh Division. "The boat proceeded slowly, almost reluctantly, it seemed; the faces in the windows blurred and the Statue of Liberty was left behind," a division historian wrote. "What could be a more fortuitous omen than the Division's own emblem smiling a 'bon chance' as the Division sailed out to sea during the latter days of March and the first of April."[19] The Liberty Division crossed the Atlantic in convoy via Halifax. After touching in England, the New Yorkers crossed the English Channel and became the first division of the national army (primarily draftees, rather than regulars or guardsmen) to reach Europe. They would undergo additional training in northern France until mid-July.

Hank Gowdy was now at the front with the Rainbow Division in the relatively quiet Luneville sector of eastern France. "Yet it wasn't so quiet," observes historian Mitchell Yockelson. "The Germans were well aware that green American doughboys loomed nearby and sent artillery fire and the occasional raid to welcome them to the front."[20] The 166th Infantry's headquarters was no safer than anywhere else. "Being in HQ Company did not spare him, or anyone, what the rest of the regiment was enduring," historian Richard Rubin writes of a doughboy in another American division. "Everyone took their turns in the front-line trenches, and . . . the fighting often came right up to HQ; after artillery and machine guns, it was the enemy's top target."[21] Gowdy recalled years later, "Yes, they tried out a lot of ways of killing a guy in that war."[22]

The Boston backstop saw his first action in an early morning raid near Badonviller. So many 166th men volunteered to go that officers selected a few from each company, the Braves catcher among them. The March 10 raid went unopposed, a good introduction for green troops. "The positions were occupied in broad daylight by the Americans, after German evacuation. A German barrage later forced a withdrawal, but the Americans returned and now firmly hold the positions."[23] The Ohioans captured no prisoners and returned without loss. According to a regimental history, twenty-three soldiers received the Croix de Guerre, a largely symbolic gesture by the French for so bloodless an action. Limited by strict censorship, war correspondents made only veiled references to Gowdy.

"The athlete whose name was deleted in Sunday's despatches is a former baseball catcher. He is different looking in a gas mask and tin hat than he was behind a wire mask and in a baseball cap." Newspapers soon confirmed that this was indeed Gowdy. "Every outfit ought to have a few fellows like Hank," his colonel had once told a correspondent. "The boys idolize him and he's got 'em all stirred up with his proposed baseball teams. He helps 'em to forget the discomforts of war."[24]

All of baseball's popular army drill instructors from 1917 were now back on active duty. Contrary to his earlier assertions, Ban Johnson no longer planned to mandate drill instruction for American League clubs again in 1918.

"I was told by army authorities that the daily drills last season stimulated recruiting to a marked degree. There is no need of that now, because of the draft," Johnson explained. "We also believe the clubs will be changed about a good deal this season, as the players are called into the army, and we would not care to stage a poor exhibition."[25] Except for a similar paragraph or two on some sports pages, the end of Captain Huston's grand preparedness scheme went largely unnoticed.

Several sportswriters and columnists who had written about Huston and the drill sergeants in 1917 were gone from the sporting scene as well. Bozeman Bulger of the *New York World* now commanded the Second Battalion of the 306th Infantry in the Seventy-Seventh division. "He went through two training camps at Plattsburg, preceded by his experience in Cuba in the Spanish-American War, and his men think him the greatest Major of them all," said the *World*.[26] In France with Eddie Grant and the others, "Old Boze" was soon transferred to less arduous duty at AEF headquarters, riding herd on the war correspondents, among whom he had many friends. "While my work is really a big job, and I go all over France, along the line," he wrote later, "I have never yet got over the keen disappointment of leaving the old battalion with which I served so long."[27]

The roster of writers and editors wearing khaki also included Lt. Grantland Rice, Capt. W. P. McGeehan, and Pvt. Bucky O'Neil, all of the *New York Tribune*, and Lt. Jack Wheeler, whose syndicate circulated sports features and comic strips. Among a dozen or more other scribes who had or would enter the army were Nat Fleischer of the *New York Sun*, Al Jappe of the *Cleveland News*, James W. Gantz of the *Philadelphia Press*, contributor J. C. Kofoed of *Baseball Magazine*, and Harry Lewis of the *Atlanta Georgian*. Virgil Jackson of the *St. Joseph* (MO) *News-Press* and *Sporting News* would be severely wounded fighting in France shortly before the armistice.

Grantland Rice had left New York City the first week of December to enlist as a private in a National Guard unit from his native Tennessee. The columnist was thirty-seven years old, and everything he knew about the army he had learned as a teenager at military school. "Why I chose the Infantry I'm not sure, except that Kipling had made it all sound romantic and tough."[28] When the army changed his regiment's designation and purpose, he suddenly found himself in Battery F of the 115th Field Artillery. "Rice is only one of a number of baseball scribes who have gone into service—note that they enter the active service, too, taking their chances with the rest of the boys," *Sporting News* noted.[29]

Rice's friend Walter Trumbull of the *New York World* enlisted as well. The pair trained together at Camp Sevier near Greenville, South Carolina. Most of the men in their outfit were Tennessee farm boys, few of whom had ever left the mountains. "Is this France?" one teary, homesick doughboy asked Rice. Like Hank Gowdy, the sportswriter soon earned a sergeant's stripes. He and Trumbull were then commissioned second lieutenants and promoted to first lieutenants. Lt. Innis Brown, late of the *New York Sun*, also transferred into their battery. The sporting gunners were known in camp as the Three Inseparables.

"As a soldier, I was no great shucks," Rice wrote decades later.[30] He cheerfully conceded to his commanding officer during a field exercise that he hadn't the slightest idea what he was doing. Rice's greatest accomplishment at Camp Sevier was carving a baseball diamond from a green forest. Time permitting, he occasionally wrote his Sportlight column for the *Tribune*. Louis Lee Arms wrote a poem for his own column about Rice, writer Franklin P. Adams, and others who had left the newsroom and press box for the armed forces:

"And what about old Grantland Rice?
He used to write his stuff blamed nice."
"Oh, he's left to take a chance
At showing Kaiserbilly's bums
That they stand no chance when a Yankee comes.
He's going to France."

"He's going to France?"

"Yep, old man, he's going to France."[31]

By the time the poem appeared in early May, Rice was headed across the ocean with his battery, sailing on the transport *George Washington* and attached to the Thirtieth "Old Hickory" Division. His war service took an unexpected turn once he reached the other side.

Capt. T. L. Huston had left the Yankees in June 1917. Now with his regiment "somewhere in France," he kept tabs on Major League Baseball from American newspapers yellowing with age. What he learned from them made him violently unhappy.

One winter day, probably in February, Huston met George V. Christie, formerly of the *Brooklyn Eagle* sports department, who was serving overseas with an ambulance unit. The captain rashly granted Christie the sort of interview that boosts a writer's career, only to withdraw permission to quote him later after he cooled down. Huston instead composed a long interview with himself. At nearly two thousand words, the piece ran in the *Eagle* and other New York papers March 24 during spring training. It detonated with a bang that would have impressed Grantland Rice's artillerymen. "As I see it from this far-off lookout station," Huston wrote, "baseball wants to do its duty by the Nation and at the same time it naturally desires to avoid the sacrifice of its entire invested rights and property."

> Everybody but the men managing baseball sees the immediate serious situation to which America is exposed. If they don't wake up from their stupor and put the national game in its rightful place in the front ranks of all patriotic movements, events combined with public opinion will force them out and put others more alert in their places. This is no time to "four flush" with the public. Beware of trifling with the situation. It's loaded. . . .
>
> The small percentage of the proceeds of the World Series donated was ridiculous and really insulting to the Nation. At least 25 per cent. should go for patriotic purposes. This would tend to take away the

bad taste always left by this annual baseball financial orgy, which is fast becoming a menace to the life of the national game, for if not abated, some fatal scandal is bound to occur sooner or later. There have already been some close shaves.

The lack of patriotism shown in baseball circles is a disgrace. Very few big league players volunteered. We have Hank Gowdy's picture draped in a silk American flag . . . stuck on our Company A's bulletin board. I hope to personally greet him when he arrives over here. Not a person connected with the business end of baseball has volunteered. Ye gods, what a mortifying and shameful spectacle![32]

Huston also criticized large player contracts at a time when, in his view, austerity was the order of the day. He stated that the American League's drill program should have been the foundation for a civilian home guard. He predicted lower Major League attendance in 1918 and urged teams to play more benefit games for soldiers and sailors. Although he praised Charles Comiskey's Red Cross donations and Clark Griffith's Bat and Ball Fund, Huston thought most other magnates had fallen far short. "Up to August 1 when I left, the National had done nothing patriotic, but I hope it fell in line subsequently."[33] Huston suggested that Governor Tener might find useful employment in France as an intermediary between military and civilian officials and that Ban Johnson might help organize the YMCA's planned baseball league in Paris.

"Gentlemen, baseball will wag along a year or two without you," Huston wrote. "Thousands of families are doing without the husband and father, so fall in. If Garry Herrmann or others so desire I'll fix them up also." Although he believed that Major League Baseball would yet rise to the occasion, the magnate ended his extraordinary broadside with a warning: "But, men of baseball, reveille sounded for you long ago. If you are deaf to that call, the nation will sound taps for you, and you will hear it!"[34]

Reaction on American sports pages was immediate. "It is a safe assertion that the published interview is not as strong as the one originally granted to Christie, but, at that, 'Cap's' communing with himself cannot be said to be in any respect lacking in forthwith, downright language that few men in his shoes as club owner would have had the courage to use," Thomas Rice wrote in the *Eagle*.[35]

To Dan Daniel at the *New York Sun*, the missive "undoubtedly is the most remarkable document yet written by a major league official. Engaged in most severe and serious work with the Engineer Corps over there, . . . Capt. Huston has far more intense opinions about some things than it would be possible for us here to develop."[36] Nonetheless, Daniels largely agreed with him, as did many others.

"The Huston warning, written many weeks ago, proves but the more the farsightedness and keen perspective of this real patriot," Bill Macbeth wrote in the *New York Tribune*. "It may be true that when he spoke Captain Huston had not been informed of the response to arms of the many major league stars who followed in the footsteps of Hank Gowdy and Rabbit Maranville. His displeasure centred, however, on those in control of the administration of the game, and on that score, at least, he has every argument for vindication."[37]

Major League owners had little to gain by publicly criticizing an officer serving in France. "Efforts to obtain official comment on Huston's letter failed in every direction except in Flatbush," Daniel wrote. Dodgers owner Charles Ebbets, the Squire of Flatbush, defended his and others' donations to the American Red Cross and similar war funds and charities. "I do not think that Huston's remarks on that score were in good taste or that they were backed by any definite information," Ebbets said. "We certainly did as well as we could last year. We intend to do better this season—that is, if some of us do not go bankrupt."[38]

After the war, *Sporting News* would recall Huston's self-interview and other letters as "attacks on baseball charging it with unpatriotism almost to the point of treason." While keeping their heads safely below the parapet in 1918, Major League magnates were privately furious. The Giants even threatened to "kick the Yankees out of the Polo Grounds."[39] Caught uncomfortably between his partner and other owners in the league, Colonel Ruppert briefly thought about selling his portion of the New York club. He soon reconsidered, and the uproar faded from the sports pages. It would not be as quickly forgotten, however.

Nobody really knew what to expect, either on the field or off it, as the Major Leagues approached their 1918 season openers. Most clubs had lost multiple players to the draft and enlistments, and worse clearly lay ahead. Hugh Fullerton expressed the widespread uncertainty about teams' abilities to compete:

> We can figure the strength and the weakness of each club, but there remains the chance that the Nation will demand the services of many ball players before the season is finished. . . . Any club in either major league is liable to lose a vital element at any minute, which adds to the uncertainty of the races and gives an incentive to the trailing clubs to keep trying, hoping that the leaders will be crippled.[40]

Uncertainty on the business side was nearly as great. Charlie Ebbets's dark aside about possible bankruptcies echoed ominously throughout the spring. Louis Lee Arms in the *New York Tribune* reported from the Giants' training camp that four big-league clubs might not survive the season. "The big leagues are in a more impoverished condition than they have been in years, and there is no telling what may happen in view of the seriousness of the war situation," he wrote, quoting an unnamed authority. "I know of four clubs now that are financially on the ragged edge, and it may be that they will have to withdraw before the season is finished, though we hope not."[41] Arms suggested that the endangered quartet were the Senators, Athletics, Braves, and Pirates.

The situation in the high Minor Leagues was even gloomier. The International and New York State circuits both sought ways to survive another season. "I do not know now whether the State league will start again," President John Farrell admitted in early March. "The contracts were sent out by all the clubs in the circuit before March 1st, as it is necessary to mail contracts to the men before that date in order to retain their services."[42] As both the New York State leader and secretary of the National Association of Professional Baseball Leagues, Farrell was well informed about conditions around the Minors. His uncertainty about his own circuit's future was chilling.

Sportswriters correctly surmised that the New York State League was waiting to see what the equally troubled Class AA International would do before deciding its own course. Sports pages reported rumors that the larger circuit would disband and reorganize. Then late on the evening of April 4, at the Biltmore Hotel in New York, the circuits jointly announced what amounted to a wartime merger.

The new International was an eight-team circuit whose shortened season would run from May 8 to September 15. The directors elected Farrell president. The cobbled-together league included Baltimore, Buffalo, Newark, Rochester, and Toronto from the International and Binghamton and Syracuse from the New York State. The eighth franchise was Jersey City, a member of the International from 1912 to 1915, but without professional baseball in the two seasons since. The seven other International and State teams that had survived 1917 were dropped. Only two of these landed in lower circuits for the 1918 season: Providence in Class B Eastern and Richmond in Class C Virginia.

"The New International League—the Dr. Jekyll of the former circuit's Mr. Hyde—has been assured a most active career for 1918 and doubtless many seasons to come," Bill Macbeth wrote in the *Tribune*.[43] Each club would carry a roster of only fourteen players and the manager. "With the imminent passage of the Sunday baseball law in this State every city in the league with the exception of Toronto will be able to play Sunday games at home. Sunday ball is not permitted in Baltimore, but that club will play outside the city limits."[44]

Most big eastern newspapers wished the new International well, but many baseball insiders saw rough days ahead for the Minor Leagues overall. "The big minors are going to have a tough time of it," predicted Dick Kinsella, former owner of a Three-I League franchise, now a scout for John McGraw's Giants. "The fans prefer the high-grade baseball and will be glad to pay the difference to take a trip to see a big league team in action rather than stay at home and see a minor league squad perform." Kinsella laugh-ingly rejected the notion of creating new lower circuits, such as a proposed Illinois State League. "There wouldn't be enough peo-ple at the ball parks," he declared, "to fill a flatiron building shoe-shining shop."[45] He was just about right.

6

New Season

The 1918 season began April 15 with two games, Athletics versus Red Sox in Boston and Yankees versus Senators in Washington. The other half of the American League and all the National were set to open the following day. Unlike a year earlier, the weather was sunny and blue in Boston. Huge front-page articles about a furious German attack on British forces near Ypres, Belgium, reminded fans in both cities why each game featured a Liberty Loan bond drive.

"Germans Hurled to Death by Thousands without Gain," screamed the *Boston Globe*, which elsewhere identified seventeen New England soldiers killed or wounded fighting in France.[1] Russia had withdrawn from the war March 3 by signing the Treaty of Brest-Litovsk. No longer fighting on two fronts, the German army had shifted divisions to the western front. "Then, on March 21, the Germans launched their great offensive," historian Martin Gilbert records. "Were it to succeed, Germany could win the war in the west on the battlefield, as she had already won it in the east at the conference table."[2]

Babe Ruth threw the first pitch in the Fenway Park opener at 3:15. "It was a perfect day, but the great drive on the other side must distract from baseball," noted a visiting Philadelphia sportswriter.[3] "It was an unusual crowd," the *Globe* agreed. "You might call it a reflective bunch. They never failed to applaud a great play, but there was a sort of conservation of appreciation apparent."[4]

Ruth earned a 7–1 victory for Boston and drove in two runs before ten thousand fans. Red Sox second baseman Johnny Evers wasn't on the field or in uniform, having failed to sign with Frazee's club. "It is the first opening day I have not played in 17 years," he lamented from the grandstand. "I would have liked very much to go in, if only for one inning, just as a matter of sentiment."[5] Newspapers speculated about Evers catching on with the Cubs or Cardinals or even Jersey City, but the Trojan wouldn't play for any other team in 1918. He instead soon found useful war work overseas.

Woodrow Wilson skipped the Senators' home opener in Washington. An avid baseball fan, the president was detained by official business, another indication of the seriousness of the war news. A District of Columbia commissioner stepped in to throw out the first ball, which in grand tradition he bounced to Washington catcher Eddie Ainsmith. In addition to the usual array of dignitaries, the crowd of thirteen thousand included soldiers, sailors, and marines from nearby military installations. They all settled in to watch Clark Griffith's team face the New Yorkers in Miller Huggins's managerial debut with the Yankees.

The game began at the unusual hour of 4:00. The Senators announced that the games to follow would begin at 4:30. "It is the intention of the management ultimately to have the games get under way at 5 o'clock, allowing a full half hour for those fans who work in the government departments to reach the park after their offices close in time to see the games start."[6]

As in Boston, everyone in the capital crowd felt the war's presence. "Sergt. Harry Marshall, who in 1916 was giving his all for the French in No Man's Land, and who now wears the uniform of the American trooper, gave a stirring appeal for the sale of liberty bonds."[7] After the speech, Capt. Antonio Resnati, an Italian military aviator, swooped low over the Georgia Avenue stadium in a gigantic Caproni triplane bomber. "Capt. Resnati's liberty bond appeal was that of dropping liberty bond posters from an aeroplane not fifty yards above the athletes of both teams toiling in our national pastime."[8] Fan responded by buying $7,500 in bonds. The flyover was more successful than the Senators' effort, as pitcher

Walter Johnson faltered in a 6–3 loss. Tragically, Captain Resnati was killed in a crash during a test flight at an army airfield in New York only a month later.

Worse, another aviation flyover June 2 would end horrifically at the American Association ballpark in Indianapolis. A U.S. Army Curtiss biplane swooped over the field before an exhibition game between service teams, a major in the backseat dropping baseballs with banners attached to the four thousand fans watching below. "The machine was 500 feet above second base when Captain [Edwin] Webb 'banked' to drop the balls. Two balls dropped earlier had caught in the controls, and the machine refused to respond; it plunged to earth in a nose dive. Captain Webb was crushed by the motor."[9] Despite this odd tragedy, the tradition of military flyovers at professional baseball games had been firmly established at Washington, Indianapolis, Waco, and elsewhere.

After the openers in Boston and Washington, the rest of the big-league clubs started the season April 16. Grover Cleveland "Pete" Alexander made his pitching debut with the Cubs on the road in St. Louis. Alexander had come to Chicago in a blockbuster deal in December, the Philadelphia Phillies trading him and catcher Bill Killefer for pitcher Mike Prendergast, catcher "Pickles" Dillhoefer, and $55,000. Betting that Alexander would be lost to the army draft, "the Philadelphia front office carried off one of the most cynical acts in baseball history."[10] The wartime extravagance had also helped stoke Captain Huston's outrage in France.

The Phillies had good reason to think Alexander might soon be wearing khaki. Although unmarried, he had asked for a draft deferment on the grounds that he supported his mother and a brother at home in little St. Paul, Nebraska, population two thousand. His local board denied that request in January. "I don't want to be called a slacker and lay myself open to criticism," Alexander told the Cubs, "but I felt as if I should have been placed in another class."[11] He was now belatedly looking for options.

Alexander talked about joining the navy and called on the commandant of the Great Lakes naval training center outside Chicago. But conditions had changed since Whitey Witt had managed the army–navy switch several months earlier in Boston. The army was now ready to receive new draftees and was less likely to let any go elsewhere. Alexander telegraphed his draft board seeking permission to enlist in the navy, with very slim odds of receiving it. In more bad news for the Cubs, catcher Killefer's draft board in Paw Paw, Michigan, reclassified him from Class 4A to Class 1A.

The opener in St. Louis went badly for Alexander. The Cards pounded him hard, winning 4–2 on nine hits and seventeen total bases. Worse for Chicago's new pitching ace, his draft board officially denied his request to join the navy. "Alexander had all winter to join the navy if he wanted to," said a captain representing Provost Marshal General Crowder in Nebraska. "Our general orders are to release no registrants to the navy after they have been called for duty in the army, and there is no reason why Alexander should be taken out of his present quota."[12]

The pitcher now stood tenth on a list of twelve men in Howard County's April draft quota. Unless he could convince someone in Washington to let him don the navy's blue jumper, he was bound for Camp Funston, Kansas, at the end of the month.

As Alexander headed out of the National League, Fred Toney tried desperately to get back in. Cincinnati's big right-hander had gone on trial for draft evasion in Nashville on April 6 with four lawyers beside him. "One of the attorneys for the defendant said Toney would admit making all the claims as to dependencies set forth in the indictment and expected to prove the truth of them all."[13]

The proceedings ended in a hung jury after five days, the judge docketing the case for retrial during the next court term. Toney had landed in more trouble during the trial, however, when it was suggested he had crossed state lines with an underage girlfriend for what the law deemed immoral purposes. With his first trial still in progress, a federal grand jury returned an indictment charging him with violating the Mann Act, commonly known as the White Slave Traffic Act. Toney posted a $1,000 bond and was released pending still another criminal trial. Temporarily free of courtrooms, and not yet compelled to join the army or report to jail, he shifted his focus to keeping his pitching job in Cincinnati.

> Long appeals which are somehow getting into the newspapers are being sent to [Reds] President Herrmann, and all signed by Toney's legal representative. His present attorney, it seems, has ordered Toney to report to the Cincinnati club, but it does not appear that he is threatening any legal proceedings. . . . Nothing definite is coming from the Cincinnati club as to its disposition in the matter, but it is a good bet that Toney never will be seen in either that or any other big league uniform again.[14]

Nonetheless, Toney hadn't been convicted of any crime, and manager Christy Mathewson's pitching staff was much weaker without him. The Cincinnati club relented. "Toney was extremely lucky when the Reds decided to take him back," Joe Vila later wrote.[15] The pitcher returned to the Reds in winning form May 5, defeating Pittsburgh 3–1 in Cincinnati. It would have been a shutout but for an error. "Cincinnati's hope now seems to be Toney, who won his first start yesterday," Hugh Fullerton noted. "The big fellow, after settling his troubles with the draft board, reported and worked hard to get off the fat that accumulated in spite of his worries. Cincinnati must be considered a dangerous factor in the National league race because of the form Toney displayed against the Pirates."[16]

Toney tossed a shutout eleven days later, defeating New York, 3–0, again at home in Cincinnati. "It was the first time the McGraw men have been called upon to face a pitcher who, in addition to the equipment of slants, speed and slow balls which every big league pitcher is supposed to possess, had two Federal court orders up his sleeve," snarled the *New York Tribune*. "The Giants wonder why Uncle Sam hesitates in putting a quietus on this Toney in the form of an injunction which will prevent him from appearing on the mound against them until the war is over, at least. The other teams in the National League must feel the same about the matter as the New Yorkers."[17] New York would have reason to reflect on those sentiments two months deeper into the season.

Cincinnati's field boss also faced another major distraction, which had nothing to do with his troublesome hurler. Christy Mathewson's popularity and pitching triumphs, of course, far outshone any that Fred Toney could ever hope to duplicate. "Matty" had amassed a staggering 373 big-league victories over seventeen seasons, all but one of the wins for the New York Giants. The final victory had come with the Reds, which he now managed. There was no more popular man in baseball, and his remarkable reputation remains untarnished after a century.

"During the Winter Matty was at Camp Sheridan [Alabama] on a visit, and while there he played checkers with the soldiers at the YMCA hut. Thousands of youths at this camp revered Christy Mathewson as the idol of their boyhood days. He was a hero during his visit, and he was such a great attraction for the soldiers that the YMCA persuaded Matty to bring the Reds to the camp for their Spring training." The YMCA and the Montgomery Board of Trade had split the Reds' costs. "Because of the great personal favor with which Matty is regarded, his ball club will have a free training trip while the other major league clubs are expending thousands of dollars to get into shape in the South."[18] "There is only one fly in the ointment," the *Stars and Stripes* noted from Paris. "An Army officer will probably umpire the games played in the camp, which means the guardhouse for all kickers on decisions."[19]

Mathewson was just as popular with American troops overseas. Barely a week into the regular season, the YMCA asked him to leave the Cincinnati club and go "over there" to take charge of the organization's baseball operations in the American Expeditionary Forces (AEF). The official in charge of the Y's work in France said "the selection of Matty was made by popular vote, the majority of men in France considering him the most desirable man to take charge of baseball among the soldiers."[20] "Come On, Matty," *Stars and Stripes* urged in a headline.[21]

It was no small imposition to ask a manager to leave his club at the start of a season and take on an enormous new job overseas, but the YMCA badly needed the help. By May 1918 some seven hundred thousand doughboys were already overseas with the AEF, with tens of thousands more stepping off troop transports every week. In March, at the request of the government, the YMCA War Work Council had begun shipping a thousand gross of Louisville Sluggers to France from Kentucky—"The largest shipment of baseball bats in the history of the game," according to the *New York Times*.[22] "Their ultimate destination," added the *New York Telegram*, "is the Lorraine sector of the fighting front in France, where they will be distributed among the American troops."[23]

The Y wanted to keep the troops active and healthy when they weren't at the front dug into their trenches. The organization was therefore recruiting a thousand business and professional men to handle its war work, including a large number of athletic directors. Who better than Christy Mathewson?

"Special cables from those in authority urge you to come over with important relation to the promotion of baseball for the entire American Army," William Sloane, chairman of the National War Work Council, wired to the Reds manager April 24. "Such an opportunity has never been presented to any man. We are hopeful, if this appeal is placed before your management, they will see in it a chance to serve thousands of Americans, now enduring the terrific strain and make a great contribution toward winning the war."[24] Sloan added that he realized the financial sacrifice involved, and he asked for a personal meeting.

Mathewson and the Reds agreed to consider the proposal. "I think Matty can be induced to accept the offer of the YMCA, and for the National League I may say that organized baseball appreciates the honor of the call from our soldiers in the trenches," Governor Tener told Dr. George J. Fisher, the YMCA official sent to Cincinnati to talk with the manager.

The drama continued for several days. Some newspapers ran articles saying that Mathewson would go and others that he wouldn't, all amid speculation that Hal Chase would replace him if and when the skipper went to France. "He will leave the Cincinnati team if the YMCA can show him that his duty lies overseas, and the men there need him to help them to win," Fisher said. "The YMCA can show him, and a cable message has been sent to France today for confirmation of the original appeal made to Matty. If necessary to convince him that he is needed in France even General Pershing will be willing to add his plea to the call of his troops."[25] Hugh Fullerton recorded Mathewson's dilemma:

> Matty evidently postponed his decision until he could have a conference with his family and study the matter. Much pressure is being brought to persuade Matty that he really is needed in France, and also volunteers are rushing forward eager to take the job. The trouble is that there is only one Matty, and no one else in sport could get the same results. They might be even better in the work, yet Matty's name would do more for baseball among the soldiers than any dozen men's work could do.[26]

Despite the excitement, the scheme slowly fizzled before the Fourth of July without any announcement or denouement from either side.

"Matty never could find out exactly what he was to do when he got there," Tom Rice wrote. "Taking charge of baseball among the troops might have meant anything from dishing out bats and balls to organizing leagues or coaching players. He declined to accept, unless the duties were outlined more specifically, and eventually the matter was dropped."[27] The YMCA had also realized that France wanted soldiers, not civilian noncombatants. "Then, too, the French people, whose viewpoint in athletics is not in accordance with our own, may possibly misunderstand our whole idea, in which event there is possibility for unfavorable reaction," an official wrote to Mathewson.[28] The plan to send "Big Six" overseas quietly died.

As Mathewson stepped back, Johnny Evers stepped forward. The legendary second baseman had wanted to enlist like former teammate Hank Gowdy, but he had failed the physical examination because of neuritis in his arm. "Hank, I will be over there some way," he had promised Gowdy.[29] In early June Evers signed up with the Knights of Columbus to become what the *Syracuse Journal* called "the generalissimo of baseball in France." Like the YMCA, the Knights of Columbus was heavily engaged in volunteer war work and was sending uniformed officials called secretaries to work among the troops in the AEF. Evers was a perfect candidate. "The famous Trojan, who was recently retired as a member of the Red Sox, was asked to take the position of second base by Manager Jack Hendricks of the St. Louis Cardinals; but he said that he believed the work in France was more essential."[30] Evers and Mathewson both would be in France by fall, albeit in different uniforms.

Besides losing growing numbers of players to the draft and enlistments, magnates and managers faced another major drain on manpower: the heavy industries that were becoming increasingly vital to the American war effort. Seattle shipbuilders snapping up Minor League ballplayers set adrift by the Northwestern League in 1917 was a harbinger of what was to happen in the Major Leagues in 1918. Workers who held essential jobs in shipyards, steel mills, and munitions plants received Selective Service exemptions, a fact that hadn't gone unnoticed by ballplayers or hundreds of thousands of other American men of draft age. Only a month into the 1918 campaign, sports fans across the country began reading reports like this:

> A unique league has arisen in the ranks of baseball with the opening of the Bethlehem Steel Corporation Baseball League which played its initial game on May 11. The season will continue for twenty weeks and as the rivalry between the various plant teams is intense a number of famous major and minor league players, for the past and present, have been signed to alternate in serving the corporation in overalls and baseball uniforms. . . . Furthermore, money is no object in the plan to secure players. While it is not authoritatively stated, nevertheless, it has trickled through the trenches that from $200 to $250 has been offered to some of the big leaguers for each game played.[31]

"Backed by the millions of Charles M. Schwab and his personal stamp of approval, the Steel league . . . is now menacing the very foundations of the organization of baseball," another article stated.[32] As the head of Bethlehem's many operations, Schwab believed in providing off-hours entertainment for workers in the corporation's steel mills and shipyards around the country. In April 1918 Schwab was also appointed head of the U.S. Shipping Board

Emergency Fleet Corporation, which oversaw all American war-time shipbuilding. The steel magnate was now one of the most influential men in the country.

"Schwab handles athletes like he does everything else, with a six-cylinder force," said a newspaper in Pennsylvania steel country. "Mr. Schwab expressed himself very emphatically in favor of wholesome hardy sports like baseball which have all the allurements necessary to attract a spectator and furnish his husky riveters amusement. Not only that but he believes in building baseball plants at all ship building places. What if the big leagues do bust up? There's Schwab."[33]

The powerful Steel League fielded teams at the corporation's plants in Steelton, Lebanon, and Bethlehem, Pennsylvania; Quincy, Massachusetts; Wilmington, Delaware; and Sparrows Point, Maryland. As arguably the best industrial baseball circuit formed since America had entered the war, it was sometimes pilloried as the Steal League, "because it has been purloining, or at least attracting, a lot of major league material to it."[34] Competing directly with the Steel League for manpower and ballplayers was the strong Delaware River Shipbuilding League, centered in Philadelphia and Wilmington. Other shipyard leagues operated in New York, Seattle, the San Francisco Bay Area, and the Gulf Coast states. Numerous other industrial circuits scattered around the country included the Head of the Lakes–Mesaba League, composed of mining, steel mill, and shipyard teams in Minnesota, and the Copper League, a mining circuit in New Mexico. Anywhere that war industries operated, industrial leagues drew ballplayers from the Minor and Major Leagues. A few military ball clubs even took part in these leagues. The League Island Navy Yard in Philadelphia, for instance, was briefly a member of the Delaware River circuit. Fort Bayard played in the Copper League, while other army teams participated in factory leagues elsewhere around the country.

Yankees manager Miller Huggins, among others, protested what he considered unfair tampering by the big northeastern industrial leagues. "A half dozen players on my club have been approached by men who presumably are conducting the welfare work for the

Bethlehem Steel Company, and I have authoritative knowledge that players on virtually all the big league clubs who thus far have played on the Atlantic seaboard have received offers similar to those made to my men," Huggins charged. He added that one shipyard had offered a New York player more "to play baseball and learn a skilled trade than his American League baseball contract called for."[35] "I think organized baseball owes it to itself to ascertain precisely what inducements are being made our men to go to the ship yards in advance of their draft call by the government. It is a fact that the repeated offers from representatives of these teams—who, I understand, are to form a shipbuilders' league—is damaging the morale of our teams and contributing to the manifold difficulties of managing a major league baseball team in war time."[36]

Cleveland manager Lee Fohl understood why a ballplayer with dependents or other responsibilities might jump to a shipyard team. "I tell you it's a great temptation to put in the way of a young fellow who is a bit undecided what to do," he said. "And I don't wonder that quite a few of them have fallen for it. What should be done is to put a bridle on the men who have been responsible for offering such contracts. They are the ones most to blame."[37]

Only a few big leaguers worked in steel mills or shipyards early in the 1918 season. Former Pirates pitcher Al Mamaux, who began the year with Brooklyn, had a job at Bethlehem's Fore River plant in Quincy. Ex-Giants infielder Hans Lobert and former Phillies pitcher Charles "Chief" Bender played on the Hog Island (Philadelphia) team in the Delaware River Shipbuilding League. Starting pitcher George Mogridge, although widely reported to be joining a shipyard team as well, remained with the Yankees instead and appeared in forty-five games in 1918.

Other familiar names were sprinkled through the steel and shipyard rosters, and the list only grew as the season continued. Giants starting pitcher Charles "Jeff" Tesreau jumped to the Steel League's Bethlehem team in June. Widely criticized for apparently seeking to avoid the draft, Tesreau told the club instead that he was "disgusted with baseball and wanted to get in to some other business."[38] On the Fourth of July, after an argument with manager

Ed Barrow, it briefly appeared that Boston pitcher Babe Ruth had jumped to the Chester team in the Delaware River Shipbuilding League, but he returned without suiting up. The Chester manager said that Ruth had asked only to play for the team on the holiday.

Charges against Steel League and shipyard teams continued all summer. "Cannot something be done to stop these robbers getting players under pretext of helping win the war?" Frank Bancroft angrily wrote to Garry Herrmann in June. "It is a joke and I don't believe the heads at Washington would sanction contract jumping and slacking if it was put to them as it ought to be." The Reds' business manager fumed in a postscript: "The Kaiser may be rotten but doubt if he would harbor a lot of crooks and hate to believe the U.S. Government will."[39]

"Divers stars have been asked to name their own terms and the agents do not take one 'nay' as final," Dan Daniel wrote later that month. "We know of a player who was approached three times in as many days. He got rid of the pest by threatening bodily harm. A pitcher for one of the New York clubs has been asked to fill out his own contract to work for a shipbuilding team."[40] Likewise Yankees business manager Harry Sparrow received a tip before a July doubleheader: "Watch sharp for a man in a gray suit and soft hat, who will try to interview the Yankee players between games. He is a shipyard agent, and his name is Petty."[41]

The fact that most players wanted to stay with their Major League clubs to protect their postwar careers made little difference to the recruiters, Daniel wrote. "When the Reds were here on their recent trip the agents planned a wholesale raid on a scale never even approached in the palmiest of Federal League days." Asked both to jump his team and to recruit two teammates as well, Cincinnati journeyman infielder Lena "Slats" Blackburne "not only refused but he nearly annihilated the unlucky agent."[42]

The Steel League's biggest bombshell had landed May 14, just a month into the season, when slugger Joe Jackson abruptly left Charles Comiskey's championship White Sox. "Shoeless Joe" had sounded unconcerned only a day earlier after learning that he would be headed into the army with the next draft call. "Well, the old boy will be out there slugging the Dutchman pretty soon," he said in Philadelphia, where his club had just played Connie Mack's Athletics. "And if I ever draw a bead on one of them birds, it'll be all off with him."[43] He reported for work the next morning at Harlan & Hollingsworth, Bethlehem's shipyard subsidiary in nearby Wilmington.

> Originally Joe planned to do some painting for the shipbuilding company. He had been decorating the offerings of star pitchers so long that he felt he would make good as a decorator in the service. He had his heart set on this work, but after the boss watched Joe wield a brush in much the same way he twirled a bat, it was decided that as a painter Joe would make a wonderful INSPECTOR.[44]

Jackson landed his plum job despite the fact that he was largely illiterate. The Harlan yard fielded teams in both the Steel and Delaware River Leagues. The slugger joined the former and played his first game June 1. He was the first big name to jump to a shipyard or steel team. Ban Johnson, for one, wasn't at all happy at what the move portended. "The American League does not desire to impugn the motives of the players who have gone into this work. Some of them are patriotic," the league president said. "But if there are any of them in class 1–A, I hope Provost Marshal General Crowder yanks them from the shipyards and steel works by the coat collar, and places them in cantonments to prepare for future events on the western front."[45]

General Crowder's office soon announced that a draft exemption for employment in a steel mill or shipyard wasn't automatic, as many believed. "Exemption is granted only through the regular channels of the army, and there is no official knowledge of the Steel League's existence."[46] Jackson nonetheless kept his new job at the Harlan yard, as did a majority of the ballplayers who followed the outfielder's example.

The Steel League and other industrial circuits became known derisively as Paint and Putty leagues. Although the games drew surprisingly well—Delaware River contests routinely drew four or five thousand spectators—the players heard about their choice of

employment from the bleachers. A former Major Leaguer serving in the navy watched as several ex-Giants played for one of
the shipyard teams. "Nothing was too mean to call them, and if
they got a dollar for every time some one called them 'slackers' or
'trench-dodgers' they must have gotten round-shouldered carrying their money home."[47]

"A star baseball player is no more entitled to extraordinary draft
law interpretation than a bum checker player," Louis Lee Arms
rumbled in the *New York Tribune*. "Only an ignorant one, who has
taken too seriously the generous approval extended the successful
sports professional, would think of such a thing, and he, perhaps,
because of his obvious shortcomings, is less at fault than his more
mentally responsible tempters."[48]

Viewed as the first of the Major Leaguers who "deserted their
teams for bomb-proof jobs in shipyards or steel works," Joe Jackson
became the particular target of unhappy writers and fans.[49] *Washington Times* sportswriter Louis A. Dougher often referred to the
slugger as "Joe the Painter," a label that stuck in the capital.[50] All
season long, in any newspaper article listing ballplayers who had
landed jobs in shipyards or steel plants, Jackson's name inevitably
came first. None of the players was popular. Owner Charles Comiskey reacted angrily when two more White Sox, Claude "Lefty"
Williams and Byrd Lynn, followed Jackson into the shipyards.

"There is no room on my ball club for players who wish to
evade the army draft by entering the employ of ship concerns,"
Comiskey said.[51] The owner praised pitcher Red Faber's decision
to join the navy. "I told him I was glad to hear it—that he had my
well wishes. That goes for every player under contract to me who
wishes to join the army or navy."[52]

"It is not pleasant to be obliged to testify that professional athletes, on the whole, have not been disposed to yield ready service
to their country," J. B. Sheridan wrote in July.[53] The sportswriter
was hardly alone in his condemnation. A Massachusetts state leg-
islator launched an investigation of what he called "camouflaged
players" in shipyard leagues, "carried on the payrolls as painters
and who carry two pails of paint a day to the real workmen and

spend the rest of the time when they should be building ships on the baseball diamond." Declared the *Sporting News*, "The 'camouflaged player' is about to get his. It won't be because of any new moral sense awakened in those in charge of the ship yards, however. They may deny they know what was going on, but the evidence is against them. As is the habit of their kind when smoked out, they make great protestations of innocence but they fool nobody."[54]

Late in the summer, *Sporting News* ran one of its harsh satirical poems, this one about young athletes who hadn't entered the armed forces as the editors thought they rightly should do:

Some more bold, fearless ath-aletes of note
Have gone to captivate the kaiser's goat
    And save the world from Hun autocracy
By smearing gobs of paint upon a boat. . . .
The boy who stood upon the burning deck,
When all about him was a flaming wreck,
    Was out of luck—he could not smite the ball
Nor swing a brush and draw a big league check.[55]

"There is a chance for some reporter to dig up a whale of a story by starting his prodding in Washington, where the government auditors have their headquarters," Tom Rice fumed in *Sporting News*.[56] This and similar calls produced few damning facts, however. An Emergency Fleet Corporation official later said that, with few exceptions, ballplayers put in a full day's work in shipyard jobs like everyone else. "Furthermore, he praises the efforts that have been made to make baseball the main recreation for the ship yard workers and says an even more expansive sport program is being planned, to include soccer, football, trap shooting and other activities."[57] The corporation did prohibit hiring ballplayers "more for the purpose of bolstering up teams than to expedite the shipbuilding programme," and announced that it wouldn't reimburse any yard that offered large salaries as an incentive.[58] The Steel League also initiated a rule that a ballplayer had to be employed at least a month before he was eligible to play.

Among the few ballplayers actually yanked back out of a shipyard was Ed Monroe of the Yankees. The pitcher had appeared in nine games for New York in 1917 and one in 1918. "Monroe deserted Huggins several weeks ago and became a member of one of the teams in the Steel League," Joe Vila wrote in late July. "He was in Class 1A and presumably was anxious to avoid a call to the colors. But it turns out that Monroe couldn't save himself from a trip to the battle front."[59] When he turned to the Steel League for protection, Louis Dougher added, Monroe was "politely, but firmly, told that it had no further need of his services. Now he is awaiting the call of the bugle."[60] The pitcher never returned to the Majors, but played two postwar seasons in the Minors.

Such minor exceptions aside, Jackson and his ballplayer colleagues complied with federal law and worked legally in shipyards, mills, and factories alongside many tens of thousands of other healthy young American males. The country badly needed the steel, ships, and weapons they all helped to produce.

"The sports writers in the cities of Major League ball are 'riding' the Bethlehem Steel Corporation League hard, contending that the players who have deserted the ranks of O. B. ball for a job in the Steel league have done so for no other purpose than to escape the draft," the *Harrisburg Telegraph* stated. Writers and managers couldn't object when the draft took their players, the newspaper contended, but were quick to complain when anyone left to work in essential industries. "Do they for one minute think that it took them to call attention to the fact that players are seeking a refuge in the Steel league to evade the draft when the country is represented strongly by agents of the department of justice and secret service upon whom devolves the duty of ferreting out draft evaders?"[61]

A few people specifically defended Joe Jackson. "I can't understand why Jackson was placed in Class One A," E. A. Batchelor, a former Detroit sportswriter turned YMCA secretary, wrote shortly after the outfielder went into the shipyard. "There are many stars of the big leagues who are married and have many times the amount of wealth Joe processes who are in Class Four."[62]

After the war, in spring 1919, Fred Lieb would write about the injustice of what he called the "war hysteria which was so severe on shipyard ballplayers." He pointed in particular to what he considered unfair criticism from Hugh Fullerton and others of Pirates southpaw pitcher Bob Steele, who worked briefly in a shipyard before returning to the National League with the Giants. "Steele, a British subject, supports a wife, a 15-month-old baby, and a widowed mother. He had three brothers in the Canadian service, one of whom made the big sacrifice."[63] But all that was months in the future. While the war still raged in Europe, shipyard and steel mill ballplayers enjoyed very little popularity or support.

"Blue stars indicate on a service flag players who have gone into the service, gold stars indicate those who have lost their lives making the fight for civilization," *Sporting News* said. "If it were not that saffron might be mistaken for a gold color it would be suggested that 'yaller' stars be imposed on service flags to demonstrate the players that have left the club to work for the 'steal' league."[64]

7

Work or Fight

Nine days after Joe Jackson's unexpected defection in Philadelphia, Provost Marshal General Enoch Crowder handed Major League Baseball an even bigger shock. He announced a new draft regulation on May 23 that Americans everywhere immediately dubbed the "work or fight" rule.

"This regulation provides that after July 1 any registrant who is found by a local board to be a habitual idler or not engaged in some useful occupation shall be summoned before the board, given a chance to explain, and, in the absence of a satisfactory explanation, to be inducted into the military service of the United States," read the statement from Crowder's office.[1]

The government aimed the regulation squarely at poolroom loafers, gamblers, and men who worked in "bucket shops and race tracks, fortune tellers, clairvoyants, palmists and the like."[2] Beyond those who worked in such shady establishments, the new regulation also applied to ordinary workers who sold food or drink in public places; elevator operators, doormen, footmen, and other attendants; those associated with games, sports, and amusements, except legitimate performers in concerts, operas, or theaters; and domestic workers and sales clerks. It didn't matter whether men working in these occupations held low draft numbers or were in Classes II, III, or IV on the grounds of dependency. "We shall give the idlers and men not effectively employed the choice between military service and effective employment," the statement read. "Every man in the draft age at least must work or fight."

The provost marshal general said the ruling would affect ball-players if strictly enforced, but the War Department hedged: "No ruling as to whether baseball players or persons engaged in golf, tennis or any other sport come under the regulations regarding idlers and non-essential pursuits will be made until a specific case has been appealed to the provost marshal general's office."[3] The *New York World* estimated that, if applied, the edict would leave just thirty-six current players in the Major Leagues.

Organized Baseball was shocked. "The blow came like a bolt of lightning from a clear sky to most of the baseball men," Fred Lieb wrote in the *New York Sun*. "Baseball officials and executives seemed to think that if the Government cared to have big league baseball terminated for the period of the war all that would have been necessary would have been a suggestion to that effect last winter."[4]

League officials and magnates made the right sort of statements in response. In effect, they said that they would close their parks if necessary, but that baseball was still valuable to the country. "I do not believe the government has any intention of wiping out baseball altogether," Ban Johnson commented, "but if I had my way I would close every theatre, ball park and other places of recreation in the country and make the people realize that they are in the most terrible war in the history of the world."[5]

Detroit Tigers president Frank J. Navin was even more candid. "Such an order would cause us to close our park," he said. "The order would leave me Donovan as pitcher, Stanage behind the bat, Spencer at first, and Jennings at short. How does that sound for a pennant winner?"[6]

Baseball continued amid tremendous uncertainty. In Richmond the Virginia League launched its season the same day General Crowder dropped his bombshell, "the last organization under the jurisdiction of organized baseball [to] get under way," according to the *Washington Times*. "To-day's opening is unprecedented in the history of baseball, in that it is the latest ever held."[7] How long the

Virginia or any Major or Minor League would keep playing was an open question. Many believed that the work-or-fight edict signaled the end of baseball for the duration.

"The condition in the majority of minor leagues . . . has been usually precarious in that the scarcity of labor in the smaller cities has robbed these leagues of their week-day support," wrote Louis Lee Arms. "They have lived by Saturday and Sunday patronage alone, and no week passes without the discontinuing of some minor league race. While, generally, the playing personnel of the minor leagues contain either younger or older players than the majors, the Provost Marshal's order would in all likelihood cause those minor leagues that have been in operation to discontinue."[8]

It would have been more accurate to write that several circuits simply hadn't resumed operations for the 1918 season. But Arms was correct about the huge pressures on the ten Minor Leagues that had taken the field. Class C and D baseball had almost vanished, with only one circuit surviving at each level. Class B had three leagues and Class A only two. The highest level, Class AA, had three leagues, including the merged and still-troubled new International. The first of these final ten went under June 15.

"The addition to the heaping debris pile of Organized Baseball is the Blue Ridge League, which started with four clubs late in May, ran a couple of weeks and then decided to quit," said *Sporting News*.[9] The popular little Class D league had played only in Maryland and West Virginia, having lost two franchises in Pennsylvania. "Increase in transportation, inability to secure good players at fair salaries and other reasons, all of which were caused by the war, in an indirect way, prompted the moguls in their action," the *Washington Star* reported.[10]

Soaring transportation costs troubled all of Organized Baseball in 1918. The sixteen Major League clubs each traveled about ten thousand miles by rail during a season, with each player getting a sleeping-car berth. "Including the war taxes, it is figured that traveling expenses this year will total more than $170,000 for the two leagues, or an average of more than $10,000 for each club," a wire service reported. "It is believed that as a result of the new rates the clubs will decide to carry not more than 14 or 16 men on the road in order to save expenses. Under former conditions managers thought nothing of buying tickets for at least 20 players."[11]

The next Minor League to suspend was the Southern Association on June 29. The directors cited lack of interest, poor attendance, and the work-or-fight regulation, but others saw an additional influence. "The Southern was doomed by the placing of army camps and cantonments in the territory of every city in the league. The fans got so they liked the army games better than they did the league contests."[12] Since franchises and players fell under the so-called war agreement of the National Baseball Association, which defined a half season as a completed season under wartime conditions, all territorial rights were protected. Still, many players soon signed with other leagues. The Red Sox snatched three men from pennant-winning New Orleans. "While none of the three are .300 hitters, they are experienced fielders and immune from a call into the army."[13] The Pirates also signed three men from Birmingham, including outfielder and future Hall of Fame manager Billy Southworth.

Three more leagues fell in quick succession, their seasons also half over. The Texas, Western, and Pacific Coast International Leagues all quit the weekend following the Fourth of July. One Lone Star sportswriter believed that public perception had as much to do with the suspension of the Texas League as financial difficulties or other business obstacles.

> When ball players were placed in the class with the riff-raff of the country and made the objects of the remarks of some of the more narrow-minded individuals, it was decided by the magnates to take action and relieve any ill feeling toward the players of the Texas League. Baseball at the onset could not have been carried on for profit this season. This was known by those interested, but to help perpetuate the game during war time as recreation for the public, the venture was made in Texas.[14]

When news of the Pacific Coast International's impending shutdown broke in the Northwest, "members of the [Portland] Buckaroos were scurrying from ship yard to ship yard today seeking the best obtainable salaries."[15] The president of the Vancouver club wired Western League president Emerson W. Dickerson, offering his players, unaware that Dickerson's circuit planned to shut down as well.

The head of the Western's Oklahoma City franchise suggested combining several Western and Texas clubs into a new "Liberty league," but Dickerson insisted on protecting territorial rights and rejected the idea out of hand. "Organized baseball would not permit this," he said. "The suggestion should be considered as a joke."[16] Still drawing his league salary, "Dick" Dickerson later signed on as a war correspondent for the *Rocky Mountain News* and the *Grand Rapids News*.

The Class AA Pacific Coast League (not to be confused with the Class B Pacific Coast International) unexpectedly threw in the towel July 14. "Exemption boards in the two states in which the league operates—California and Utah—have ruled that the players are subject to the 'work or fight' rule, and the league has decided to abide by this decision rather than appeal to higher authorities," said a league statement.[17] The critical event, however, was the imminent financial collapse of the Vernon club, which the six-team circuit was unable to weather. "Magnates gathered hurriedly in Los Angeles . . . and found the situation so bad as regards Vernon affairs that, when it was coupled with the threats of the work or fight order, the draft and the ship yards, they concluded the jig was up."[18] Pacific Coast officials also mentioned the same poisonous atmosphere reported in the Texas League.

"The crowds were beginning to taunt the players with 'Why don't you go to work?'" Los Angeles Angels owner Johnny Powers told writers. San Francisco manager Charlie Graham said the situation was just as bad in the Bay Area. "Not only did the draft board rule that ball players must work, but a police sergeant with fifteen officers entered the ball grounds several days ago and asked every man between 20 and 31 why he was not working. . . . Then we got a telegram from Salt Lake saying that the draft board there had ordered all the players to work or go to war. Matters were getting tighter all the time."[19]

The league wrapped up its season with a best-of-nine championship series between frontrunners Los Angeles and Vernon, which also helped the latter club financially. Los Angeles won the series in seven games. For battalions of Minor Leaguers, however, failure or suspension of individual leagues no longer mattered, as was apparent in a statistic published about the same time in New York.

> When John H. Farrell, who is secretary of the National Association of Professional Baseball leagues as well as president of the International League, was in Rochester a day or so ago, he said that more than 800 minor league ball players were with the colors. Secretary Farrell's latest bulletin gives the names of more than two score of players who have recently enlisted or been called for service.[20]

The updated list of those who had entered the armed forces included ballplayers from twenty-four franchises around the country.

The United States meanwhile had held a second national Registration Day, exactly one year after the first. All American males who had turned twenty-one in the interim were required to appear. General Crowder didn't sugarcoat his message. "Many of these men [who registered in 1917] are now on the battlefields of France, and on to-morrow, the 5th of June, that voice will have found its echo when one million more will rally to their support," Crowder's statement read. "Those who are of such an age and condition in life that they may, without detriment to the economic support of the army, actively oppose themselves against our enemy on the European battlefields are indeed privileged. Most of the men who register to-morrow will be so classified."[21]

Ballplayers who had come of age since June 5, 1917, registered alongside everyone else. A month later, the National Commission advised all Major League clubs how their eligible players could request deferred draft classifications. "The Commission strongly recommends the use of an affidavit in every case and submits herewith a form that should be used after consultation with club officials, who will properly introduce and make the most of such other features, as the large number of dependents on the players and other such evidence that may impress the Board."[22] With so many players already gone, and more reporting for military training every week, the Major Leagues and the few remaining Minors waited anxiously for a definitive ruling on whether General Crowder's work-or-fight regulation applied to baseball. If it did, the future would grow far darker.

The situation seemed headed toward a resolution when a draft board in Fort Worth, Texas, notified Cardinals shortstop Rogers Hornsby that he must either take up an essential job or immediately be classified 1-A. The St. Louis club appealed the ruling and told Hornsby to keep playing until his case was settled. "Hornsby has received offers from several industrial plants to leave the St. Louis club, but he says he will stick to the profession that has made him famous as long as possible," the *Washington Herald* reported. "Hornsby is said to be drawing $7,500 in salary. He is the sole support of his mother. If he is compelled to seek essential employment, will he receive the same amount of money?"[23]

The case of pitcher James "Rube" Parnham also seemed a likely test. After two seasons with Connie Mack's Philadelphia club, Parnham now toiled for Baltimore in the International League. Although he was married and classified 4-A, his local board had ordered him to seek essential employment. "Parnham's case is a model on which the whole baseball matter may be threshed out. There are scores of ball players who come under the same conditions, and it would be an excellent way for organized baseball to find out just how far the government cares to go with the case."[24]

Events moved faster in the nation's capital than in either Texas or Baltimore, however. Another player emerged in Washington as the new central figure in baseball's work-or-fight drama. "Decision in the case of Eddie Ainsmith, the Washington catcher, who last night received a work or fight notice, will be taken as a guide by local draft boards throughout the country and definitely settle a question that has proved a source of great worriment to magnates as well as players," *Washington Star* sportswriter Denman Thompson wrote July 12.

Ainsmith's notification to engage in a useful occupation or shoulder a gun was served on him by local board No. 9 of the District, where he registered June 5, 1917, after the player had appeared before the board in company with Manager Griffith and, to show cause why his draft status should remain unchanged, stated that base ball was his profession, was the only calling in which he was fitted to earn a good living, and that if compelled to give it up a financial hardship would be worked on his dependents. Ben Prince, chairman of the board, and his associates, ruled that under the regulations, the only action open to them was to order Ainsmith to obtain more productive employment or be reclassified from 4A to 1A. There was one dissenting vote.[25]

Ainsmith had replaced Gabby Street behind the plate as Walter Johnson's regular catcher. The contrast between the two receivers seemingly was the stuff of melodrama. One man asked to stay home and continue playing baseball. The other had been fighting in France with the First Gas Regiment since the big German offensive in March. Still Ainsmith was a tough, amiable player who had caught more games for Johnson than anyone, and certainly was no courtroom villain. He was, however, perhaps unlucky in having supplanted popular, patriotic Street.

Ainsmith's appeal would go all the way to Newton Baker, President Wilson's capable and innovative secretary of war, who "looked as if he ought to be teaching Latin in some girls' academy."[26] Other players' appeals progressed at lower levels. A board in East Orange, New Jersey, considered the case of Yankees pitcher Joseph "Happy" Finneran. "Finneran, whose classification in the draft was 4A, . . . advanced the plea that he had a wife and child dependent upon him for support and that, being skilled in base ball alone, there was no other work he could do by which he would be able to support them as well. In consideration of this the board granted him permission to remain with his team and continue to earn his livelihood by playing professional base ball."[27] The Senators and the rest of baseball hoped Secretary Baker felt the same way.

As the Major Leagues awaited the big decision, Fred Toney popped back into the news. Still facing trials for draft evasion and violating the Mann Act, he was having a very poor season in Cincinnati. The New York Giants purchased his contract July 22 from Cincinnati, a move generally interpreted as an attempt by manager John McGraw to strengthen his pitching staff. "Were it not for his 1917 record, 'Muggsy' McGraw would not consider him for a moment," Louis Dougher wrote in the *Washington Times*.[28] Toney compounded his problems by trying to hold out for a portion of the purchase price, reportedly as high as $10,000.

"While the major league officials are trying to talk the Secretary of War into granting them a respite, Fred Toney balks at being sold by Cincinnati to the Giants," Dan Daniel wrote in wonder. "Especially is this hard to understand when that man is a pitcher who has lost nine games in ten starts and is confronted with the probability of making every start an early and winning one in shipyards and the like."[29]

Toney finally suited up for the Giants on August 1 to face Jim "Hippo" Vaughn and the Cubs at the Polo Grounds. "The first intimation that Toney was a full-fledged Giant and had finally signed the 'papers' was flashed to the press box when the big fellow walked in front of the grandstand to warm up."[30]

Vaughn and Toney had faced off in an epic game the previous season, in which each pitched a no-hitter through nine innings. Toney's Reds had then won 1–0 in the tenth. The New York papers stayed silent now about what sort of reception Giants fans gave their new right-hander. Chicago hitters ran Toney ragged as Vaughn threw a one-hit, 5–0 shutout. "Toney moves over the ground with just about as much grace as an army tank, and when the Cubs started to deposit bunts on the infield lawn, monstrous Frederick found himself getting in the way of his own feet."[31]

Vaughn beat Toney again four days later in the final game of the Cubs series, effectively ending the Giants' hopes of overtaking Chicago for the National League pennant. Toney next appeared out of the bullpen to face his old club, the Reds. He would ultimately win six games for the Giants and improve his record to 12-12 for the season . . . after which he still faced two federal criminal proceedings.

Baseball's anxiety over Secretary Baker's work-or-fight decision meanwhile continued for several days, prompting speculation that he might delay his ruling until after the season. "Relief from the suspense under which all connected with base ball now are laboring is what is most earnestly sought. No matter how it is brought about, it will be welcome," Denman Thompson wrote. "It is not merely the mental stress being suffered by men having their all invested in the game. The players who have only the diamond to rely on for the support of their dependents, who have received or know they soon will receive orders making it obligatory for them to find something 'useful' to do, are leaving their teams in increasing numbers."[32]

A decision on the appeal of Edward Ainsmith, order No. 1239, serial no. 1137, local board no. 9, District of Columbia, finally arrived July 19. In a long and thoughtful statement, Secretary Newton reviewed the history of the appeal and of the work-or-fight regulation itself. He addressed the three main arguments for excluding baseball from the regulation. Paraphrased, they were these:

1. Baseball was a large business that the regulation would destroy.

2. Ballplayers devoted so much time to attaining their high level of skill that they couldn't maintain their families' standard of living in other occupations.

3. Stopping the national pastime would cause social and industrial harm far outweighing any military loss from exempting players.

Baker rejected all three.

"The situation of professional base ball differs in no wise from other civilian peace-time business which by reason of the stress of war and its demands upon the industries and energy of the country must be content to bear whatever burden is imposed by temporary inactivity. . . .

It has been necessary for us in this country to institute processes of rapid industrial training, and it is quite inconceivable that occupations cannot be found by these men which not only would relieve them from the onus of non-productive employment but would make them productive in some capacity highly useful to the nation. . . .

The country will be best satisfied if the great selective process by which our Army is recruited makes no discriminations among men, except those upon which depend the preservation of the business and industries of the country essential to the successful prosecution of the war."[33]

The war secretary denied Ainsmith's appeal and affirmed the ruling of the catcher's local and district boards. "Base Ball Ruled a Non-essential," read a front-page headline in the *Washington Star*, echoing others all around the country.[34] "Base ball received a knock-out wallop yesterday," Denman Thompson wrote. "But although shaken from stem to stern and hanging on the ropes the sport has not yet taken the count and it is possible the magnates may take some action to continue the game even if it is but a shadow of its former self."[35] Dan Daniel believed the blow to baseball had been delivered from France. "It came from Major Til Huston, part owner of the New York Americans, in his now famous scathing rebuke to his fellow owners and his severe arraignment of the players and others connected with the clubs."[36]

With rosters in flux, numbers were hard to pin down. The National Commission had informed General Crowder privately in mid-June that of 309 active Major League ballplayers (an average of 19 per club), 258 fell under the work-or-fight order, "if the Amended Selective Service Regulations issued by you are to be strictly enforced."[37] Bill Macbeth of the *New York Tribune* now pegged the figures at 247 out of 318. "With comparatively few exceptions, all sixteen clubs will be completely riddled as the result of the ruling of the Secretary of War," Macbeth wrote. "Indeed, the Philadelphia National League club stands to lose all sixteen of the men now on its payroll."[38]

Fred Lieb put the figure slightly lower in the *Sun*, at 236, but was no more optimistic than Macbeth. "An attempt may be made to continue the league races with veterans over the draft age, and boys under 21, but such baseball would be 'major' only by courtesy," Lieb wrote. He estimated that at least 90 percent of the ballplayers were married, most with dependents. "A change in employment will mean a great monetary loss to the average ball player, the great majority of whom know no trade and can do little besides play ball." Clearly angry, the sportswriter fired a broadside at the government:

> Whether the baseball fan deserved more consideration from Secretary Baker was a question for the War Secretary himself to decide. It was a remarkable fact, however, that baseball was drawing better than it did last year, and the Yankees had visions of a banner season. Despite the fact that the club had lost five straight games, close to 12,000 persons paid to see last Thursday's double header with Detroit.
>
> A patriotic impulse to obey the Government's latest order seems to actuate all baseball magnates, but most of them cannot hide a feeling that the Government was unnecessarily hard on a sport which has served as the nation's summer recreation for the last generation, and all for the purpose of adding about 250 unskilled laborers to war plants.[39]

While expressing their disappointment, baseball's leading men delivered appropriate remarks to the writers. "I do not know if the game could be continued with men outside the draft age, and surely we do not want to continue it if that is not the will of the administration," Ban Johnson said for the American League.[40] "If it is the desire of the President that there be no more base ball I will gladly abide by his wishes," manager Clark Griffith agreed in Washington.[41] Cleveland owner James Dunn went further and announced the Indians' immediate shutdown. "We will play a double header with Philadelphia to-morrow and will then close the ball park for the balance of the season at least," Dunn said the day after the secretary's statement. "It is our desire to comply promptly with Secretary Baker's ruling on baseball."[42]

"If baseball comes under the classification of a non-essential occupation we will most gladly make the sacrifice of our business interests in the country's welfare," said John Tener. "We feel, however, some provisions should be made that would give us time to determine whether or not the clubs can proceed under the suggestion made by Secretary Baker or whether we will close out our business entirely, and we will request the War Department to make its ruling more definite as it concerns this point."[43]

Tener's point was pertinent and important. Secretary Baker hadn't said exactly *when* his ruling would take effect. The calendar was already three weeks past General Crowder's original effective date of July 1. Like Governor Tener, Brooklyn owner Charles Ebbets thought James Dunn and others might be moving too hastily to shutter the Major Leagues.

"It is hard to tell how many men will be taken by the application or how fast they will be taken, but in any and every event I am in favor of continuing," Ebbets said. "It will be found that in the long run the financial loss to the second division clubs will not be as great as might be supposed at first glance, and that will be atoned for by the protection of property rights and the heading off of law suits in the future." Ebbets suggested that clubs further reduce their rosters to seventeen or eighteen players. "It is sure that we are not going to play to empty parks, and as conditions adjust themselves we might do pretty nearly as well as if we kept on going on the present basis."[44]

Stars and Stripes in Paris wasn't interested in the exact date on which the work-or-fight order would take effect. Strongly influenced by Lt. Grantland Rice, shanghaied onto the paper from his artillery duties, editors no longer cared to cover sports at all.

Rice had landed with his battery at Cherbourg in the spring. "I started to the front with my bunch but didn't get very far before an order came through reassigning me to Paris and *The Stars and Stripes*," he later wrote.[45] He resisted the assignment the only way he could. "Lieut. Grantland Rice, hired to be sporting editor, promptly canned the sport page for the duration of the war and went off to report the front," an editor recalled, exaggerating only slightly.[46] Rice's version was that he had visited the front to learn what sort of sports news the doughboys wanted.

"Wandering around a day later from one battery or company to another we found that most of the troops, largely volunteers, were against all sport back home," he wrote in 1943. "They were bitter against star ball players, fighters and motion picture actors who had remained behind. 'Slacker' was the only word they used, heavily embellished. I reported the situation after a week's survey and the sporting page of the *Stars and Stripes* was promptly canceled."[47]

The army newspaper announced the shutdown in the July 26 issue. "Lieutenant Grantland Rice, the sport writer, himself recited the funeral oration for the sporting page when it was buried for the duration."[48] The piece was unsigned, but it reflected the style and elegance of Rice's old column.

> Back home the sight of a high fly drifting into the late sun may still have its thrill for a few. But over here the all absorbing factors are shrapnel, high explosives, machine gun bullets, trench digging, stable cleaning, nursing, training back of the lines and other endless details throughout France from the base ports to beyond the Marne.
>
> Sports among the troops must go on—for that is part of the job. Sport among the youngsters back home must go on—for that, too, is part of the training job.
>
> But the glorified, the commercialized, the spectatorial sport of the past has been burnt out by gun fire. The sole slogan left is "Beat Germany." Anything that pertains to that slogan counts. The rest doesn't. And that is why this is the last sporting page THE STARS AND STRIPES will print until an Allied victory brings back peace.[49]

Despite shuttering the sports page, Rice didn't successfully wrangle a return to his artillery unit until autumn.

In the United States, three of the four surviving Minor Leagues decided not to wait for clarification of the government's work-or-fight timetable. The Virginia League suspended operations after its games July 20, the day following Secretary Baker's announcement. "The players can't play to empty stands, you know," said an official from the Class c league. "And we cannot keep on under the present arrangement; it would be a matter of continually asking the sporting populace to patronize a thing which they do not wish to patronize." "Of course, allowance has to be made for the fact that the larger part of the crowds of last year has been drafted into the service," added the *Richmond Times-Dispatch*. "And the rest are, consequently, kept too busy to go to the games."[50]

The Eastern League and the American Association padlocked their turnstiles the day after the Virginia's action. "In view of Sec Baker's decision . . . there is nothing left for minor baseball leagues except to close up shop," said the president of the Eastern, a Class B circuit. "There is no doubt but that the Government considers baseball nonessential and we hasten to comply with the Government's wishes in this matter."[51]

By far the largest loss was the Class AA American Association. Only two weeks earlier, it had actively signed players from the shuttered Western, Southern, Pacific Coast International, and Texas Leagues. "As is generally known, the baseball business is anything but a success this season, due to the war situation," President Thomas Hickey had said, "but in view of the fact that our organization will go thru with its season we have decided to give the public the highest standard of the game possible."[52] Now his circuit, too, was finished.

"Secretary Baker's decision was a surprise to us," Hickey admitted. "We have had encouraging attendance and had expected to finish the season. Naturally, however, we will abide by the government's wishes."[53] The Kansas City Blues were awarded the pennant. "It is understood that the enforcement of the work or fight order against professional baseball players will mean an exodus of ball players from the American Association to shipyards and other war industries at Duluth and Superior."[54]

The only Minor League now left playing was the new International League, the reorganized and merged Class AA circuit that had very nearly not begun the season at all. Its leaders alone took time in deciding whether to abandon the field. "It was rumored in Newark that Joe Lannin, former owner of the Boston Red Sox and a baseball enemy of AL President Ban Johnson, had convinced other New International League team owners not to close shop, intimating that if the majors did, places would be made for their players in the International," Louis Lee Arms reported.[55] Lannin, perhaps the most influential owner in the circuit, later declared that his circuit "would finish the original schedule regardless of the present crisis in baseball."[56] The league owners voted July 25 at a special meeting in New York to keep playing. The circuit would, in fact, last out the season, although the Syracuse franchise would run into trouble the first week in August and be moved to Hamilton, Ontario.

As the last Minor League still operating, the International borrowed a tactic from the shipyard circuits and tried to turn turmoil in the Majors to its own advantage. With the Syracuse-to-Hamilton shift still in progress, Newark manager Tommy McCarthy sent telegrams to Cleveland outfielders Tris Speaker and "Smoky" Joe Wood and to Brooklyn pitcher Rube Marquard, offering them good salaries to finish the season with his club. "The International will stick and will be a real big league," McCarthy wired. "Better get in out of the wet while the getting is good."[57]

The Duluth team in the Head of the Lakes–Mesaba industrial circuit had tried the same tactic while the big leagues were still waiting to learn when the work-or-fight order would take effect. Officials of the Minnesota club fired off a telegram to Washington's Walter Johnson on July 24, offering him at least $300 per game to pitch for them if the Major Leagues disbanded. The pitcher was married with two small children and so was in Class IV of the draft. Telegrams also went out to Cubs pitcher Claude Hendrix and Browns catcher Hank Severeid. The league's Superior team likewise tried to recruit shortstop Dave Bancroft of the Phillies. Duluth's offer was but the latest of many that Johnson had already received from shipyard and steel leagues.

"I'd rather not talk about these offers I have refused," "Big Train" told sportswriters in St. Louis. "The other boys are getting them, and while I love baseball, I'd prefer to wait until we receive the decision as to the future of the game from Washington before I announce my plans. Really, now, I don't know what my future plans are." A Washington reporter saw it this way:

> It is not improbable that if baseball is declared non-essential Johnson will return to his home in Kansas and swing the plow on the farm. Walter has accumulated sufficient funds to carry him through life without worrying about the price of his breakfast tomorrow. Like many athletes, Walter is adopting a "watchful waiting" policy.[58]

Fig. 1. Capt. T. L. Huston pushed
his baseball preparedness program
in the early months of 1917. Huston
and Yankees manager Bill Donovan
participated in the military drills during
spring training. Library of Congress.

FIG. 2. Although often at odds with the Yankees' co-owner, President Ban Johnson enthusiastically supported Captain Huston's drill program for the American League. Library of Congress.

FIG. 3. Maj. Gen. Leonard Wood and Maj. Halstead Dorey supported Huston's preparedness program. They attended the Yankees' 1917 season opener at the Polo Grounds. Library of Congress.

FIG. 4. Sgt. Smith Gibson
(*right*) commanded the Yankees
as they marched onto the
diamond at the Polo Grounds,
led by Captain Huston (*left*),
Major Dorey, and Colonel
Ruppert. Library of Congress.

FIG. 5. Chicago White Sox
owner Charles Comiskey was
the first American League
magnate to adopt Huston's drill
plan. Library of Congress.

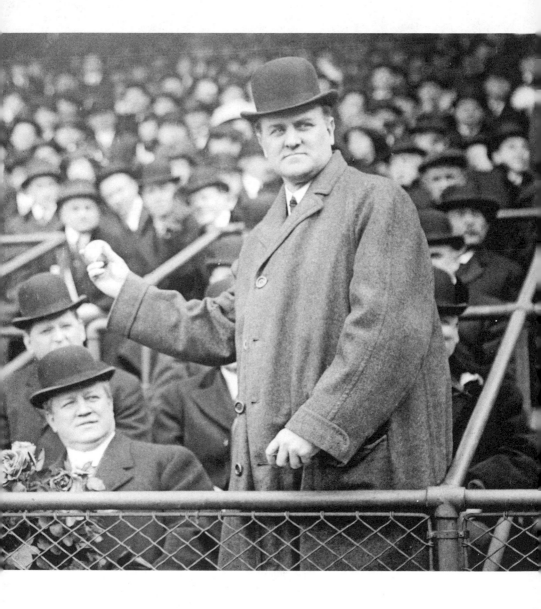

Fig. 6. Governor John Tener, president of the National League, neither adopted nor publicly opposed Huston's preparedness plan. Library of Congress.

FIG. 7. Clark Griffith, manager and part-owner of the Washington Senators, founded the Bat and Ball Fund, which grew much bigger than he anticipated. Library of Congress.

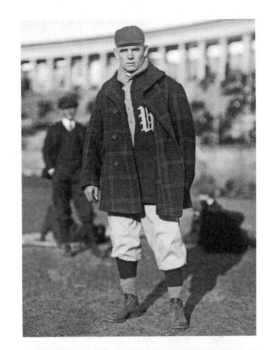

FIG. 8. Billy O'Hara, former New York Giant, was wounded in France serving with the Twenty-Fourth Battalion, Canadian Army. Library of Congress.

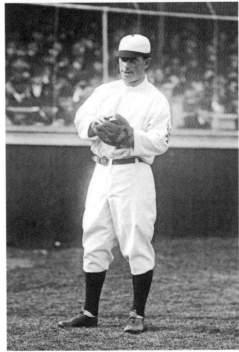

FIG. 9. Eddie Grant, former
Giants infielder, was a New York
attorney when America entered
the war. He became a captain in
the Seventy-Seventh Infantry
Division. Library of Congress.

FIG. 10. Harry McCormick, star
New York Giants pinch hitter,
trained with Eddie Grant at
Plattsburg before being assigned
to the Forty-Second Infantry
Division. Library of Congress.

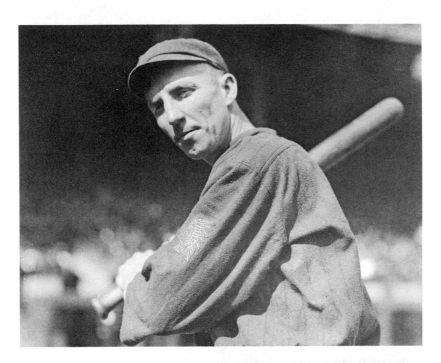

FIG. 11. Catcher Hank
Gowdy, batting hero for the
"Miracle Braves" in the 1914
World Series, was the first
active Major Leaguer to enlist
in 1917. Library of Congress.

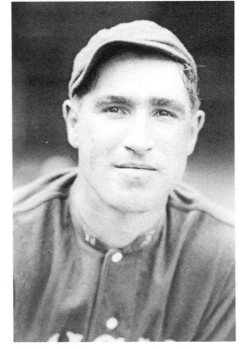

FIG. 12. Chicago White Sox
pitcher "Death Valley" Jim
Scott enlisted in an officers'
training program and missed
the 1917 World Series.
Library of Congress.

FIG. 13. Gabby Street, former
Washington Senators catcher,
underwent an operation to
enlist in the army after the 1917
Minor League season. Library
of Congress.

FIG. 14. The Chicago White
Sox, seen here walking into the
Polo Grounds, captured the
1917 World Series from the
New York Giants in six games.
Library of Congress.

FIG. 15. Hank Gowdy chatted with Giants manager John McGraw at the Polo Grounds during the 1917 World Series. Gowdy soon left for France with the Forty-Second Division. Library of Congress.

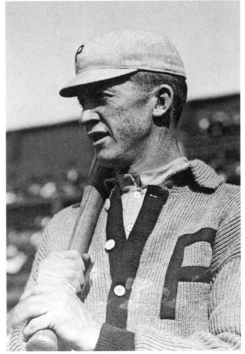

FIG. 16. Grover Cleveland Alexander was traded from the Philadelphia Phillies to the Cubs during the offseason. Chicago's gamble didn't pay off, as Alexander was drafted into the army early in the 1918 season. Library of Congress.

FIG. 17. Cincinnati Reds pitcher Fred Toney was arrested and tried for draft evasion and violating the Mann Act, but nonetheless played Major League baseball in 1918. Library of Congress.

FIG. 18. The YMCA wanted Cincinnati Reds manager Christy Mathewson to head its baseball operations in France. "Matty" is seen here with Red Cross workers. National Archives.

FIG. 19. Provost Marshal General Enoch Crowder's name was familiar to every young American male. His "work-or-fight" order profoundly affected the Major Leagues in 1918. Library of Congress.

FIG. 20. Secretary of War
Newton Baker approved the
"work-or-fight" order and helped
to determine the early start of the
1918 World Series. Library of
Congress.

FIG. 21. Joe Jackson, the Chicago
White Sox's great slugger,
shocked fans and magnates alike
by jumping the team to work
and play ball at the Harlan &
Hollingsworth shipyard.
Library of Congress.

FIG. 22. Charles Schwab, head of Bethlehem Steel and the U.S. Shipping Board Emergency Fleet Corporation, was among the most influential men in the country. He strongly supported shipyard baseball. Library of Congress.

FIG. 23. Walter Johnson and Eddie Ainsmith formed a strong Washington Senators battery. A shipyard league tried to recruit Johnson, while Ainsmith appealed his draft status. Library of Congress.

Fig. 24. Red Sox player-manager Jack Barry enlisted as a yeoman in the Naval Reserve. He managed an outstanding team at the Boston Navy Yard in 1918. Library of Congress.

Fig. 25. The Anglo-American Baseball League played in England in 1918. King George V (*left*) met navy team captain Mike McNally of the Boston Red Sox before the July 4 game at Stamford Bridge, Chelsea, as Adm. William Sims (USN) looked on. Jim Leeke Collection.

FIG. 26. Harry Hooper, the Red Sox's retiring captain, helped convince striking players to take the field for Game 5 of the 1918 World Series. Library of Congress.

FIG. 27. John Heydler, acting National League president, was another peacemaker at the 1918 World Series. He later permanently replaced Governor Tener. Library of Congress.

FIG. 28. German-born Sgt. Robert Gustave Troy (*left*) was killed in action on October 7, 1918, fighting with the Eightieth Division. "Bun" had pitched one game for the Detroit Tigers. Library of Congress.

FIG. 29. Johnny Evers (*center*), a
uniformed Knights of Columbus
athletic secretary, and Hank Gowdy
(*right*), of the Forty-Second Division,
chatted with American sailors in Paris,
summer 1918. Jim Leeke Collection.

FIG. 30. Sgt. Grover Alexander and
several other Major Leaguers fought
in France with the 342nd Field
Artillery. Roy Grove's illustration
was part of a larger panel about the
pitcher's war service. Jim Leeke
Collection.

FIG. 31. Lt. Col. T. L. Huston of the Sixteenth Engineers (Railway), after long service in France. Jim Leeke Collection.

FIG. 32. Color Sgt. Hank Gowdy, Forty-Second Division, posed for this photo at home in Columbus after the war. Note the division's famous rainbow patch on his left shoulder. Jim Leeke Collection.

A committee of baseball magnates called on Provost Marshal General Crowder in Washington on July 24, asking that enforcement of the work-or-fight rule be extended to October 15, which was after the date on which the World Series normally would end. General Crowder met with Secretary Baker later that day to give him recommendations. The baseball world then held its breath.

"This suspense is awful!" the *Washington Herald* sighed on July 26, when Baker still hadn't issued a statement. The newspaper hopefully pointed out that Baker had once been Cleveland's mayor and now lived in Washington, and perhaps he wouldn't care to ruin the pennant chances of either city. "The decision has been written and all it awaits is the Secretary's signature. No one knows definitely whether it's a death warrant or a lease on life—until the end of the present season, at least—for the sport."[59]

The suspense ended that evening. "I think it would be an unfortunate thing to have so wholesome a recreation as baseball destroyed if it can be continued by the use of persons not available for essential war service," Secretary Baker said in a long, well-reasoned statement. "It does happen that baseball is more integrated than any other occupation in our country, at least in the sense that its successful conduct depends upon the preservation of all the major league teams scattered throughout the country, while in most occupations the work-or-fight order has merely a series of local and more or less personal effects." Baker denied the magnates' request for an extension to October 15, but settled on September 1 as the date for the work-or-fight rule to take effect for ballplayers. "The decision met the baseball magnates half way," the *Washington Herald* concluded.[60]

"I suppose that the league seasons will close on Sept. 2, which is Labor Day and a legal holiday," said Cincinnati magnate and National Commission chairman Garry Herrmann. "The day after ball players will have to start to work. It is expected that all the ball players will have secured positions in essential industries by that date, so they will lose no time getting busy for the Government as soon as the season ends."[61]

The key word in Herrmann's statement was *suppose*. Again, no one knew exactly what Secretary Baker had in mind. This new uncertainty set off another conflict within the Major Leagues. "Ban Johnson, and those with him, want a world's series. The National Leaguers want a world's series. All the magnates want the money. So far, they are united," Louis Dougher wrote in the *Washington Times*. "Here steps in the interpretations of Secretary Baker's ruling. General Crowder forgot to provide the magnates with a map, suitably adorned with crosses showing where the body lay, and so the magnates don't know what it's all about."[62]

Johnson and the American League believed that the 1918 season, including the World Series, had to finish by September 1. In Johnson's view, this meant ending the season August 20 to leave enough time for the championship series. Governor Tener and the National League, however, believed that September 1 was the end date (extended by another day for the Labor Day holiday) only for the *regular* season, with the World Series to follow.

Compounding the problem was yet another dispute between Johnson and Tener, this one over the services of pitcher Scott Perry. In protest of Johnson's actions in the convoluted case, Tener for a month had refused to serve on the National Commission, effectively stalling all its functions. Hashing out a solution to the World Series was therefore bound to be contentious. The parties scheduled separate meetings—the NL in New York, the AL and the National Commission both in Cleveland. The fireworks erupted in the city on the lake August 3, when Johnson met unaccustomed opposition within his own league. Pittsburgh owner and emissary Barney Dreyfuss sparked the crisis when he arrived with precise instructions from the National League.

"My league has given me no alternative," Dreyfuss said. "We intend to play through Labor day. If the American league quits sooner, that's its privilege, but I can tell you positively there will be no world's series."[63] Three rebel American League magnates agreed with that view—Clark Griffith, Charles Comiskey, and Harry Frazee.

"If the club owners wish to take a chance on acting contrary to the ruling of the war department, that is their business," Johnson snapped back. The opposing trio retorted, "The declaration by President Johnson that we are taking a chance on continuing the season, inferring we were defying the war department, is an unwarranted misstatement of facts." They added in a statement that although Johnson had always acted honestly, "he has bungled the affairs of his league in this particular case. . . . He has tried to close our gates several times this season, but from now on he is through spending our money. From now on, the club owners are going to run the American league."[64]

When other American League magnates gave way, Johnson capitulated and agreed to play through Labor Day. It was a stinging defeat for the league founder and president, one that many sportswriters mistakenly believed he could not survive. Johnson found an unlikely defender in John McGraw, who thought he deserved better. "Johnson is big enough to take care of himself in the present controversy," the Giants manager said. "He is a smart base ball man and I can't figure how his enemies have a chance to down him. These base ball quarrels are unfortunate just now, when the game needs help from every one."[65] Nonetheless, if not the end of his long reign, the defeat in Cleveland was perhaps the beginning of the end of the Ban Johnson era.

The two leagues now hoped to begin the World Series on September 4. The date was later than Baker's order had seemed to indicate but a month earlier than in peacetime. "The continuance of only two teams beyond September 2 will be required," the National Commission said, "and as the series ends automatically when a team wins four games it is practically certain that not more than six games will be required, and at most eight or ten days will cover the time which the contesting players will lose in entering the Government's service or essential employment."[66]

In late August Secretary Baker granted a request from the National Commission and officially sanctioned the series. "I will write to General Crowder and tell him that I would be glad to have the local draft boards informed that I am in sympathy with an extension to the 15th of September for such persons as will be involved in the world series."[67]

There seemed little doubt all along, however, about which two teams would play for the championship. "This will . . . give 'dope-sters,' for the first time in their lives, a chance to pick a pennant winner in July," the *Washington Herald* commented on July 27. "For in the American league the Boston Red Sox hold a commanding lead, and in the National organization the Chicago Cubs are on top. If both clubs keep up their present pace, it looks as though they will meet in the annual classic."[68]

Governor John Tener wouldn't be around to enjoy the World Series as head of the National League, however. On August 6 he asked that his resignation as league president, first tendered in December, now be accepted. Sportswriters generally thought the request was helpful in difficult times. "The resignation of President Tener will clear up the involved situation in the National Commission and expedite the work of that organization in preparing for the proposed world's series, scheduled to begin September 3 or 4."[69]

8

Calibers

The number of Major Leaguers serving in the armed forces had risen sharply since spring and continued climbing during the final weeks of the shortened season. "It is almost impossible to keep the record of the baseball players in the service, as it increases daily," J. B. Sheridan noted in early July, "but it seems that about 120 major leaguers have joined or been drafted into the army or have joined the navy."[1]

Sheridan's figure represented nearly eight men for every big-league franchise, before the work-or-fight order went into effect. Shipyards and steel mills increased the manpower drain. Clubs improvised and finagled to put barely recognizable teams onto the field. Often they turned to the shuttered Minor Leagues in search of former Major League players who were now safely beyond the draft age.

The *El Paso Herald* announced, "The old timers are flocking back into the majors at a fast clip since the war has taken out so many youngsters, and it would be possible to put in the field an 'All Aged' team that would hold its own with some of the clubs now in the majors."[2] High on this imaginary roster was surely Nick Altrock, forty-one, pitching again for Clark Griffith's Senators. Many players in their thirties, who might otherwise have retired, hung on for one more season.

Occasionally, too, the flow reversed, as a shipyard or industrial team lost a player to the Major Leagues. Frank Truesdale, a thirty-four-year-old former Browns and Yankees infielder, leaped all the way to the Red Sox from the Copper League. "It is there that the men play ball with the thermometer registering 100 degrees in the shade, with the mesa for a background and the cactus taking the place of safety razor signs," Dan Daniel marveled. "It is from there that Truesdale is coming to join the pacemakers of the American League. What a jump!"[3]

Fred Lieb found the state of the American and National Leagues sadly laughable.

> Were it not for the plight that professional baseball finds itself in, the lineups of some of the big league teams these days would read like a comic sheet. Even the most hard hit magnate will admit that the present baseball lineups are ludicrous. One may feel sad for Miller Huggins, yet cannot help from breaking out with a loud guffaw over Ham Hyatt playing first base for the Yankees with Silent John Hummel his first assistant.
>
> When John McGraw is compelled to play Jay Kirke on first base it is more amusing than sad, but still more funny is the sight of the Yankees and Chicago White Sox scrapping for the services of John Picus, alias Jack Quinn. The leading humorist of all the season has developed so far has been Pitcher [Roy] Sanders of Pittsburgh, who purposely passed the venerable Mickey Doolan in a pinch. Purposely passing Mickey, hitting around .150, gives you a pretty good tip on the present caliber of big league baseball.[4]

Hyatt, Hummel, Kirke, and John Picus Quinn all were in their early to mid-thirties, and each had been out of the Majors for the past three seasons. "Doc" Doolan of the Brooklyn club had played for the Cubs and Giants in 1916 and for the International League's Rochester club in 1917, but he was now thirty-eight. Sanders, who had intentionally walked Doolan, was twenty-five and in his second Major League season. Of all these players, only Quinn remained in the Majors after the war—playing until 1933, when he pitched his last game for the Cincinnati Reds at the remarkable age of fifty. Another pitcher, Charles "Babe" Adams, thirty-six, had been out of the Majors for two seasons when he returned to the Pirates from the Kansas City Blues. He, too, remained in the big leagues, last pitching for Pittsburgh in 1926.

"It was the greatest process of disinterment ever known," Lieb wrote of the 1918 campaign nearly a quarter-century later, when the Second World War again drained baseball's manpower. "It was distinctly on the ghoulish side. Old players who had done nothing but wield a pool cue for 10 years were suddenly resurrected and pushed out on the diamond."[5]

If the Major Leagues were in a lamentable state, military baseball had never been stronger. Infused with talent from leagues of every class, fine army, navy, and marine teams drew large crowds both Stateside and overseas. By summer, perhaps the best of these teams had already come and gone like a baseball comet.

"The flat-footed and flapjack-hatted gentry composing the baseball team of the Boston Navy Yard—they were once nearly all members of the Boston Red Sox, but you couldn't tell it to look at them now—are going to have their first workout this week in the Harvard baseball cage," *Stars and Stripes* announced in early March. The manager, of course, was former Red Sox player-manager Jack Barry, now promoted to chief yeoman. According to the army newspaper in Paris, his ballplayers called themselves the Wild Waves.[6]

Counting himself, Barry had fourteen big leaguers on his roster, including ten from the two Boston clubs. Among them were future Hall of Famers Walter "Rabbit" Maranville of the Braves and Herb Pennock of the Red Sox—although, curiously, Pennock never actually pitched for the team. Barry also had a handful of Minor Leaguers and collegiate players, plus Connie Mack's son Roy McGillicuddy as treasurer and former Red Sox secretary John Lane as business manager. The navy nine was so rich in talent that Barry played Whitey Witt out of position in right field because Maranville was holding down shortstop.

"The Navy Yard team is a wonder, and would class well with any major league club in the country," Hugh Fullerton wrote. "There are several major league owners who would listen to an offer from the Government and trade their entire teams for that bunch."[7] Red Sox owner Harry Frazee, in fact, had attempted over the winter to secure the return of his men to the field by arranging prolonged furloughs—despite very public statements to the contrary.

"Most of the boys are in the navy, and all cheerfully responded to the call when the season closed last fall," Frazee had written to Franklin D. Roosevelt, an assistant secretary of the navy. "I do not have to say to you that if I am without the services of all these players during the season of 1918 my club will not only be out of the running professionally but that my business investment will be practically wrecked."[8] The navy hadn't seen the matter Frazee's way, however, and prohibited furloughs for sailor ballplayers to rejoin their teams for long periods.

For six weeks in May and June, the Wild Waves rampaged through military and collegiate teams. Forty thousand fans saw them beat Hal Janvrin's Camp Devens team at Braves Field, one of several times the National League club donated use of its park to military teams. Fifteen thousand people saw Barry's squad beat the Brooklyn Navy Yard in New Haven, and ten thousand witnessed their tough win over an Atlantic Fleet team at Norfolk, Virginia, on Memorial Day. Altogether, during eight wins without a loss, perhaps one hundred thousand people saw the Wild Waves play a class of baseball that the weakened Major Leagues were hard-pressed to match.

Barry's one great problem was that most of his ballplayers were rated as yeomen, several as petty officers. That fact was still too much for some detractors. "The case of the Barry yeomen ball team has attracted most attention and criticism, but it is not to be supposed that it was any more flagrant in violation of what the nation expects of the men who wear its blue or khaki than other cases," *Sporting News* huffed.[9] The admiral commanding the First Naval District largely agreed with the critics. He placed several restrictions on his great Navy Yard nine before the season began, then transferred several ballplayers after the second game—which didn't bother Maranville, who was eager to go to sea. When the navy began enlisting women as yeomen, the admiral broke up and scattered his ball team with the season barely begun. The navy cited "exigencies of the service" in announcing the move several weeks later.[10]

"It was surely a ball club to conjure with," said a newspaper in upstate New York, "especially when it is considered that the best of the service clubs contained only one or two stars at the most."[11] Without a team to manage, Barry gave up his chief petty officer's rank and entered an officers' training program at Harvard along with Red Sox and Wild Waves pitcher Ernie Shore.

The navy had another power baseball team on Lake Michigan. "Down in Chicago at the Great Lakes naval training station they have a ball team that is said to have the White Sox and the Cubs and everybody else cleared off the map," an Iowa newspaper said in July. "The Great Lakes nine is said to be one of the strongest military ball teams in the country."[12] Chief Yeoman Felix "Phil" Chouinard (*schwee-nahrd*), a former White Sox and Federal League outfielder, had managed the team since its formation in 1917. His roster included White Sox pitcher Red Faber, Washington infielder Joe Leonard, Red Sox infielder Fred Thomas, and a handful of Major League journeymen.

Great Lakes's natural interservice rival was Camp Grant at nearby Rockford, Illinois. The army team's star was young Pittsburgh Pirates pitcher Hal Carlson, who went on to have a fine National League career following the war. Army-navy games between these two teams routinely attracted a great deal of publicity and ten to twelve thousand fans.

The Great Lakes team also traveled to play on the East Coast during the summer. There it beat a strong Atlantic Fleet team, which following the disbandment of the Boston Navy Yard team had welcomed Rabbit Maranville, Del Gainer, Whitey Witt, and other former Wild Waves. The Rabbit was now a gunner's mate assigned to a fourteen-inch gun aboard the battleship USS *Pennsylvania*. Witt was on the battleship *Arkansas* and Gainer on the battleship *Minnesota*. Chouinard's club faced the Atlantic Fleet team again in a three-game series the first week in August. Great Lakes won the third and deciding game of what newspapers called "the

Calibers

naval baseball championship" on August 5 before a large crowd at the Cubs' Weeghman Park in Chicago.[13]

After the Major League season ended in September, Chouinard was replaced as Great Lakes manager by Lt. (JG) John "Doc" Lavan, the Washington Senators shortstop, who was also a physician. "Lavan is an officer and Chouinard is not and of course an officer could not play under and take orders from one below him in rank," *Sporting News* explained. "Also Lavan has had more major league experience, which is said to count."[14]

On the West Coast, Chief Yeoman Duffy Lewis, Jack Barry's former left fielder on the Red Sox, managed a good team at the naval training center at Mare Island near San Francisco. His roster included Pirates pitcher Earl Hamilton and Cubs catcher Harold "Rowdy" Elliott. Lewis's squad played various military teams in Northern California. "Lewis has his eyes on some big league stars still in the East and subject to the draft, and is being ably assisted by Boatswain Dan O'Connor in sending telegrams to the athletes in an endeavor to land them for his aggregation before they report to the National Army."[15]

Duffy's squad lost a hard-fought, five-game championship series in June to a Marine Corps squad managed by Sgt. Rod Murphy, former captain and third baseman of the Oakland Oaks in the Pacific Coast League. Five thousand fans saw the final game at Cyclodrome Park in Vallejo. Lewis later took a navy all-star team on the road, defeating an army all-star team before sixteen thousand fans at Camp Fremont near Palo Alto. The team kept playing, eventually adding infielders Charles "Swede" Risberg and Fred McMullin of the White Sox, along with Detroit pitcher Howard Ehmke. (The two Chicago players were later banned from Organized Baseball for their roles in the Black Sox scandal of 1919.) Doc Lavan hoped his Great Lakes team would have an opportunity to face Lewis's club in October. "A victory over Mare Island and the naval title goes undisputed to the big inland Station of Lake Michigan."[16]

The army likewise fielded many strong nines, especially after the Major League season ended. Cleveland pitcher Guy Morton managed the Camp Pike team at Little Rock, Arkansas, which claimed "the strongest army team in America."[17] Morton's roster included Brooklyn second baseman Ray Schmandt, catcher Herold "Muddy" Ruel and infielder Aaron Ward of the Yankees, and pitcher William "Big Bill" Fincher, formerly of the Browns.

One army team that could have given Jack Barry's Wild Waves an unforgettable contest was the 342nd Field Artillery nine at Camp Funston. "The spring season found the regiment well stocked with some of the best baseball players in the country, and the Divisional Team itself used eight of our players," states a regimental history, adding that the 342nd's athletic prowess "was largely instrumental in cementing it into a unit."[18] The star pitcher was that famously reluctant soldier and would-be sailor Grover Cleveland Alexander. Other units had tried to "secure him as if he had been a new type of machine gun or the latest invention in long range cannon," according to *Sporting News.*

> The artillery was successful in landing him, it seems, not because Alex himself had any particular choice, but the artillery at Funston happened to have the best ball team in camp and an addition like the One and Only Alex was calculated to make it even more famous. Grover was assigned to the 342d Field Artillery, which already had the pick of soldier athletes, and it is announced he probably will be assigned to clerical work to save his strength for athletics.[19]

Sporting News spared the pitcher the criticism it generally directed toward the navy's yeomen ballplayers. "He went to the Army camp ready to take his chances," the publication wrote of Alexander. "That he should land in a favored position was inevitable and consistent with the principle that the government believes for the best interest of the military service, the principle laid down by General Wood when he said: 'Men must be taught to play before they can fight efficiently.'"[20]

The 342nd's roster included Alexander; pitcher Win Noyes of the Athletics; pitcher and utility man Clarence Mitchell of the Dodgers; pitcher Otis Lambeth of the Indians; infielder Chuck Ward of the Pirates and (briefly) the Dodgers; and several good collegiate and independent-league players. Unlike many other military ballplayers, these men belonged to a combat unit. The regiment sailed from New York at the end of June, arriving in France via England in mid-July. The baseball team, with the Cubs star on the mound, "did some touring during the summer and cleaned up everything in sight, as it naturally would do with the great Aleck on the mound."[21] By fall, however, Alexander and his teammates would be far more concerned with surviving German artillery barrages than playing any game of baseball.

The War Department had prohibited players from taking extended leaves or furloughs to rejoin their old teams. Grover Alexander didn't throw another pitch for the Cubs before shipping out to France. Boston's Hal Janvrin never rejoined the Red Sox while serving in the Signal Corps at nearby Camp Devens. Still, a few former Major Leaguers did suit up while off active duty for short periods. Navy players seemed especially able to jump temporarily back into the big leagues.

Brooklyn pitcher Jeff Pfeffer, for example, while training at Great Lakes, once ventured into Chicago to watch his old teammates play the Cubs. "He was cheerfully received, and was implored to get back and show his old speed. Pfeffer answered Manager Robinson's request by asking for a uniform," the *New York Tribune* gleefully reported. "Many of his sailor mates recognized him in his playing togs and cheered him wildly. He was also roundly cheered by the five thousand spectators when he was announced as the Dodger pitcher."[22] The tall right-hander threw a nifty 2–0 shutout.

Chief Yeoman Bob Shawkey pitched two Saturday games for the Yankees at $100 apiece, forcing him to miss scheduled turns for the League Island navy team down in Philadelphia. The decision had "an altogether retrogressive effect on the great twirler's popularity in Philadelphia naval circles."[23] Reassigned to the battleship USS *Arkansas*, the right-hander later concluded that the navy had actually done him a favor. Shawkey wrote to Harry Sparrow after the armistice of "dodging torpedoes from Hun submarines, on board the *Arkansas* up near the Arctic Circle, and of other exciting experiences in foreign waters."[24]

126

Walter Maranville, in addition to serving at sea on the USS *Pennsylvania* and playing ashore for the Atlantic Fleet club, appeared in eleven games for the Braves during a two-week leave in July. The shortstop was "enthusiastically greeted by the fans, who recognize the midget as a real warrior," *Sporting News* reported.[25] "The Rabbit has been across to the other side as convoy to escorts twice and says it's [a] great life and that he thinks it would do some ball players who kick on Pullman berths and $5 a day hotels good if they would take a swing at it."[26]

Brooklyn's Leon Cadore, now an army lieutenant, pitched twice for the Dodgers in June while on furlough from Camp Gordon, Georgia. The second game came on Cadore Day at Ebbets Field. "At the suggestion of admirers of the Brooklyn team, C. H. Ebbets announced last night that several women will be at the entrance of the park soliciting subscriptions for a fund which will be expended in purchasing an officer's outfit for Cadore."[27] Brooklyn won both games the soldier pitched.

While their respective units were segregated, African American army teams occasionally played their white counterparts. Longtime Yankees pitcher Ray "Schoolmaster" Fisher led a team from Fort Slocum, New York, in a May benefit game at the Polo Grounds versus the 349th Field Artillery team from Camp Dix, New Jersey. "The Camp Dix outfit was composed entirely of colored players, many of whom were well known to the fans, having pastimed hereabouts with the famous Lincoln Giants."[28] Fisher went the distance in a shutout, with Brooklyn Royal Giants alumnus Jess "Mountain" Hubbard appearing in relief for Camp Dix. "While Fisher showed all his former major league ability, the feature of the game was the twirling of the rangy Hubbard. . . . Hubbard had a total of fourteen strikeouts, retiring the side in both the third and ninth frames in this manner in order."[29] The *New York World* said the game "served to demonstrate the high plane of the national pastime which our soldiers are capable of holding."[30]

Few military teams participated in organized leagues in the United States, but the AEF assembled a huge circuit in France. The Paris

Base Ball Association, sometimes called the American Soldiers Baseball League by newspapers back home, fielded thirty teams outfitted with gear supplied by Clark Griffith's Bat and Ball Fund. Most of the ballplayers involved weren't front-line infantrymen but rear-echelon troops attached to Service of Supply units.

"The league comprises teams made up of men of all the different branches of the service in the country—the aviation service, the engineers, the military police, the soldiers and sailors' club, the Red Cross, the YMCA, and the quartermaster's department."[31] All played at a huge athletics complex in the Paris suburb of Colombes. "The field is over 50 acres in extent, and at least ten games can be played at the same time," *Stars and Stripes* reported. "A monster grand stand with a seating capacity of over 25,000 persons surrounds part of the field. The practice games will be played on various local gridiron fields, but all league battles will be staged at Colombes on Sunday afternoons."[32]

The AEF had several other circuits around France as well, including a large YMCA league in Tours. "There are 16 clubs in this league, as many as there are in the American and National combined," the army newspaper reported. "Five other teams are playing in the same town, but there was no room for them in the circuit and they are holding an overflow meeting of their own."[33] Segregated African American soldiers cheered very good ball clubs of their own. Perhaps the best was the 312th Labor Battalion team, formed after the armistice at Saint-Sulpice. Soldiers there called the club the Clean-up Squad, "with particular reference to the manner in which it has walloped the tar out of all contenders in that section for diamond honors. . . . There is no league for colored players at the base, so the team has to play independent ball."[34]

When the YMCA and the Bat and Ball Fund couldn't supply enough equipment for all the soldier teams in France, the army turned to local manufacturers. Although the French-made bats and gloves were somewhat successful, the baseballs proved generally disappointing. They were likely to disintegrate on contact into "a white puff resembling a burst of shrapnel."[35]

Unlike Stateside cantonments and naval bases, the AEF leagues included few Major League ballplayers. Before disbanding its sports page in July, *Stars and Stripes* mentioned only former Senators Gabby Street and Mike Menosky, along with several Minor Leaguers and collegiate players. Hank Gowdy, Eddie Grant, Harry McCormick, and other former big leaguers played only in pickup, regimental, or inter-company games when not in the trenches. "The baseball giant . . . has been educated to baseball and very little else, and consequently, when he becomes a soldier, is the ordinary fighting man, and goes with as little delay as possible to the quarter where he is most needed," the *Times* of London explained.[36] *Sporting News* might have phrased it differently but certainly would have agreed with sending ballplayers to the front.

The situation on the other side of the English Channel was very different. The U.S. Army normally had about fifteen thousand Air Service men training and studying at British flying fields, most of them technicians and aviators. Along with sailors serving in London, they constituted the nucleus of the Anglo-American Baseball League, a military circuit in England. The league was smaller than the Paris or Tours circuits, but vastly more influential for the United States. Thirty wealthy American businessmen formed the circuit early in 1918, American and Canadian forces fielding four teams each. The league played on weekends and holidays at venues in and around London, often on diamonds laid out at the Highbury and Stamford Bridge football (soccer) stadiums. The American squads represented U.S. Army and U.S. Navy headquarters in London and two Air Service fields outside the city.

The U.S. Navy squad boasted two former Wild Waves: pitcher Herb Pennock and infielder Mike McNally. Naval officers had transferred both men to London headquarters the moment they arrived in Ireland, bound for other duties. "Minooka Mike" was soon named the team's captain, despite the presence of two officers on the roster. The U.S. Army team had former Detroit Tigers and Federal League pitcher Capt. Edward F. "Doc" Lafitte, a dentist assigned to a hospital outside London that specialized in repairing soldiers' damaged faces. Both squads had a number of good Minor Leaguers as well. The league's spokesman and chief umpire was

Walter Arlington "Arlie" Latham, a colorful, controversial character known as "the freshest man on earth" when he played third base for the St. Louis Browns and other clubs in the 1880s and 1890s. Latham also had coached—and occasionally gotten into a game—for John McGraw's New York Giants as recently as 1909.

On the Fourth of July, at Stamford Bridge, Chelsea, Pennock and Lafitte met in a special holiday game. The occasion marked Great Britain's first-ever observation of its former colonies' Independence Day. When King George V announced that he would attend, the event immediately gained international attention and became the most important sporting event of the Great War.

City newspapers enthusiastically boosted what they called the "baseball match" and printed helpful guides so Londoners might vaguely understand the game. An enormous crowd of Allied soldiers, sailors, and ordinary Londoners trooped out to Chelsea on the sunny midsummer afternoon. The league later said that attendance was thirty-four thousand. McNally, who had played in the 1916 World Series, estimated fifty thousand, which may have been more accurate. King George V attended with Queen Mary, Queen Mother Alexandra, and Prince Albert. The king was prevented from throwing out a ceremonial first pitch, stymied by tennis netting hastily strung to protect the royals from foul balls. Instead, he walked onto the field, where Adm. William Sims (USN) introduced him to McNally and the army team captain. George V then personally handed an autographed Spalding baseball to umpire Latham, who had earlier taught the monarch how to throw it.

The game was as good as anyone had dare to hope, exciting even Londoners who barely comprehended the action. "I don't know what he did, but I'm for him!" Queen Alexandra exclaimed as the navy's Harvard-educated catcher slid across the plate to score.[37] Both pitchers were dazzling, Pennock taking a no-hitter into the ninth before finally defeating Lafitte and army, 2–1. The American teams delivered a raucous display of vigor and athleticism at a time when doughboys were only beginning to reach the front lines in meaningful numbers. The thrilling afternoon cheered war-weary Britons and helped to solidify the great transatlantic alliance.

The game "took us completely away to those distant times when we could rejoice under a blue sky, without looking for Zeppelins and Gothas," commented the *Times*.

> The afternoon was crammed full of extraordinary moments. It passed in such a pandemonium as was perhaps never heard before on an English playing-field; not even on a football ground. The United States seemed to be shouting in chorus, and Great Britain joined in, a little breathless, but determined to make a good show of lung power. . . . The pitching of Pennock, for the Navy, and Lafitte, for the Army, was the feature of the game, and these two players, who are famous in the United States, worthily upheld their reputations.[38]

McNally would recall for the rest of his life shaking hands with the British monarch. Pennock and Lafitte chatted briefly with King George about the game afterward. No other ballplayers would play such important roles in their country's international relations until Babe Ruth's great All American tour of Japan in 1934.

"If Waterloo was won on the playing fields of Eton," a British newspaper concluded, "it may be that it will be said hereafter, in the same symbolic sense, that the Great War was won on the baseball ground at Chelsea."[39]

9

World Series

"Nineteen eighteen was a weird and badly twisted season, one almost beyond the pale of the ever elastic dope," Grantland Rice wrote later. "Form was badly mixed and the entire situation out of focus."[1] But when the season ended on Labor Day, the curtailed pennant races ended in exactly the way most fans and sportswriters had expected in July.

The Cubs had bested John McGraw's champion Giants in the National League, while the Red Sox had dethroned Charles Comiskey's White Sox in the American. Although Chicago had lost its expensive gamble on Grover Alexander, and second baseman Pete Kilduff had enlisted in the navy early in the season, the Cubs' roster otherwise had remained surprisingly intact. In Boston, after losing Jack Barry and nearly his entire starting lineup, Harry Frazee had restocked his club by buying four players from the Athletics and signing any others he could. "Neither the Cubs nor the Red Sox comprise a great club, but without doubt they are the best in their respective leagues," Fred Lieb wrote in the *Sun*. "Both clubs have retained more players of class than any other teams in their leagues, which is one of the reasons they are on top."[2]

The sixteen Major League clubs wrapped up their campaigns as their players prepared for essential work outside of baseball. The Yankees split a doubleheader with the Red Sox to finish in fourth place. "They tucked the weak, tottering baseball season away in camphor up at the Polo Grounds yesterday afternoon," the *New York Times* reported. "The game is interned for the period of the war, along with a lot of other less useful things."[3] "Giants, Yankees and Dodgers all have been paid off, some of them undoubtedly for the last time, and the players are scattering to the far corners of the country, most of them to munition making plants, ship-yards, steel yards, the farms and other 'essential industries,'" the *Sun* added the next day.[4]

In Washington, Clark Griffith's Senators lost the morning game of a doubleheader to Connie Mack's Athletics. Late in the second game, forty-one-year-old coach Nick Altrock pitched, played first base, and blooped an inside-the-park home run featuring a comically drawn-in outfield, "a generous cutting of all the corners and a fancy high dive into the plate."[5] Walter Johnson appeared in relief to end the season in front of the home fans. "Big Train" clinched an 8–3 victory pitching to catcher Eddie Ainsmith.

"Never in Washington has the baseball season ended as it did yesterday," sportswriter John Dugan wrote in a front-page piece for the *Washington Herald*. "The afternoon shadows of the stands had lengthened across the fields and the setting sun witnessed three thousand American soldiers standing at attention, as a military band played 'The Star Spangled Banner,' and twelve thousand persons stood in the stands, bareheaded, thrilled, happy, yet sad."[6]

The season also ended on Labor Day for the International League, the sole Minor circuit still standing. Toronto had captured the championship following an exciting pennant race that few fans had followed except in the box scores. "The International League magnates have lost money, but they have shown greater gameness in the face of difficulties than those of any other circuit in the country, not even excepting the majors," the *Washington Times* declared.[7] Toronto fans believed their American counterparts could learn from the Canadians.

New York sportsmen find it strange that baseball is more popular in Toronto than in any other city of the New International League. Indeed, they hint that the public patronage of the professional game 'in war-scarred Canada' is better than in some of the large American cities where the 'big leagues' are established. The reasons are natural ones. The country has discovered, after four years of war, that it is neither desirable nor necessary to walk through life to the strains of the dead march. . . . Our neighbors will discover, after they have endured the long pain of war, that base ball will revive; that crowds will be easily secured for anything that will take the mind away, even momentarily, from the contemplation of horrors.[8]

Not every player or team saw the season out to its melancholy conclusion. Once the White Sox had fallen from the pennant race in August, second baseman Eddie Collins enlisted in the Marines—the devil dogs, as German soldiers called them. "There's been a lot of criticism about ballplayers seeking bomb-proof jobs, but this can scarcely be said about a man who voluntarily joins the '*teufel hunds*,' who have a reputation of always being in the middle of it when there's dangerous work to be done."[9] The future Hall of Famer wouldn't have time to ship overseas or see action, however, before the armistice.

Cleveland owner James Dunn didn't wait until the season's official end, either. Immediately after the work-or-fight order, his club had announced plans to shut the ballpark July 21, but Dunn was talked into continuing. The Indians now closed their season a day early by skipping a road doubleheader with the Browns. Finishing second in the American League, the Cleveland players "preferred to disband at once and start useful work tomorrow instead of running a chance of violating Gen. Crowder's orders."[10] The Browns actually took the field on the holiday to claim both games by forfeit. Bill Macbeth angrily wrote in the *New York Tribune* that Dunn's departed club had "disgraced baseball in its refusal to keep scheduled obligations at St. Louis Labor Day."[11]

Dunn was unrepentant and offered a gloomy assessment of Organized Baseball. "I don't know what my colleagues think about continuing next year, but if I must build up a team of schoolboys and old men I will not open my gates," he said. "I am not in favor of minor league baseball in a big league town. We had better let the amateurs have the field to themselves until the war is over, when the game will come back to its own."[12]

At least two other owners appeared to agree that the Major Leagues wouldn't return in 1919. Charles Ebbets had already announced plans to convert his park into a vast cold-storage warehouse. "Immediately after the final home game of the curtailed season . . . special structures will be erected upon certain portions of the field, and these, in conjunction with space in and under the grandstands, utilized for storage purposes."[13] Giants owner Harry Hempstead was considering something similar at the Polo Grounds. Washington Park, former home of the Brooklyn Tip-Tops in the Federal League, was already in use as a government warehouse. "If the movement extends to the other ball grounds throughout the country it means there will be no professional baseball next year," a wire story stated.[14] Owner Ebbets estimated that the space beneath his grandstand would provide enough storage for one hundred thousand cases of goods. "It is heartbreaking to the fans, of course," another wire service added, "but they realize that it is not a good-by, but an au revoir, to baseball."[15]

The players on the fourteen clubs not playing in the World Series now headed for home or to new jobs. Rogers Hornsby paused to marry his fiancée before reporting to work as a plate-setter (and part-time ballplayer) at the Harlan yard in Wilmington. White Sox catcher Ray Schalk took a job at the Great Western Smelting Company in Chicago and set out to learn the industry. "Baseball has been pretty good to me, but now I realize how little I knew about business, so I'm glad I can learn while I'm still young," he said. "For eight years I did nothing to speak of except to play ball. I don't know whether I'll ever play any more professionally or not."[16] Other players had similar doubts about giving up newly learned skills, but the great Chicago backstop returned to the White Sox after the war and played in the Major Leagues until 1929.

Managers also found new jobs. Yankees skipper Miller Huggins was appointed assistant athletic director at Pelham Bay Naval Training Station and reported for duty early in October. Jack Hendricks of the St. Louis Cardinals signed on as an athletic secretary for the Knights of Columbus. "I have been anxious for some time to do my bit on the other side," Hendricks said. "I feel like a youngster, although I have a son now in an officers' training camp."[17] He briefly served in France toward the end of the war. The Tigers' Hughie Jennings also became a K of C secretary, but didn't have an opportunity to work "over there."

Ban Johnson had announced the World Series schedule August 24, before the Cubs and Red Sox officially clinched their pennants. The first three games were slated for Chicago and all remaining games for Boston. Johnson made the announcement for the National Commission, not as the American League president.

Playing the first three games of a seven-game series in one city was unusual, but did have a precedent. The Cubs had done it in 1907, winning a five-game series with the Tigers. Now a coin flip determined that Chicago again would host the long opening series. The home-and-home format also eliminated the need for an extra round-trip of nearly a thousand miles by rail if the series went to the limit. While logical, the plan upset Red Sox owner Harry Frazee, who said he wouldn't abide by it.

"Such a schedule is not only very unfair to the Boston club, but it is an insult to Boston fans and to the best baseball town in the American league," Frazee fumed. The magnate wanted the first two games played in one city—preferably Boston—followed by two in the other, as had been the case during Boston's championship run in 1916. Frazee didn't specify where any additional games should be played. "The national commission will not pay any attention to Harry Frazee," Johnson retorted. "Frazee probably forgets that it is necessary in these times to relieve the railroads of all unnecessary burdens. In normal times we would arrange a schedule such as Frazee demands, but it was impossible this year." "It is possible that Chicago got a 'break' by being awarded the first three games, but it was not our doing," said Cubs business manager Walter Craighead. "Frazee's attitude is not in keeping with the times, when everything possible should be done to relieve the transportation systems."[18]

The 1918 series also differed in other significant ways. The National Commission decided "to materially reduce the prices of admission in order to enable the patrons to attend the games at reasonable prices." In 1917 a box seat for a single game had cost $5. Now a box seat for all three games cost just $9—or $9.90, including war tax. A one-day bleacher seat was fifty-five cents. The players would earn less, too. Under an agreement between the leagues and the National Committee reached the previous winter, each of the players on the winning and the losing clubs was to receive $2,000 and $1,400, respectively, instead of a fixed percentage of gate receipts, as in earlier seasons. The White Sox's winning share in 1917, by comparison, was nearly $3,700, and the Giants' losing share about $2,400. "It is estimated that owing to the reduction of the admission charges the gate receipts will fall nearly 50 per cent," one newspaper reported. "Umpires and all others, aside from the players, who share pecuniary benefits from the series will have their compensation cut in half."[19]

Knowing the payout and the precise limit of Secretary Baker's work-or-fight extension, the Red Sox handed Frazee another setback. "The Boston players before coming East waited upon Harry Frazee with the ultimatum that they would not engage in the titanic struggle even for the proscribed rich spoils of $2,000 per man win or $1,400 per man lose unless the Boston magnate would agree to pay pro-rata season's contract salary in full up to September 15," Bill Macbeth wrote in the *New York Tribune*. "The Red Sox carried their point, needless to say. Also, needless to say, the Cubs will do likewise when they hear of the Hub coup."[20]

The Cubs and Red Sox headed west by rail for the Windy City after ending their seasons in the East. Many fans across the country had bigger things on their minds than baseball and simply shrugged at the championship series. The government had scheduled a third Registration Day for September 12. Young men from eighteen to twenty-one were required to register, along with older men from thirty-four to forty-five. The change vastly expanded the pool of manpower available for military service.

It is estimated that at least 12,278,758 men will register, compared with nearly 10 million between 21–31 June 5, 1917. Of those who enroll . . . it is estimated that 2,300,000 will be called for general military service and will be in France before July 1st. The idea is to take the eligible men 31–37 first, then 37–45, then 19–20 and leave the 18-year-old boys to the very last.[21]

Few sportswriters saw signs of fan interest in the World Series. Tickets sales for the opening games in Chicago, while brisk, fell short of previous years. "There is none of the wild clamor and fighting for tickets that have marked other World's Series, but the early sale of box and reserved seats has been quite large," Hugh Fullerton wrote from Chicago. "To-day a block of box seats will be sold at open sale, breaking another World's Series record, and the three ticket speculators I called upon yesterday to inquire concerning tickets yelled, 'Nothing doing!' They do not want them at any price."[22]

Interest in smaller cities and towns was equally slight. Fans in Maysville, Kentucky, had always avidly followed the World's Series. "But this year there has been absolutely no interest taken in the affair and there are very few people who know that the series started today. There is nothing in the series that would cause Maysville people to be very much interested."[23]

American soldiers and sailors overseas would receive news from the series if they cared to read it, although not in the weekly *Stars and Stripes*. The Federal Committee on Public Information was set to cable a daily report and the score of each game to Paris for publication in the European editions of the *New York Herald* and *Chicago Tribune*. "The cooperation of this agency is the result of the official approval of the series by the Federal government, as expressed by the Secretary of War and Provost Marshal General Crowder."[24]

The opening three games in Chicago weren't slated for Weeghman Park, the Cubs' home field, but for the White Sox's bigger South Side facility. The two owners had struck a deal. "The Old Roman, Charles Comiskey, who can have the mayoralty any time he asks the honor, never overlooked any bets, nor is he now,"

Macbeth informed his New York Tribune readers. "Commy made himself strong with local fandom by tendering his spacious South Side Park for the use of the rival Cubs. It means more money, provided there happens to be enthusiasm enough to crowd a ground as cramped as the cigar box of the North Side on which Weeghman's team plays its games."[25]

The weather was equally uncertain. After two dry months that some likened to a drought, rain threatened the series' opener, scheduled for Wednesday, September 4. "No one would be greatly surprised if a whole week's activities were to be washed away," Macbeth wrote on Monday. "And that would be a real disaster, for this particular series needs all the press agenting it can possibly get, with no interruptions of any kind, to place it among the classics of the years gone by when baseball was considered an essential everywhere."[26]

The rains arrived as predicted to wash out Game 1. "Even the weather bureau was crossed by the storm which blew into Chicago yesterday morning and spilled so much water on the south side ball park that the impending battle was called off before 11 o'clock," I. E. Sanborn wrote in the *Chicago Tribune*. "As the disturbance came on the wings of an east wind, it looked as if the elements were conspiring to aid the eastern representatives—namely: Red Sox."[27]

The assembled sportswriters passed the rainy day discussing the same topics that no doubt occupied the Boston and Chicago ballplayers—departed friends, the work-or-fight order, and what they would do following the series. "That intense interest in the big baseball classic, so apparent in other years, was not present," the *Chicago Tribune* reported. "Instead, the writers seemed to feel sort o' ashamed of themselves for being here while the boys 'over there' (among them several members of the Writers' association) are engaged in the biggest game the world ever had."[28] The scribes even mused about forming a unit of their own. Compounding the gloom already surrounding the series, the day also brought news of the first violent wartime death of a ballplayer widely known in a Major League city.

Two big leaguers had already died in the armed forces, although neither in combat. The first was Seaman Newton S. Halliday, an infielder who had appeared in one game for the Pirates in 1916 and later played for the Great Lakes navy team. "Newt" died of pneumonia at the big naval station April 6. The second casualty was Cpl. Ralph Sharman, a rookie outfielder for the Athletics in 1917. He drowned in the Alabama River on May 24 while training with the Ohio troops at Camp Sheridan. Now Pittsburgh pitching prospect Marcus Milligan was gone, too. The aviation cadet died from injuries suffered in an air crash September 3 at an army flying field outside Fort Worth, Texas. The accident also killed his flying instructor. Milligan had never appeared in a regular-season game for the Pirates, but magnates and sports editors paid homage as if he had been a star. The youngster had played in the Virginia and New York State leagues before spending the 1917 season with Class A Birmingham. "He caused many a thrill in the Southern League [*sic*] and was just about ripe for regular duty in the majors when he offered his services to the higher cause," a Pittsburgh sportswriter wrote.[29]

"Milligan is the first prominent ball player to give his life in his country's service," said National Commission chairman Garry Herrmann. "His death which places the first golden star in the National League's service flag proves the patriotism of the professional ball players."[30] The twenty-two-year-old was buried in Anniston, Alabama, where his mother and sister lived. A newspaper there offered a moving editorial: "Mark Milligan did not get to face the Hun, but he is a hero nevertheless; for he sacrificed a brilliant career to enter the army, he underwent great hardships to train himself for service abroad, and he died for you and me just the same as if he had been to France."[31]

The World Series finally started a day late, Thursday, September 5. The official attendance was 19,274—more than could have shoehorned into Weeghman Park, but less than two-thirds the capacity of Comiskey Park. Large swaths of seats lay empty. Charles Comiskey tried to give the attendance figure a positive spin. "When you stop to think that most of our boys between 21 and 31 years of age are gone, and most of those at home too busy to get away, I think the attendance was large," Comiskey said. "Then, too, there are few out of town patrons because of the high railroad rates and busy times. I don't know that there has been as big a crowd as that present at a ball game in Chicago this year."[32]

Fans who did turn out saw a tremendous pitchers' duel between Boston's Babe Ruth and Chicago's Hippo Vaughn. Ruth won, 1–0, in what baseball historians Cecilia Tan and Bill Nowlin rank among the greatest Red Sox games ever played. Still, despite the brilliant play, the park remained eerily quiet. People paid less attention to the field than to six army airplanes doing dives and spins nearby. "The effect of the war was everywhere apparent, especially in the temper of the crowd, which, largely local, saw the home team drop the first game without a protest," the *Boston Globe* reported. "There was no cheering during the contest, nor was there anything like the usual umpire baiting."

The one roaring moment came during the seventh-inning stretch. Boston rookie Fred Thomas was playing third base. Thomas had managed to enlist in the navy despite a rejection by the army because of his diabetes. Now serving at Great Lakes, he was on a two-week leave to rejoin his club for the series. When a military band struck up "The Star-Spangled Banner" at the stretch, the sailor didn't remove his cap or hold it over his heart like the civilian ballplayers. He kept his cap on, turned toward the flag, and delivered a crisp military salute.

The crowd noticed Thomas "as he stood erect, his eyes set on the flag which fluttered at the top of the flagpole in right field. First the song was taken up by a few, but others joined and when the end of the song came, a great volume of melody was rolling across the field. It was at the very end that onlookers exploded into thunderous applause and rent the air with a cheer that marked the highest point of the day's enthusiasm."[33] Although the song had been played many times in ballparks since America had entered the war, and indeed occasionally had been played at baseball games as early as the Civil War, the rendition today became a turning point. "The Star-Spangled Banner" would be played at every subsequent World Series game and season opener. Playing it before *every* Major League baseball game would begin during the Second World War, after the song became the national anthem.

Game 2 followed on Friday. Although attendance ticked up slightly, gate receipts fell. "It seems there was a lot more bleacherites present and fewer box seat patrons." Unlike the opener, the contest provided "such a thrilling afternoon that the crowd forgot to watch the aeroplanes doing nose dives."[34] The Cubs evened the series by beating the Red Sox, 3–1, overcoming a Boston rally in the ninth. The Red Sox then regained the advantage in the third contest on Saturday. Hippo Vaughn again took the mound for the Cubs, and pitched well in a 2–1 loss to Boston's unpopular submarine pitcher, Carl Mays. The game ended when Fred Thomas muffed a catch at third, but threw out Chicago's Charlie Pick at the plate. Attendance improved to about 90 percent of capacity at Comiskey's ballpark, with the total dampened somewhat by sprinkling rain and threatening skies.

Altogether, paid attendance for the three games totaled 66,368, with receipts barely topping $100,000. "For the first three games last year the attendance was 97,616 and the receipts $219,368," the *Chicago Tribune* noted.[35] The abysmal figures added up to trouble and dominated the ballplayers' talk during their long train ride to the Northeast. The two teams left Chicago at eight o'clock Saturday night on the Michigan Central line. By the time they chugged into Boston in a heavy rainstorm twenty-six hours later, the championship series had taken a lamentable if not unforeseeable turn.

"When the world's series players arrived here late tonight," the *Chicago Tribune* reported in a dispatch datelined Sunday, "it became known that they had got together on the train and appointed a committee to interview members of the national baseball commission, expected here tomorrow, and to voice the dissatisfaction of the Boston and Chicago players over the proposed reduction of their receipts from the first four games to $1,200 each for those on the winning team and $800 for the losers."[36] The *New York Times* added that if their original agreement wasn't carried out, the players said they "would refuse to play any more games."[37]

The *Boston Globe* tried to explain the situation while downplaying prospects for a strike. "The National Commission had stipulated that the students [*sic*] on the winning team would receive $2,000 and the losing athletes $1,400 each, provided the players' share for the first four games amounted to $150,000," sportswriter Edward Martin wrote. "It will not amount to $75,000, and out of that must come 60 percent to be divided between teams that finished second, third and fourth in the two major leagues."[38]

The ballplayers chose catcher Bill Killefer and outfielder Leslie Mann from the Cubs and outfielder Harry Hooper and infielder Dave Shean from the Red Sox to represent them in a special meeting with the National Commission on Monday morning. The quartet would act as the players' representatives throughout the dispute. The money question was especially important to Killefer, who expected to report to the army soon after the series ended. After the athletes and commission agreed to keep talking, the World Series resumed on Monday afternoon.

Twenty-two thousand fans saw Game 4, the first contest at Fenway Park. Among them were fifty-four wounded American soldiers and sailors from Boston City Hospital. Two of the soldiers wore the French Croix de Guerre. Fans stood to cheer them all when they arrived and would cheer them again as they escorted the warriors out of the park after the game. The wounded troops were lucky in attending Game 4, "the most exciting and desperately fought game of the 1918 world's series."[39]

Babe Ruth again took the mound for the Red Sox, despite a finger that was grotesquely swollen "due to some mysterious altercation on the train from Chicago to Boston, one that put his fist into contact with either a solid steel wall, a window, or the jaw of another passenger."[40] The Babe defeated the Cubs, 3–2, pitching into the ninth inning before shifting to left field and giving way to reliever Leslie "Bullet Joe" Bush. Ruth's record of 29⅔ scoreless World's Series innings, dating back to the 1916 championship series with Brooklyn, had ended with Chicago's two runs in the eighth. Boston's big pitcher also tripled to help his own cause against Cub starter George Tyler. Chicago reliever Phil Douglas took the loss, giving the Red Sox a commanding 3–1 lead in the series.

That night, the unhappy ballplayers tried again to meet with the National Commission to discuss their share of the gate receipts. "But the commission had ducked, in its customary backstairs policy; had gone to see a portrayal of the drama 'Experience,' the young lady of the Copley Plaza switchboard informed every one," wrote Macbeth, up from New York to cover the series. "The jaded committee, sometime about 1 a.m., retired to repose against the prospective battle of the morrow without having crossed the trail of a single commissioner."[41]

Despite the desperate win-or-go-home scenario for the Cubs, Game 5 on Tuesday was completely overshadowed by the crisis. Both teams refused to play unless they reached an agreement with the National Commission. Stuffy McInnis, Boston's first baseman, was the only uniformed player on the field at the scheduled starting time of 2:30. "Minute after minute and half hour after half hour the issue remained at a deadlock," Macbeth wrote. "The commission refused to see the strikers. The strikers in their civilian clothes played pitch in their quarters."[42] A Philadelphia sports editor described the scene in a sardonic poem.

'Twas on an autumn evening
    A goodly crowd was there,
That nigh filled Frazee's ball park,
    A mile from Copley Square.
The commission cut the divvy,
    The players chewed the rag,
But no one hit a baseball
    And no one touched a bag.[43]

The commission members and city officials grew anxious about the mood of the large crowd in the stands. "A squad of mounted policeman came on the field half an hour after time for starting the game for the purpose of quelling any unruly spirits who resented the long delay, but their services were not required."[44] The crowd remained quiet and bemused throughout the delay. When the ballplayers and the commission finally began talking in the umpires' room, pleas by Ban Johnson and Garry Herrmann left the players largely unmoved. Macbeth credited the commission's newest member for breaking the deadlock.

"John A. Heydler, acting president of the National League, a man of sober judgment and more sober deportment, saved the situation," the *Tribune* scribe wrote. "While his conferrees [*sic*] of the National Commission were babbling about their self-importance John was working frantically and in secret for the good of the game to which he has devoted a brilliant life. He suggested that the issue involved should remain in status quo pending a reference to those clubs of the first division interested in a division of the spoils. He pointed out to the players' committee what a travesty on the name of sport would result from not satisfying the sport-loving thousands already chafing at the delay."[45]

The ballplayers held the weaker position and had no choice but to give way or go home. Many reports pointed to Hooper, the Red Sox captain who would retire after the series, as the man who swung the players around to playing. Herrmann then tried to shake Hooper's hand, but Red Sox manager Ed Barrow brushed him aside. "We have wasted enough time already," Barrow barked. "To the field, everybody!"[46]

Hooper spoke for both teams to waiting sportswriters. "We will play, not because we think we are getting a fair deal, because we are not," he said. "But we'll play for the sake of the game, for the sake of the public, which has always given us its loyal support, and for the sake of the wounded soldiers and sailors who are in the grandstand waiting for us."[47] The sentiment was a fine one, but too little and too late. The publicity was brutal for everyone.

"But for presence at Fenway Park of a number of Pershing's veterans, some minus legs, others without arms, and all wounded, the fifth game of the 1918 world's series might never have been played," snarled the *Washington Times*.[48] "'For the good of baseball, we will play,' said these 30-odd young gentlemen the other day after they had held a crowd of 25,000 waiting in the bleachers for an hour while they and their owners wrangled over the division of the proceeds—after they had wasted 25,000 man hours, made trebly precious by war needs, not counting their own," *Stars and Stripes* sniped from Paris.[49]

The *Chicago Tribune* acidly reported that during the delay at Fenway—"while players and promoters were fighting over pennies"—American soldiers had carried two wounded comrades down to the boxes on their shoulders.

> As the wounded men were borne to the seats reserved for them the big crowd jumped to its feet, bared heads, and under the leadership of a fan down in front, gave three cheers for the boys who have been in the only game that counts. Those cheers nearly raised the roof off the Fenway plant. They were echoed back from the pavilions and bleachers with a will when the fans out there learned the cause of them. Still the players of the two teams imagined themselves heroes.[50]

Many sportswriters were equally unhappy with the National Commission. Macbeth wrote of "the many rebuffs the players experienced from the high and lofty National Commission Poo Bahs, when nothing more than a heart-to-heart conference was requested at first."[51] Even *Sporting News*, so often disdainful of ballplayers whose wartime actions or choices had offended its editors' sensibilities, angrily indicted both sides.

> However, we decline to join in the general chorus of roasts for the diamond heroes [at Fenway], badly as they acted. They had some cause for a grievance. . . . The players are blamed for forcing the issue the way they did. But how else were they to force it? Having never been consulted by the magnates in their beneficent plan to dispose of the players' money, and not being given to reading anything in print except their batting averages, they had a very hazy notion of what had been done for them or to them.[52]

Perhaps the only person to benefit from the brief strike was John Heydler. He would be elected as Governor Tener's permanent replacement as National League president in December.

Former Boston mayor John F. "Honey Fitz" Fitzgerald, whose one-year-old grandson, John Fitzgerald Kennedy, would one day be elected president of the United States, announced to the fans that the game would be played. Their reaction was muted. "When the players came on the field an hour late some of the fan started 'booing' them, but the majority cheered the athletes and drowned out the 'boos.'"[53]

The game began with little warm-up by either team. Hippo Vaughn's excellent pitching for the Cubs was largely overlooked amidst the strike debacle. Throwing nine scoreless innings in his third complete game in six days, he lowered his earned run average for the series to a magnificent 1.00—among the best mound performances in championship history. Yet the shutout was his sole victory in the World Series and earned him only a grudging, backhanded headline in the hometown *Chicago Tribune*: "Cubs Grab Victory under Shadow of Dollar Sign, 3-to-0."[54]

The Red Sox clinched their fifth world's championship on Wednesday, September 11, in Game 6. It was another close-fought 2–1 affair. Boston scored both of its runs on a muffed fly ball to right in the third inning. "Boston is the luckiest baseball spot on earth, for it has never lost a world's series," wrote the *New York Times*.[55] The club wouldn't win another for eighty-six years. "If the Cubs could have cut out the fourth inning in the series they would be world's champions," noted the *Chicago Tribune*.[56] "Chicago's once loyal fans had a feeling of relief that baseball was over, rather than a feeling of sorrow in the loss of the championship," the newspaper added in another column. "When the ninth inning was posted on the various score boards about town the common expression among those present was: 'Well, it's all over. Now those fellows can go to work.'"[57]

The club owners had promised the players' representatives before Game 6 to lobby the National Commission and league officials for an increase in the players' pool, enough to deliver something nearer the payout the two teams had anticipated. "The division of the pool under national commission rules is so far below normal, however, that it is doubtful if the club owners will be able to make up the deficit, without going into their own pockets for the expenses of the series, and the players are not avaricious enough to expect that."[58]

The fourteen Red Sox regulars and manager Ed Barrow each received $1,108.45 for their winning series work. They voted $750 for Fred Thomas and smaller sums for trainers, groundskeepers, players in the armed forces, and others. "The check did not include 10 per cent which it had been voted to donate to charitable organizations, and the players instructed Capt. Harry Hooper to obtain the amount from the commission and distribute it among Boston war charities."[59] During their long train ride back to Chicago, the losing Cubs voted twenty-two shares of $574.62 apiece for their regulars, with lesser amounts to other players who had contributed and $140 apiece for the five men away on military duty. The Chicago team, too, contributed 10 percent to war charities. The two teams' hopes that they might see extra shares from their respective leagues were never realized.

Charles Weeghman, at least, was happy. The Cubs chief offered Charles Comiskey his "very sincere thanks" for the free use of his South Side park during the series. "Although of different and rival leagues," Weeghman wrote to his rival owner, "the wholeheartedness of your invitation and the many courtesies extended to us during the series have added to your nation-wide reputation for good sportsmanship and to our admiration of you"—sentiments that the Old Roman's own ballplayers emphatically would not share while throwing the series during the Black Sox scandal a year later.[60]

As the other fourteen teams had done two weeks earlier, the Red Sox and Cubs now quickly disbanded. "'Babe' Ruth says he has seven offers to go to work and because he's going to accept one of them he will do no through-the-ice fishing up at South Sudbury this Winter," the *Globe* reported.[61] Ruth accepted a job with the Bethlehem plant in Lebanon, Pennsylvania, and briefly played exhibition ball for the company team. He remained a civilian throughout the war, but in 1924 greatly boosted an army recruiting push by enlisting as a private in the New York National Guard—and, of course, reporting for duty personally to General Pershing.

Following the World Series, most of the Babe's teammates scattered to their homes, new jobs, or military camps. Sam Jones, Joe Bush, Everett Scott, Walter Mayer, and Hank Miller, however, along with George Burns of the Athletics and "Pep" Young of the Tigers, put together a travel squad to play exhibitions along the East Coast under the Red Sox name. Harry Frazee quickly complained of what he called this "fracture of a national commission order against barnstorming."[62]

From Chicago, Bill Killefer and four other Cubs soon headed into the army. Rollie Zeider retired from baseball and returned to his farm in Indiana, while Fred Merkle went back to his own farm in Florida.[63] Other teammates took up new jobs in power plants, shipyards, and chemical companies. Professional baseball was finished for the duration, and none too soon in the opinion of many. From his regiment in France, T. L. Huston expressed a common weariness and frustration.

"I believe that baseball will be very much better off if it is permitted to lie dormant until at least 1920," the Yankees co-owner wrote to sportswriter Tom Rice. "It needed a rest. The slate can be wiped off and a new start made. The fans had absolutely gotten tired of the incessant wrangling between the club owners themselves and between the club owners and the players." Huston added what fellow magnates might have considered a warning: "When this great war is over our United States will be run by the soldiers who fought to save it and the national game will probably enjoy the same blessing."[64]

10

Strain of Battle

The Major League season ended a month early, but baseball continued elsewhere into the fall. The shipyard leagues even staged a championship series that overlapped the World Series. The Harlan & Hollingsworth team from Wilmington won a one-game playoff with Chester Ship for the right to represent the Delaware River Shipbuilding League in this best-of-five series. Harlan's star in both the playoff and championship was Joe Jackson.

The former White Sox outfielder played the entire season for Harlan's nine in the Steel League before shifting to the Delaware River team for the championship run, no doubt at the company's request. It was one more cause for outrage. "Just what the eligibility rules of the Shipyard League are we do not know," sputtered Philadelphia sportswriter Edgar Wolfe, "but Chester must have committed murder if . . . the acts of Harlan in reinforcing its team with players from another league solely for the decisive championship contest can be considered innocent."[1]

Jackson played center field and went three-for-three in the playoff victory. Harlan's opponent in the championship series was Standard Shipbuilding of Staten Island, winner of the New York Shipyard League pennant. The series began September 7 at the Phillies' ballpark. Jackson came off the bench to spark a ninth-inning rally and 3–2 victory. The series then shifted north to the Polo Grounds for Game 2. Harlan won again, 2–0, as Jackson sat out the game with a foot injury. Harlan went for the sweep September 14 before forty-five hundred fans in Philadelphia. Jackson doubled and homered twice off former Cardinal and Dodger Dan Griner in a 4–0 shutout.

"When Jackson hit his second home run, which virtually clinched the game and series for Harlan, the Wilmington fans went money mad and showered him with greenbacks," the *New York Sun* reported. "For more than five minutes he was kept busy walking to the boxes and pulling in bills. After he had his fist full he walked over to a box directly behind home plate and handed them to his wife."[2] Mrs. Jackson pocketed about sixty dollars amid the raucous scene.

Military teams were still playing baseball as well. The Brooklyn Navy Yard and Camp Merritt, New Jersey, played one game September 15 at the Polo Grounds to decide the metropolitan service championship. "Since the beginning of the baseball season great rivalry has existed among the baseball teams at the various army and navy camps," declared the *New York Times*. "Although there has been no league, the consensus of opinion is that Camp Merritt has the strongest team in the military end of the service and that the nine at the receiving station of the Brooklyn Navy Yard is the best of the seamen teams."[3]

Former Brooklyn pitcher Jeff Pfeffer pitched a 1–0, three-hit shutout for the navy over Rube Bressler of the Cincinnati Reds for the army. "Had it not been for Casey Stengel, another well-known Brooklynite, Bressler might have been staving off defeat yet, but Casey broke up the pastime in the third inning with a timely single which sent Gene Sheridan, who, by the way, is one more former Robin, over the plate with the only run of the game," the *Times* reported. "More than 7,000 persons wildly greeted the effort of Stengel, and even then acclaimed the Navy supreme."[4]

Service nines had developed several regional rivalries across the country. Teams from the Fourth and Fifth Naval Districts, headquartered in Philadelphia and Norfolk, respectively, played a short series to determine which squad would meet Great Lakes later in a navy championship. The districts split a pair of games at the Athletics' park that coincided with the start of the Major League World Series. One Fourth Naval District player prowled Shibe Park at the same moment that his brother was playing in the big contest at Comiskey Park. "'Brick' McInnis made the hit that won the game in the same fashion that his brother, 'Stuffy' McInnis, made the hit that won to-day's game for the Boston Red Sox in Chicago."[5]

The Norfolk nine ultimately went to Chicago for three scheduled games at Great Lakes. Both clubs were loaded with Major Leaguers. Great Lakes won the two opening games, September 23 and 24, before large crowds of sailors at the big lakeside station. The commandant was then forced to cancel Game 3 amid an influenza epidemic sweeping army bases and navy stations nationwide. Three thousand new cases had been reported in just twenty-four hours, and sixty-eight men had already died at Great Lakes.

> Just when the fans were getting interested in Army and Navy baseball along comes that Spanish influenza thing to call off most of the schedules arranged. More than 25 camps have been put under quarantine because of the influenza outbreak and on one day last week more than 20,000 cases were reported. Up to that time there had been several hundred deaths in the camps, the Great Lakes naval training station showing the heaviest list of victims.[6]

The navy consequently disbanded the talented Great Lakes team, news that gave some satisfaction to a *Sporting News* correspondent. The influenza epidemic, he wrote, "has caused the Great Lakes naval training station all star baseball team to disband and the players, some of whom according to reports never handled anything more deadly than a baseball bat, are being assigned to real service that scatters them to various other stations. Some of them even may go to sea."[7]

Far from being a poor joke in the *Sporting News*, the Spanish flu with its attendant pneumonia was extremely deadly. The epidemic was even worse overseas. The American Expeditionary Forces reported seventy thousand cases by the first week of October, many among troops fresh off the transports from America. "The death rate from influenza rose to 32 per cent of cases for the AEF and was as high as 80 per cent in some groups," General Pershing wrote later.[8] In the United States, the disease killed several Major and Minor Leaguers in less than a month, including civilians and servicemen alike.

In Philadelphia, current or former Phillies Sherwood Magee, Bradley Hogg, Joe Oeschger, and Dave Bancroft (plus three of their wives) fell seriously ill in early October. The four ballplayers were working in area shipyards following the early end to the baseball season. All recovered from the illness. Babe Ruth fell ill at home in Baltimore, but likewise recovered. Former St. Louis Cardinal catcher Harry Glenn died October 12 at the army aviation mechanics school in St. Paul, Minnesota. Former White Sox, Indians, and Braves outfielder LaVerne "Larry" Chappell, who had enlisted in the hospital corps with several teammates from the Salt Lake club of the Pacific Coast League, died November 8 at Letterman Army Hospital in San Francisco.[9]

The epidemic also killed several Minor Leaguers. John W. Inglis, a New York State League catcher and outfielder, succumbed October 7 at the navy's Pelham Bay training station. Pitcher Dave Roth, a veteran of the International and three other leagues who had gone undefeated over the summer for Sparrows Point in the Steel League, died October 11 in Baltimore. Pitcher Harry Acton, another former New York State player, died October 12 at Camp Sherman. All these men earned gold stars on baseball's figurative service flag.

The flu epidemic only compounded the dangers that soldiers and sailors faced during the war. Baseball's first rank of fighters had now worn khaki for nearly eighteen months. Yankees co-owner T. L. Huston, the earliest of them all, had been in France with the Sixteenth Engineers (Railway) for more than a year. The regiment was a support unit, but saw plenty of action.

"The latter part of March we left the middle east part of France for the British front and stayed there about two months," Huston wrote in a censored letter to Tom Rice in late September. "We saw all the spectacular part of the big drive, especially the push in Flanders, where the Hun was trying to get a hold of the big coal fields of France, near —. Had they done so this war might have been different. While we were not right in the front line trenches, we were building light railways in the rear, and were subject to shell fire and many airplane raids."

Huston no longer commanded a company, having been promoted twice, most recently to lieutenant colonel, "but half of the men in the regiment still call me captain." His old outfit, Company A, was scattered across southern France, while Huston had taken charge of building a massive hospital at Mesves, "possibly the largest one in the world. Our regiment has just received orders to prepare for service with the [American] First Army, which very likely means we will soon be on the go back to the front, at the prospect of which we are all delighted, because when you get a taste of the excitement at the front it has a fascination for you, in spite of war's horrors."[10]

Hank Gowdy and the Forty-Second Rainbow Division had been in France almost as long as Huston's engineers. The catcher's 166th Regiment had seen action at Luneville, Baccarat, Esperance-Soulain, Champagne-Marne, Aisne-Marne, St. Mihiel, Essey, and Pannes, and soon would be engaged in the great Meuse-Argonne offensive. "Lank Hank" had penned a few lines about the war in July to former big-league pitcher Ed Reulbach. "We have been kept busy and have been at the front now just about four months," Gowdy wrote. "Just returned from gas school. Am acting as regular gas non-commissioned officer and it's very interesting. A Boche plane was brought down here yesterday. It was on fire and two Germans just about burned up. One of them jumped out." Gowdy asked Reulbach to visit his family if he ever got to Columbus. "I surely did miss the Florida trip this spring. About the time the boys were going South we were getting a little polite hell."[11]

Stars and Stripes had published a breezy interview with the army's best-known color sergeant later in the summer. "I don't mind admitting I'll be ready to change the gas mask for the catcher's mask and to take my chance against Walter Johnson's fast one rather than one of the fast ones from Fritz," Gowdy said. "At that, Fritz hasn't got much more speed than Walter has and no better control. But he's noisier and meaner, and I guess we'll have to drive him from the box, or help in doing it." "Lank Hank looks just as he did in the old days," the army paper added. "His uniform isn't the same color or shape and neither is the mask he wears, but the change hasn't affected that world-embracing grin nor the cheery call along the road."[12]

Gowdy also ran into Johnny Evers during the summer. Evers was overseas working for the Knights of Columbus. The Ohioan likely wasn't aware of the compliment the Trojan had paid him in the spring, shortly before his retirement from baseball. "When the train carrying the Boston Red Sox east stopped at Columbus, o, the home of 'Hank' Gowdy, . . . the players, headed by Johnny Evers, Gowdy's old teammate, stood up and gave the world's series hero a silent toast."[13] Now the former Braves teammates were reunited in a Paris café.

> "When I met Gowdy he just had come out of Chateau Thierry," said Evers. "He had been sent along with the rest of his outfit to Paris to recover from the strain."
>
> "What, Johnny Evers!" was Hank's greeting to me. "You here! You darned fool! Go back!"
>
> "Yep," says Johnny, "Hank advised me to get right out of there and go home."
>
> "Yet three weeks later," said Evers, "I got a letter from Hank in which he told me about being right in the thick of the fighting and the whole tone of the letter showed how he enjoyed it. The strain of battle can't long affect the courage of a fellow as nervy as Gowdy."[14]

But soldiers experience combat differently, and few were as seemingly unchanged as the Boston catcher. Lt. Harry McCormick had also fought with the Rainbow Division in the spring and summer, but had come away far more emotionally damaged than Gowdy. Sportswriters were surprised to see the former Giant back in New York in August, when he took in a Yankees game at the

Polo Grounds. "Two weeks ago Monday Lieutenant McCormick was in action 'somewhere in France' in a town mentioned in the big headlines every day," a Philadelphia newspaper reported. "He is here under orders, the nature of which is secret, but he hopes and expects to go back to the front as soon as his duty on this side of the ocean is finished."[15] "A Hun shell fell close enough to 'Moose' to muss him up a little," Dan Daniel added in his *New York Sun* column. "Lieut. McCormick just radiated optimism and enthusiasm. He has been assigned to duty on this side for a while."[16]

McCormick told the scribes little about the war except that soldiers were unhappy with Major League Baseball. "The talk of the soldiers is that the ball players should have volunteered in a body and made up one big organization and gone into the country's service to fight right at the start," the lieutenant said. McCormick pointed out that *Stars and Stripes* had dropped its sports page for the duration. "The soldiers like to play ball. They are interested in baseball, but it's in their own organization. You can't get enough baseballs to go around over there. Governor Tener sent me two every week, and they were worth their weight in gold. The soldiers get plenty of chance to play, but they want to play it themselves. They don't take any interest in men playing it here any more."[17]

Writers were vague about what McCormick was doing in the United States. Some said he was on leave and intended to rejoin his unit. Others mentioned his so-called secret orders. Fred Lieb came closer to the truth than many. "A shell exploded near him and impaired his sight. He was sent home and arrived in New York last week. He also has suffered from shock," the sportswriter wrote in the *Sun*. "McCormick wears a chevron on his sleeve, indicating that he was wounded, but looks tanned, hearty and hard as nails. For the present he will be on duty on this side of the water." In fact McCormick was suffering from shell shock, what is known today as post-traumatic stress disorder (PTSD). He never returned to France, to combat, or to the infantry. The army promoted him to captain and quietly reassigned him to the supply department at Camp Kearny, California, where he assembled a good baseball team. While the Rainbow Division fought on, McCormick largely dropped from public view. "His New York friends were of the opinion that McCormick was still in France," Bill Macbeth wrote shortly before the war's end.[18]

Six months after the armistice, Hugh Fullerton chatted with Hank Gowdy about serving in France. Their talk turned to what the sportswriter (but not Gowdy) termed "yellowness." The catcher mentioned a ballplayer whom he either didn't identify or whose name Fullerton purposely withheld, although clearly it was McCormick.

> He was one of the greatest pinch-hitters that ever stepped to a plate. He kept himself in perfect physical condition, went to bed by the clock, took his exercise the same way, ate regularly and carefully and as a result he had no nerves. He could walk to the plate in the tightest game in the world and seem as cool as if he was batting fungoes and his hitting was wonderful, especially in the tight places. We all admired his nerve and his coolness. He was one of the first to get into the war and that proved his courage.
>
> But almost as soon as our troops got into action he blew all to pieces, with the thing they call shell shock. How do you account for that?[19]

Neither man could account for it in 1919, but our understanding of PTSD has greatly expanded during the wars and decades since. During World War II, McCormick deflected a question about his combat service with a quip: "Just say that I was the bravest guy in the whole Army when I had some of my own men along with me—and the biggest coward in the world when I was out in No Man's Land alone."[20]

Baseball's greatest combat hero during the war was Pvt. Hugh S. "Hughie" Miller, a former first baseman whose name was familiar only to the most diehard fans. He had appeared in one game for the Philadelphia Phillies as a pinch-runner in 1911. Afterward, Miller had bounced around the Minors until signing with the new Federal League club in his hometown of St. Louis. He played for the Terriers throughout 1914 and in seven games during 1915. Sportswriter J. B. Sheridan wrote that Miller was "a very quiet player.

Indeed, it was held against him that he always kept his head down, never said a word, and while he played good ball, he also played 'dead' ball. His friends are wont to hold that Miller would have been a very successful player had he shown any 'life.'"[21]

Miller began to show that life by enlisting in the Marines two months after America entered the war in 1917. A year later he was at Chateau-Thierry, one of nearly eight thousand marines attached to the army's Second Division, fighting to stop a dangerous German push toward Paris. Suffering from a high fever, Miller sneaked out of a hospital June 6 to rejoin his company at a place called Belleau Wood. The battle there soon entered Marine Corps lore. "The fighting during most of this period was intense," Pershing wrote. "The German lines were favorably located on commanding ground and were made more formidable by the extensive use of machine guns, especially in Belleau Wood. The success of this division against an enemy determined to crush it was obtained with but little assistance from the tired French divisions on its flanks."[22]

"They thought the Germans were going to Paris sure, but were willing to let the marines block 'em off the home plate if they could," Miller wrote home to a friend. "Did they? Well, about 5,000 leathernecks held up 50,000 Boches and made them face toward Germany in no time."[23] His actions earned Miller the Distinguished Service Cross.

His citation read, *"Hugh S. Miller,* private, Company K, 6th Regiment, United States Marine Corps. In the Bois de Belleau, France, on June 6, 1918, he captured two of the enemy single-handed. Although ordered to the rear twice because of illness, he returned to his command voluntarily and continued to fight with it vigorously throughout the advance."[24] General Pershing personally pinned the medal on Miller's chest. "Hail Hugh Miller, Hero with Marines," *Sporting News* trumpeted.[25]

Sports pages across America heaped headlines and praise on the warrior they had barely noted as a ballplayer. Miller wouldn't have known much about his new fame. After recovering from his illness, he rejoined his company and was wounded in action July 18: "I was hit by a machine gun bullet, which entered my shoulder, and was laid up in the base hospital almost a month." He recovered and again returned to his company. He then received a second, far more serious wound September 12. "A Boche airplane which was flying high, almost out of sight to the naked eye, dropped a bomb down on us and it exploded near to where I was," Miller wrote. "Part of the steel struck me in the leg below the hip and tore the flesh away and broke the bone."[26] The explosion felled several other marines, including Miller's officer.

The severe injury kept Miller in a military hospital until well past the armistice. Surgeons saved his leg, but he had limited mobility the rest of his life. With the Distinguished Service Cross (later changed to a Navy Cross, an equivalent decoration for marines), a medal from the French, and a citation for gallantry in action, Hughie Miller "after all is said and done is about the greatest living hero in the war that baseball has produced."

Brooklyn pitcher Leon Cadore also fought in France. He was a first lieutenant, one of the white officers commanding the African American 369th Infantry Regiment. Nicknamed the Harlem Rattlers or Hellfighters, the outfit earned a fine combat reputation fighting beside French troops, and they "spent more time on the front lines than any other AEF unit."[27] "On occasions too numerous to count we were in the thick of the fighting and the noble work done by these Negro troops was wonderful," Cadore later wrote. "Every man in my regiment fought with the courage of a lion."[28]

"Several times I thought it was all over with me" the pitcher once admitted to a sportswriter. "One day, while resting in a trench, a hand grenade dropped at my feet. But luckily it failed to explode."[29] Cadore led nighttime sorties out through the wire. "Oh, a couple of us went out in No Man's Land one night and bagged a few prisoners that gave us a little valuable information," he recalled of one raid. "None of us were wounded or killed. It wasn't much, you know." ("Cutting through the barbed wire an' squirmin' right into the German trenches an' bringing back a squad of Heinies— wasn't anythin'!" one of his men added.)[30]

A few soldiers in Cadore's outfit had played professional ball before the war with independent African American teams. "Needless to say when we were in the thick of the fighting in the Vosges and the Champaign we got mighty little time for baseball," Cadore said. "We had to play it with hand grenades."[31]

Dozens of other big-leaguers fought in France as well. Grover Alexander of the Cubs and several other big-league ballplayers in the 342nd Field Artillery all saw combat with their batteries. Pittsburgh Pirates pitcher Elmer Ponder flew as an Air Service pilot and became an ace shortly before the armistice. Outfielder "Leaping Mike" Menosky of Washington, pitcher Hal Carlson of Pittsburgh, and pitchers Sherrod "Sherry" Smith and Johnny Miljus of Brooklyn all fought in France. Cleveland Indians outfielders Joe Harris and Elmer Smith and pitcher Ed Klepfer also saw combat; Harris was nearly killed when caught between American and German shellfire. When Klepfer earned a commission in France, Harris plaintively asked, "Can you imagine me having to salute Big Ed?"[32]

Even Frank "Brownie" Burke, a diminutive vaudeville performer and former mascot for the Cincinnati Reds, served in the AEF. Despite standing just four feet six inches tall, far below regulation height, Burke talked his way into uniform to become the "smallest man in the armies of the United States."[33] He was a corporal, a clerk attached to the headquarters of the Ninetieth Division, which went into action in the St. Mihiel sector.

Former sportswriters saw plenty of action, too. Among the youngest was Lt. James Saunders O'Neale, twenty-six, formerly of the *New York Tribune*. He had played football and captained the baseball team at Columbia University and was a nephew of U.S. Secretary of the Treasury William McAdoo. O'Neale was wounded in action August 25 while fighting with the 305th Infantry Regiment, Seventy-Seventh Division. He sent a cheerful letter from a base hospital, assuring his wife that he wasn't seriously hurt. "He wrote that the 305th went 'over the top' at 4:30 a.m., the morning of the 25th, and that he was crawling toward the German lines when a bullet struck him in the lower left side. He added that he lay for thirty hours in 'No Man's Land' before he was rescued."[34]

New York newspapers reported O'Neale's death a month later. After the armistice, a captain from the same regiment told the *Brooklyn Eagle* in Paris that only 35 of 250 men had returned safely from the August attack. "Poor Jimmie O'Neale unexpectedly died," he said. "He was on the road to recovery when complications set in. Isn't it too bad."[35]

Even civilian Johnny Evers came under fire in France while in uniform for the Knights of Columbus. The "Crab" had gone over to teach and talk about baseball with doughboys behind the front at American camps and bases. Later he instructed French *poilus* in the national pastime as well. One day Evers visited Lt. Joe Jenkins, a White Sox catcher in 1917, in a line of trenches recently captured from the Germans outside Verdun. A large German shell exploded about 150 yards away, sending a young soldier leaping like a rabbit for the safety of a dugout. "I followed just like that rabbit's brother," Evers recalled. "I was picking myself up from the bottom of the dugout when Jenkins stuck his head in the doorway and laughed, 'Ha! Ha! Ha! Johnny! What're you afraid of! Don't you know that shell is gone! You never see the one that hits you!'"[36]

Once he returned home, Evers spoke movingly of meeting an army chaplain who had found a soiled baseball in a dead doughboy's overcoat pocket while searching him for personal effects. "I'd like to have that ball," Evers said. "Not for a million dollars," the chaplain replied. "I'm too big a fan, and this is too precious to me. It will be more precious to others. If I can find them when we get back that boy's baseball belongs to them. If not, then I'll keep it as one of the biggest prizes of my life."[37]

American troops flooded into France at a frantic pace. Troop transports unloaded masses of soldiers onto French docks and immediately reversed course and steamed back to the United States to embark more. By September 1918 some 1.7 million doughboys formed the AEF. There were nearly 2 million by the armistice two months later. Several of the biggest names from the Major Leagues made it "over there" near the end of the fighting, arriving with a quickness that would have amazed ordinary officers and doughboys.

With ten days to go in the regular season, Cardinals president Branch Rickey and Reds manager Christy Mathewson received commissions in the army's Chemical Warfare Service, also commonly called the Gas and Flame Division. Boston Braves president Percy Haughton was already a major in the same branch. Rickey became a major and Mathewson a captain. Tigers slugger Ty Cobb also received a captaincy once the regular season ended on Labor Day. All of these men had families and likely could have avoided military service had they wanted.

"The men were not commissioned because they were ballplayers, but because they were healthy, live specimens of American manhood and the type of leaders we need in the service," Maj. Gen. William Sibert, chief of the gas service, assured the newspapers. "They were not selected because of any knowledge of chemistry, but will be used solely as leaders with gas troops or with organizations having gas administering units."[38] Louis Lee Arms explained their duties:

> All of these men will go into the lines to fight, for there is no hint of 'swivel chair' luxury in the offensive and defensive branches of this service, and these are the ends with which the non-chemists, such as Cobb, Mathewson, et al., will be identified. They will go to school in France, and school will be conducted in the shadows of the trenches, where big guns constantly roar. Completing their courses they will become staff officers, and their actual work of fending off gas attacks and planning chemical onslaughts will begin.[39]

Arms's account was correct. All but one of baseball's Gas and Flame officers arrived for duty in France before the armistice, earlier than others who had enlisted or were drafted at the same time. The exception was St. Louis Browns first baseman George Sisler, who had a rocky transition from baseball into the armed forces. Following the season, numerous sports pages reported that Sisler, a University of Michigan engineering graduate, had turned down Rickey's offer of an immediate lieutenant's commission to work instead in either Bethlehem's Lebanon plant or an unnamed shipyard.

"The reason ascribed by St. Louis correspondents to Sisler's refusal of a commission sounds unbelievable," Arms wrote. "It is that he balked when informed that he would have to withstand the cost of his uniform, the same as all army officers."[40] Louis A. Dougher defended the ballplayer in the *Washington Times*, insisting that Sisler had been "placed in a wrong light by some unknown masquerading under his name" in the shipyard. "He denied ever playing with a shipyard team and rightly scorned to reply to the second rumor [about the uniform]. . . . It's really too bad!"[41]

But the reports held an atom of truth. Sisler had hesitated accepting the offer from Rickey, his friend and mentor. The opportunity passed before he made up his mind. Sisler then turned down an offer to work and play Steel League ball in Lebanon and enlisted on his own in the chemical service. He earned a second lieutenant's bar after training at Camp Humphries, Virginia, and was designated for overseas service. The war ended before he could sail for France. "And now that I look back upon my experience," Sisler wrote the next spring, "I regret that I failed to act a little quicker, before luck broke against me."[42]

Christy Mathewson, in contrast, reached France the last week of September. He was soon hospitalized with influenza. To a *Brooklyn Eagle* writer who slipped in to see him, the stricken Reds manager looked like "a big boy in bed for punishment. . . . I cannot tell you of his work, or anything like that, but he seems on edge to get to it again. He is a hero among the sick and wounded officers here, and for that matter, the boys are pretty much excited about having him around."[43]

Captains Mathewson and Cobb were later involved in a deadly training accident near AEF Headquarters at Chaumont. Soldiers marched into a sealed chamber, where they were supposed to don their gas masks upon seeing a hand signal. Unbelievably, the exercise involved real poison gas. Most of the men missed the vital signal, including Cobb and Mathewson. In his 1961 autobiography, Cobb described a frantic struggle to pull on their masks and scramble to safety. Both ballplayers inhaled gas, and eight men died.

"Ty, when we were in there, I got a good dose of that stuff," Mathewson wheezed. "I feel terrible." Cobb suffered from a hacking cough and a colorless discharge from his chest for weeks afterward, but suffered no lasting damage. Mathewson's lungs were permanently weakened, a fact not generally known during the war. The gas exposure likely contributed to his early death from tuberculosis in 1925. "I saw Christy Mathewson doomed to die," Cobb remembered.[44]

Having repulsed the dangerous German offensives during the spring, the Allies were now poised to counterattack and pierce the enemy's weakened defenses. The push began the day after the World Series with an attack by Pershing's First Army on the German salient at St. Mihiel, France. Hank Gowdy's Forty-Second Rainbow Division was one of six Yank divisions in the battle, which ended in victory September 16. First Army then shifted fifty miles to the northwest for a larger offensive, the Meuse-Argonne, named for a river on the right and a forest on the left of the Americans' line. General Pershing vividly recalled the pivotal moment in his memoirs:

> The Meuse-Argonne offensive opened on the morning of September 26th. To call it a battle may be a misnomer, yet it was a battle, the greatest, most prolonged in American history. Through forty-seven days we were engaged in a persistent struggle with the enemy to smash through his defenses. The attack started on a front of twenty-four miles, which gradually extended until the enemy was being assailed from the Argonne Forest to the Moselle River, a distance of about ninety miles.[45]

Allied divisions also launched a massive offensive, sometimes called the Fifth Battle of Ypres, two days after the Yanks. The Germans slowly began to give way. "The first four days of October saw the Allied armies advancing on all sectors of the Western Front."[46] Lieutenant Colonel Huston and his Sixteenth Engineers supported the American push.

"In October we were ordered to the American First Army and were a short time on the light railways in the general neighborhood of Varenness and Montfaucon," Huston wrote. "During the battle of the Meuse the regiment reconstructed the standard gauge line down the Meuse from Verdun to Sedan as far north as Stenay. It was still engaged in this work when the armistice was signed. The men were under shellfire by day and were bombed and made the subject of machine gun fire from airplanes constantly during the nights. Again low visibility reduced the efficiency of the Hun planes, but they appeared to have pretty well located us when the armistice occurred."[47]

Gabby Street was also in the big push. Walter Johnson's old catcher had seen his first action with the First Gas Regiment in the spring near Amiens and Luneville. By September he was near St. Mihiel. At zero hour, 5:30 on the morning of the twenty-sixth, he and his men were at the base of Hill 267, just outside the Argonne. Street blew a blast on his whistle and shouted, "C'mon, men! Let 'er go!"

> Adverse winds prevented the gas barrage, but Sergt. Street and his men laid down a smoke screen for the 138th (St. Louis) Infantry of the 35th Division, and a few moments after 5 a.m., the gallant 138th plunged into the Battle of the Argonne. On and on, ahead of the artillery calculations at times, and without artillery support, they moved forward, Street and his men with them.[48]

The regiment fought through the day and those that followed. October 2, Street and his men dragged a gun into a shell hole. A German pilot strafed them with a machine gun, wounding the old catcher. "He lay on the field fourteen hours before the stretcher-bearers reached him, and while helpless the enemy put over a gas attack, the effects of which are discernible on his neck and chin, which he no longer has to shave."[49]

Sergeant Street passed through an evacuation hospital and two base hospitals before the armistice was signed. With his wounds and gassing, Street had legitimately earned the nickname that St. Louis fans would use for him when he managed the Cardinals from 1929 through 1933: "Old Sarge."

Captain Eddie Grant was in the Meuse-Argonne offensive, too. His Seventy-Seventh Division had taken over a quiet sector in

Lorraine from Hank Gowdy's Forty-Second Division in mid-July, the first step toward serious action. "I look forward to staying here to the end," Grant wrote in his diary July 30. "All I hope is that I am lucky enough to do that."[50] The New Yorkers moved in August into a position along the Vesle River near Reims, where they experienced their first heavy shellfire. In September the division advanced to the Aisne River as "a feeling of confidence swept through its ranks; the knowledge of might and will to exercise it properly had sprung into being."[51]

In early October Grant was fighting in the Argonne Forest. On the third, the Seventy-seventh division was furiously trying to reach a small mixed force commanded by Maj. Charles S. Whittlesey, Grant's classmate and friend at Plattsburg and Harvard Law School. Whittlesey and his men were surrounded by the Germans; Americans would soon know them as the Lost Battalion. "The history of the next three days covers one of the most heroic periods in the story of the 77th Division. There was no such thing as rest or relief, no concern for food and water, no regard on the part of anyone for the wet, the cold, and the exhaustions that all were suffering from. . . . The heart of King Richard had been thrown far into the enemy lines and way must be won to it."[52]

Captain Grant and Company H of the 307th Infantry Regiment fought to reach Whittlesey on the morning of October 5. "'Just put your head down and batter your way through' was about the only order that could be followed," the divisional history states.[53] Utterly exhausted, Grant could barely lift a tin cup of coffee to his lips. Sportswriter Damon Runyon, then a correspondent with the First Army, described the scene:

> Finally with a terrific effort, he gulped down the coffee, when the command came to move.
>
> He stepped off at the head of his company as briskly as ever. On the way through the forest, fighting at every step, Grant came upon stretcher bearers carrying back the major commanding the battalion, who had been wounded. The major called to Grant:
>
> "Take command of the battalion!"

Eddie Grant was then one of the few officers left. The major had hardly spoken when a shell came through the trees, dropping two lieutenants in Grant's company. Eddie shouted:

"Everybody down," to his men, without hunting cover for himself. He called for more stretcher bearers for the two lieutenants. He was calling and waving his hands when a shell struck him. It was a direct hit.

Officers and men say Eddie's conduct during the fight was marvelous. He never slept while the drive for Whittlesey's position was on.[54]

In a *Stars and Stripes* article that ran without a byline, Sgt. Alexander Woollcott offered a slightly different version. Woollcott put the captain's death late in the afternoon and added that men in Grant's company had tried to send him back to an aid station to rest an hour earlier.

But he had paid no heed to them.

Now, with the whole battalion under his command, he was moving forward when a big shell exploded, killing several men in the company just ahead and badly wounding his own adjutant.

"Flop, everybody!" the captain called out to the men of Company H, but because his lieutenant had been hurt, he himself remained standing so that he could shout down the forest path. "Stretcher, stretcher, stretcher!" That was the last word he said, for there came a second shell and a piece of it tore its way into his side and killed him instantly.[55]

A sergeant crawled to the captain's body but couldn't remove it from the field under the heavy fire. He and three other soldiers later crept out and retrieved the corpse under the cover of darkness.

"We buried him in a place where several of his fellow officers lie buried, which had been prepared by the Germans in the Argonne Forest as a small cemetery for their dead," an army chaplain wrote to Grant's old manager, John McGraw. "Captain Grant was the most popular man in the 307th Infantry, well beloved by his men, who would follow him wherever he led the way. He had no fear of death, going where duty and honor called him. Now he lies near the spot where he poured out his life's blood that liberty and justice may prevail."[56]

Whittlesey and his battalion held out until relief broke through October 8. "I can just see and hear that boy when he heard that my battalion was trapped in the woods, saying, 'Well, if there is any chance to get my old friend "Whit" out of that hole, I want to be the man to do it,'" Whittlesey said later of Grant. "When that shell burst and killed that boy, America lost one of the finest types of manhood I have ever known."[57] "His is the first gold star on baseball's service flag," a newspaper wrote of the former Giant. "He died for his country and for the world. No greater epitaph awaits any man."[58] Grant's body was later reinterred in the Meuse-Argonne American Cemetery under a soldier's simple white cross.

It was an especially deadly week for the American army in France and for the ballplayers serving in it. German-born Sgt. Robert Gustave Troy died two days after Grant, on October 7, of wounds received in action with the 319th Infantry Regiment, Eightieth Division. "Bun" Troy had pitched in one game for the Tigers in 1912, his only game in the Majors, which he lost to Washington's Walter Johnson. Troy's body was returned to the United States in 1921 for burial with full military honors in his hometown of McDonald, Pennsylvania.

Five days after Troy, army pilot Lt. Alexander Thomson Burr died in a training accident in southwestern France. The aviator was a former Williams College student who was "rated high as a pitcher but who was snatched up by the big leagues before he could represent the Purple on the diamond."[59] In 1914 Tom Burr had played two innings in center field for the Yankees without a plate appearance or the chance to make a play in the field. His plane collided October 12 with another during gunnery training and crashed in flames into Lac de Cazaux. The army recovered Burr's body from the lake twelve days later, but the other pilot was never found.

Reports on the deaths from combat and disease of numerous Minor Leaguers appeared in *Sporting News* and local newspapers. No comprehensive list was kept, and many of Organized Baseball's casualties went unnoticed except by their families. An exception was the battlefield deaths of two ballplayers mourned in their hometown of Lockport, New York, and still occasionally remembered today.

Lifelong friends Cpl. Leo Dolan and Sgt. Matt Lanighan were members of Company I, 309th Infantry Regiment, Seventy-Eighth Infantry Division. "Dolan and Lanighan are well known athletes. They formed a battery for the Fibre Industrials. Both left here in September 1917. They received their training at Camp Dix, New Jersey, before embarking overseas."[60] Lanighan, a catcher, had never advanced beyond industrial and semipro leagues, but Dolan had pitched for Columbus, Georgia, in the South Atlantic League in 1917. In the army, the pair played together on their regimental team at Camp Dix. "Dolan was a splendid type of young man, tall and powerful. His partner, Lanighan, was also of imposing physique," their local newspaper recalled. "Their friends have no doubt that they distinguished themselves in action and fought with the same team work and determination that gave them fame on the baseball field."[61]

The 309th fought in the Meuse-Argonne offensive. Combat on October 16 was fierce. "Our company and in fact our whole division got shot up quite bad and lots of the boys are among the missing," a wounded sergeant wrote home to Lockport. Dolan was mortally wounded in the stomach, and Lanighan killed outright. "It was hard when you looked around and saw your old friends lying all over the ground and among them were Leo Dolan and Matt Lanighan from my home town," the sergeant wrote. "The rest of the boys are still alive and anxious to go back and get revenge."[62]

"The two boys were inseparable pals," the local newspaper recalled after the armistice. "They carried the companionship of the ball field into their social lives and were always together. In the army they were allotted places in ranks side by side and thus they went into the battles of France."[63]

"I buried a private, Peter Dolan of Lockport, NY, in high honors and helped to lower him into the grave," a Jewish army chaplain wrote to friends in Niagara Falls, not far from the doughboy's hometown. "If any of my friends get to Lockport [it] would be doing me a favor to tell his people or the Knights of Columbus that there was a K of C card in his pocket. He died on the eve of victory."[64]

Pvt. Thomas A. Quinlan, a former Major and Minor League outfielder, was at the front, too. A replacement in Company K, Twenty-Eighth Infantry Regiment, First Infantry Division, he had been overseas for less than two months.

"Finners" Quinlan was a good ballplayer. He had played eight seasons in the lower circuits, paying his dues for fifty-five games with the Cardinals and White Sox in 1913 and 1915, respectively. Quinlan nearly captured the Pacific Coast League batting title while with Salt Lake City in 1916. The Bees then traded him to Columbus in the American Association in spring 1918, in exchange for Larry Chappell. Quinlan didn't report to Columbus, however. One article said he didn't want to play ball anymore, and another said that he was simply awaiting his draft call. Instead, he enlisted that July. As night fell in the Argonne on November 9, Quinlan couldn't have been aware of Chappell's death a day earlier in San Francisco. It was only two days until the armistice, although the troops didn't know it for sure.

As fighting continued, a high-explosive German artillery shell detonated near the southpaw outfielder. "I lasted only one inning in the big game," Quinlan said ruefully later.[65] "The shell that 'got' Quinlan not only tore off his throwing arm, but it put out his right eye and inflicted minor wounds on the head and face," a wire service reported.[66] He passed through casualty stations and field hospitals until he reached an American Red Cross military hospital in Paris. St. Louis Cardinals manager Jack Hendricks, now a K of C secretary, visited him there. "And there are a lot more ball players, many of them well known in the minors, who more than did their bit," Hendricks said.[67]

"There isn't much to tell about my being wounded," Quinlan said weeks later. "A German shell just dropped near me, and you can see what it did. The doctors and nurses are taking good care of me, and the Red Cross is keeping me supplied with everything I want. So they needn't worry about me at home." Quinlan offered no complaints and said he would get along all right with a glass eye and a prosthetic arm. Another wounded doughboy said of the disabled ballplayer, "That Quinlan is game."[68]

Despite thousands of dead and wounded, the U.S. Army pushed ahead in its great offensive for forty-seven days. In the end, the doughboys and the ballplayers prevailed.

"The battle of the Meuse-Argonne was not the sole reason the Allies won the war, but it was certainly the deciding factor," states historian Mitchell Yockelson. "Pershing's forces broke the back of the mighty German Army in the most heavily defended section of the western front."[69]

11

Armistice

Gunner's Mate Walter Maranville was busy on board USS *Pennsylvania* at Norfolk, Virginia, as the battleship took on stores in preparation for setting to sea. The ex-Braves shortstop told shipmates November 10 to get ready for big news the next day. "Everyone kept asking me what the big news was going to be. I said, 'Wait until tomorrow; I will tell you then.' At six-thirty the next morning we got word that the armistice had been signed." The ship's captain soon called Maranville into his cabin, a rare and daunting summons for an enlisted sailor. He demanded to know how the Rabbit had come by such sensitive information.

> I said, "I didn't know anything about the armistice being signed. The reason I said the big day is tomorrow and they would hear great news is that today is my birthday." With that the skipper laughed so much he almost fell out of his chair. When I reached deck the boys already had heard of my birthday, and did they give it to me! That was one birthday I will never forget.[1]

Lt. Grantland Rice remembered the day, too. He had spent part of October at the front with his battery, but November 11 found him at Third Corps headquarters, on the French coast near the Belgian border. "Everybody, from buck private to brigadier, immediately got drunk—on anything and everything, from cognac to sterno," Rice recalled decades later.[2]

Capt. Christy Mathewson had reached the front just three days earlier, after recovering from his influenza and accidental gassing. He was assigned to the Twenty-Eighth Infantry, the "Iron Division." Most of these men, like the captain, hailed from Pennsylvania. The Gas and Flame officer was with them in the trenches when the war ended, having never seen combat.

"It was at his request that he was attached to a division from his native State," the *New York Times* reported. "Since the armistice was signed, Mathewson's duties have been to mass the shells loaded with mustard gas which have been left behind by the Huns and inspect the dugouts for gas and bombs. In one sector alone, Matty has informed his friends in recent letters, he and his assistants came across sufficient mustard gas to kill an army."[3]

Sgt. Pete Alexander and other Major Leaguers in the 342nd Field Artillery had a much closer view of the armistice than Mathewson, Rice, or Maranville. They had no champagne to share between them on the day the war ended. "I was a gunner the day the armistice was signed," Alexander said later. "I had charge of the fighting of one of the guns of our battery which was sending over shells toward Germany. In fact I took it all the way through. I did pretty near everything in the battery. . . . None of our men was gassed and none was wounded, though we went through some heavy shelling at times. But I guess it wasn't heavy compared with what some of the others got."[4]

Sgt. Chuck Ward of the Dodgers believed he knew which gunners had fired the last big American shell of the war. "Chuck writes that his battery of the 342nd field artillery did, because he held the watch to prove it," *Sporting News* reported. "That battery, according to Ward, shot its last load at 59 minutes and 59 seconds past 10 o'clock, and peace came at 11. He'd like to know how anybody could shoot later than that."[5] A regimental history later stated that the 342nd actually fired its final rounds at precisely ten seconds before the hour, the last of nearly 2,500 shells expended since nightfall.[6]

Stable Sgt. Clarence Mitchell, likewise of the Brooklyn club, shared a few additional details about the regiment's hard campaign. "I am sorry I can't explain my experiences while on the front, as that is forbidden," he wrote to Charles Ebbets Jr., son of the Dodgers' owner and secretary of the Flatbush club. "I will say, however, that we were in real hard fighting for 51½ days, and with no let up at all. . . . Our men did very good execution with the big guns."[7]

Sgt. Otis Lambeth, also of the 342nd, believed the Great War had changed all of them. "There's one thing about this war. It takes all a fellow's nervousness away," the Indian pitcher cabled to a Stateside newspaper. "I don't care how the Red Sox and Tigers try to ride me any more. And I won't be a bit afraid of getting beaned in the future. Maybe [manager] Lee Fohl and the bunch in Cleveland will be glad to hear this."[8]

With the country at peace, everyone suddenly was in a hurry— the magnates to reopen their gates in the spring, the ballplayers to return home and exchange their khakis or blues for home whites and travel grays. "I am proud of my present uniform, but it sure will feel good to get those old togs on again," Yeoman Herb Pennock of the Red Sox cabled from England. "It will be one big day when we head for home and the Statue of Liberty. Tell the fans my fast one is faster than I ever thought it could be and wish them a Merry Christmas."[9]

Many Major League magnates were chipper as well. John Heydler of the National League, Harry Hempstead of the Giants, and Barney Dreyfuss of the Pirates met for lunch in New York on November 21. Despite many uncertainties and unknowns, they were optimistic. "They feel cheerful regarding the outlook for 1919. . . . Dreyfuss said that he didn't believe any club would have much trouble in getting fifteen players or more of caliber, though the developments of the next month would have to be awaited to give the clubs some definite idea of how matters stand."[10]

Ban Johnson, as usual, disagreed. "Major league clubs would be at a great disadvantage in attempting a resumption of baseball next spring," the American League president said a few days before the armistice. "The players are widely scattered in the Army and Navy service of their country and those immediately available would not appeal to the patrons of the game for reasons too obvious to name."[11] Hugh Fullerton was frankly worried, too, no matter when baseball resumed. "The reconstruction period in baseball," the sportswriter warned, "promises to be as lively as the reconstruction in Europe, with as many rebellions."[12]

The government quickly began discharging servicemen still in the United States, including several ballplayers. Tris Speaker of the Indians and Wally Pipp of the Yankees, both training as naval aviators, became civilians again just two weeks after the armistice. Jack Barry soon left the navy officers' school at Harvard, but Ernie Shore stayed a while longer and received his ensign's commission in December. Ten ballplayers at Great Lakes received discharges before Christmas.

Ballplayers in the AEF would take much longer to get home, but the Major Leagues soon had good news. Johnson received a letter from the army chief of staff December 4, saying there was no reason why the game shouldn't resume a regular schedule in 1919. "The wholesome effect of a clean and honest game like baseball is very marked and its discontinuance would be a great misfortune," wrote Gen. Peyton C. March.[13]

"The demobilization of ball players in the army who had not been sent overseas is already under way and it is probable that before the end of the current year most of the players called last summer will be mustered out of the service," a wire report stated. "Reports have been received in New York of the demobilization at Camp Pike, Ark., which means the return to civil life of two former members of the Yankees and one member of the Robins [Dodgers]. All were young players who had shown great promise."[14]

Capt. Ty Cobb, as aggressive in securing army transportation as in batting and stealing bases for the Tigers, somehow managed to return from France before Christmas, long before his fellow Major Leaguers in the Gas and Flame Division. "The chance to shoot gas into these Germans is gone," Maj. Branch Rickey lamented from France, "and our detachment is as a bunt in a 9 to 0 ball game." Much like Captain Mathewson, Rickey had been hospitalized with pneumonia after arriving overseas and hadn't seen any action. "No, I'm not homesick and can stick it out with good spirit and cheer as long as there is any use for me over here," he wrote, "but the first time they call for volunteers to return home I'll be the first one over the top to say, 'That's me,' and I am not ashamed to say it because there are two million other Americans over here who feel the same way about it."[15]

Lt. Col. Til Huston reached Newport News, Virginia, on the *Ryndam*, a liner turned transport, just as the tumultuous year was ending. He was back in Manhattan by January 2, besieged by newsmen who wanted to hear about his war in France. Huston said he had no hair-raising tales to tell them. "Although I met several newspaper men over there," he quipped, "I was not gassed. It isn't true that the major league baseball players were in disfavor among the soldiers. The soldiers were so busy fighting that they didn't take time to criticize any one but the Germans. Baseball stands in high favor among the soldiers. Since the armistice was signed they have talked about nothing else but the game. They are all anxious to get back home to see a good ball game. . . . I expect to continue my interest in baseball," he said, "and let me say right now that my stock in the Yankees is not for sale."[16]

The future looked less certain for Color Sgt. Hank Gowdy of the Forty-Second Division and Sgt. Grover Alexander of the field artillery. Their units were assigned to occupation duty in Germany, and no one had any good idea when the athletes might be discharged. It seemed possible they might miss most or all of the 1919 season. It was bad news for the Braves and the Cubs, which were eager for their stars to return. The Major Leagues offered what assurances they could. "After five years of war blight," John Heydler said when elected president of the National League on December 10, "the big leagues will emerge again and give the nation some of the best baseball in history during the coming season."[17]

With the armistice also came a revised attitude toward shipyard ballplayers. Connie Mack, for one, had spoken out for them even before the peace. He particularly defended his Athletics, about whom Mack had received good reports from Philadelphia area yards.

"There is not a Class One ball player at a shipyard or steel plant,"

the Philadelphia skipper said. "Those in the essential employ-
ments are Classes Three or Four and haven't been called. They
were put in those classes for the reason they belonged there. . . .
When these men went into essential employment they were obey-
ing the work or fight order. That's the reason the pennant races
were closed a month early, so ball players could be doing just what
they are doing today. Yet, some persons insinuate that a ball player
who abandons all the comforts of life to put on overalls at 5 in the
morning is unpatriotic."[18]

Five days after the armistice, the *New York World* published a long
article by writer-illustrator Robert Edgren about ballplayers working in shipyards along the Pacific Coast. Edgren had written positively about them during the summer and been in the minority. He
pointed out now that the federal government, in fact, had encour-
aged the formation of industrial-league baseball to provide recreation for exhausted workers.

> Incidentally nearly all of the minor league players were snapped up by
> ship yard club managers, who kept the wires and the mails busy carry-
> ing telegrams and letters urging ball players to accept jobs. Scores of
> big league players were brought from all over the country. These men
> didn't go into the ship yards to play baseball and be listed as working
> men by way of camouflage. They went to work like any one else and
> were freely accepted into the membership of the various unions. They
> worked six days a week and played baseball on Sundays. If they had any
> time for practice at all it was only after supper, when, as a rule, they
> were too tired to play ball. The result, of course, was that big league
> form suffered. But the enthusiasm over baseball in the ship yards grew
> steadily. The ship builders' league is playing better ball than the Coast
> League did and has more followers.[19]

Early in 1919 one of Joe Jackson's old Chicago teammates, Alfred
"Fritz" von Kolnitz, staunchly defended the slugger. Now an army
major who had been injured during training, the ex-White Sox utility man believed that Jackson was as well qualified to hold a shipyard position as anyone. "During the draft period, I will venture,
there were thousands of men walking the streets in civilian clothes

with exemption papers in their pockets with far less claims than Joe," von Kolnitz wrote to sportswriter George S. Robbins shortly before 1919 spring training. "I know that Joe lost practically all of his savings a few years ago in an unlucky investment. He is dependent upon his salary for the support of his family. It has always been a puzzle to me why Joe was picked out of the hundreds of shipyard workers and persecuted. You know and I know the main reason. He was a star in his profession and the small mindedness of some people makes them delight in blaming any one high up when they can criticise."[20]

While not as understanding or forgiving as Mack or von Kolnitz, owner Charles Comiskey quietly reversed his banishment of shipbuilding players. "The first thing Kid Gleason, new White Sox manager, did when he got on the job was to pay a visit to the shipyards where Byrd Lynn, Lefty Williams, and Joe Jackson were at work and to arrange for them to return to the Pale Hose next season," a Memphis sportswriter noted in mid-January. "And this is the trio which President Comiskey said would never put their gunboats in his park again."[21] The three ballplayers all eventually returned to the club for the new season. Even *Sporting News* managed to view Jackson in a changed light.

> But times and sentiments change. Our war madness of six months ago has subsided to a great degree and we have learned—many of us having undergone the experience of enforced military service—to take a new view of the man, even though he be a ball player, who exercised his legal rights to consider first his family dependents. Joe Jackson can therefore, if he desires, return to the White Sox with no stigma attached to him. . . . After all, it was this or that: The government said work or fight; the magnates—at the moment—said play ball. The players obeyed the higher order. There's nothing more to be said.[22]

Changing sentiments, his peerless play in the shipyard leagues, and von Kolnitz's letter all helped to ease Jackson's return to the White Sox during the spring. Many of his shipyard colleagues rejoined their clubs as well.

Even Fred Toney was ultimately welcomed back into the big leagues during the season after serving time in jail rather than in the army, navy, or an essential occupation. The Giants hurler pleaded guilty January 1 in federal court in Nashville to violating the Mann Act and was sentenced to four months' imprisonment. Three days later a jury acquitted both Toney and the county official who allegedly had assisted him on the separate charge of conspiracy to evade the Selective Service Act. "The fact that the star pitcher is uneducated and unable to read or write is thought to have been largely responsible for his trouble."

"I think I have just as good an arm as ever hung on a man's body, but less brains than any man in the entire league," Toney said later from his cell in Robertson County, Tennessee. "I attribute all my trouble to my lack of education and the fact that I have been taken advantage of." The pitcher said he was through with baseball, but soon changed his mind—the Giants still needed his arm.[23]

When the convicted felon reported to the team a few days into the season, New York sportswriters would respond with wisecracks rather than outrage. Perhaps they also believed that Toney was as limited a person as he claimed to be. "Toney will need little work to get into condition," Fred Lieb wrote. "The pitcher was not confined very closely while the State of Tennessee was boarding him and was able to warm up every day with other guests. A week or so of practice should put him in condition to take his regular turn in the box."[24] Toney pitched five more seasons in the Major Leagues.

The ballplayers, managers, and writers in the armed forces started for home in ones and twos over the winter. No special program returned them any sooner than other sailors or doughboys. Sportswriters made a point of interviewing them for columns or feature articles, especially when they had returned from overseas.

Chief Yeoman Bob Shawkey popped into the Yankees' front office January 3. He didn't regret his reassignment to the battleship *Arkansas* as punishment for pitching his two Saturday games for New York the previous summer. "I left Philly last July and saw the finish of the war, the last struggles of the U-boats, and then the surrender of the German fleet," Shawkey said. "The surrender was the greatest sight I ever saw. Imagine getting a ticket for that as punishment for pitching two games for the Yankees."[25]

Huston, who had beaten Shawkey into the office by only a day, gave the pitcher a hearty welcome. "I'll bet you never regretted that you got in," Huston said. "I can't see how it is that all the players weren't in."[26]

Capt. Christy Mathewson reached New York in mid-February on the converted liner *Rotterdam*, too late to manage the Cincinnati Reds again in 1919. Garry Herrmann had hired Pat Moran to fill the post in late January, but Mathewson expressed no bitterness or regret. "My contract with Cincinnati terminated before I left for France last September," he said. "I am under orders to go to Washington immediately, and as I see no further use of instructing any one how to throw gas, I expect to ask for my discharge and get back to civil life. The only persons I know of in need of gas are the umpires."[27]

Matty soon returned to the New York Giants as John McGraw's assistant and coach for young pitchers. "McGraw will stay at the helm this season and perhaps next," the *New York Times* reported, "but he says that he has almost come to the end of his managerial career after nearly twenty years in the major leagues and is anxious that his successor should be the player who perhaps stands higher in the estimation of baseball fans than any other man the game has ever produced."[28] Mathewson's compromised health deteriorated, however. He never managed again before his early death in 1925.

First Lt. Grantland Rice began his journey home with former press-box colleague Jack Wheeler on the *Ryndam*, the same ship that had brought back Huston. A flu epidemic broke out aboard the packed ship three days out of St. Nazaire. "It was a heart-rending sight, watching those men and boys dying like flies—knowing they were sinking but struggling that much harder to get home," Rice wrote decades afterward. "Jack and I spent most of our time making our final papers on the listed dead—a list that grew daily. . . . A thankful, subdued Lieutenant Rice landed with an equally subdued Lieutenant Wheeler at Newport News, Virginia, on a drizzly day in February 1919."[29]

Rice rushed home to New York City, only to learn that a lawyer the sportswriter had entrusted to safeguard his securities in 1917 had lost everything in bad investments. The man had taken poison and died. "I blamed myself for the poor fellow's death; I shouldn't have put that much temptation in his way."[30]

Infielder Joe Harris of the Indians and pitcher John Miljus of Brooklyn, both of the 320th Infantry Regiment, almost didn't make it home at all. Having survived the fighting, they nearly died together in an April traffic accident when their army truck rolled over near Le Mans. "Harris sustained a fractured skull, two broken legs and three fractured ribs, but his companion was more fortunate, his injuries being confined to several nasty gashes and a bad shaking up," *Stars and Stripes* reported. "The two men were on their way to St. Aignan for embarkation to the United States."[31]

"I was with both of the boys several times in France and learned they had narrow escapes while in action," wrote Pittsburgh sportswriter Charles J. Doyle. "Joe was the sergeant in charge of a Stokes gun, and Miljus was his corporal. After the armistice was signed the two Allegheny county boys were sent to an officers' training school, but they preferred to come home at the earliest opportunity."[32] Both players got home while the season was under way. Harris returned to the Indians' roster in 1919, while Miljus pitched for AA Toledo before returning to Brooklyn in 1920.

Homecoming stresses like these, combined with the inevitable effects of prolonged combat, prompted many baseball insiders to wonder how well the returning ballplayers would fare back in the Major Leagues. Giants manager John McGraw was profoundly sympathetic, but skeptical about the prospects for such men as Grover Alexander. "I am afraid that Aleck and the other boys who have seen active service on the battle front will find it impossible to play the old game as they did before they went through that experience," McGraw said. "The life which they have led for the last few months has been sterner than anything they ever knew before, and while they have gained the glory which is the due of all our fighting men they have lost something, I believe, which they can never get back. That which they have lost is the physical condition and the mental poise so necessary to the major league ball player."[33]

The Minor Leagues were set to return after the most disastrous season in their history. The circuits bickered, as always, with the Major Leagues and with each other, but the outlook was bright. "In the Southern States the spring training exhibition games attracted more patronage than at any time for many years past," John Farrell of the National Association said in the spring, "and the attendance at the opening series of these games between the Chicago Nationals and the San Francisco club in California was the greatest in the history of baseball on the Pacific Coast."[34]

The entire top tier of the prewar Minor Leagues—the Class AA American, International, and Pacific Coast and Class A Southern and Western circuits—all roared back to life. The American Association and Pacific Coast League would even play a post-season 1919 championship series, won by the PCL's once fatally troubled Vernon club. The Eastern League, with the change of a single franchise, rose from Class B to Class A.

Class B saw the return of the Texas and Indiana-Illinois-Iowa (Three–I) circuits, joined by the new eight-team Michigan-Ontario League. The New York State League, however, was finished. Two other leagues—the Northwest International (formerly the Pacific Coast International) and the New England—began the Class B season but were unable to complete it, ending in June and August, respectively. The Virginia, South Atlantic, and new four-club Western Canada Leagues comprised Class C, while the sole Class D representative was the new Florida State League. All four circuits completed their 1919 campaigns.

From Maine to California and from Canada to Texas all the reports were to the effect that professional base ball was enjoying an extraordinary season; and when the curtain fell upon the dozen minor league races the reports were uniformly to the effect that each had enjoyed its most prosperous season. This generous attendance everywhere can only be attributed to the fact that the mass of our people sought relief after two years of war, with its consequent anxieties and privations, and found it in the open air and in the field of sport.[35]

Overall 1919 was a good year for the Minors.

The Major Leagues began a shortened, 140-game season in Boston on Saturday, April 19. This was also Patriots' Day, the traditional day for running the Boston Marathon. Baseball fans dressed for topcoat weather, sunny but cold.

Boston met Brooklyn at Braves Field in a split doubleheader, the first game in the morning, the second in the afternoon. National League president John Heydler came up from New York to see the season start. An estimated six to ten thousand fans turned out for the morning contest, including five thousand soldiers and sailors admitted for free by the ever-generous Braves. "Those up on baseball superstitions declare that the Bostonians did not have a chance from the start owing to the presence of that potent jinks [*sic*] a horseshoe floral piece, which was hung near their dugout."[36] The service members witnessed the return to the Major Leagues of eight of their recently discharged brethren, including Brooklyn starting pitchers Leon Cadore and Jeff Pfeffer and Braves shortstop Rabbit Maranville. The two hurlers proved less rusty than the infielder.

"A hearty greeting, extended Rabbit Maranville on his first appearance on the home diamond after his days of life on the briny deep, inspired the midget to do his best, but he had the same affliction as his brothers in arms," the *Boston Post* reported. "He didn't look exactly the Rabbit of other days, making misplays of an unaccountable sort. At times he could flash in his ancient estimable manner, but that was only at remote periods."[37] "The Rabbit was not quite up to form in his hitting but will come along all right later," the rival *Globe* added. "He did some nice fielding, participating in three fast double plays."[38]

Cadore went ten innings to win the morning game, 5–2. "Battle experience on the plains of Picardy evidently made no impression on that Brooklyn pitcher as he gave the locals no manner of a lookin [*sic*] until the game was well along to its closing stages. Cadore was as tough a nut to crack as could well be found until he met up with a slip in his defence and a mass attack."³⁹ One of two Maranville errors on the day contributed to the first Brooklyn win.

The afternoon game was slated to start at 3:15, but a large, late-arriving crowd jamming the concourse on Gaffney Street prompted the Braves management to push the first pitch back thirty minutes. Twenty thousand fans eventually filed in, nearly filling the ballpark. "The floral jinks was increased at this game, when the crew of the battleship *Pennsylvania* presented Rabbit Maranville with a huge floral token."⁴⁰ Brooklyn swept the doubleheader as Pfeffer went the distance and won the second game 3–2 despite his wildness in the eighth.

The Dodgers caught a train home that night to play a scheduled exhibition with the Yankees at Ebbets Field on Monday. No other regular games were scheduled in the Major Leagues until Wednesday, April 23, Opening Day for everyone else. A chance encounter in Chicago on Tuesday neatly symbolized the unique occasion.

> A little bit of the Argonne forest was transferred right to the loop in Chicago last night at dinner, when Lieut. Joe Jenkins happened to be seated at the next table to Sergeant Grover Cleveland Alexander. Both had chased the boche through that historic wood in France.
>
> Aleck arrived yesterday afternoon, after visiting his mother in Nebraska. He will pitch the first ball today at the opening game of the season at Cub park.
>
> Jenkins left last night for St. Louis, to appear with the White Sox today against the Browns in their opening game. With Jenkins was Red Faber, recent petty officer at Great Lakes Naval station, and John Collins, outfielder, also going to St. Louis to join the Sox. With Alexander was Sergt. Killefer, captain of the Cubs, who will be back of the bat in the north side opening.⁴¹

Rain delayed the Cubs' opener until Thursday. The afternoon was so chilly that the club reduced the opening ceremonies. Alexander, in a Chicago uniform, quickly trotted to the mound to throw out the first ball, "without half the crowd knowing who it was. Those who did see him hurl that first ball thought he did it in such stylish form that he will be on the rubber for a regular battle in a few days."[42]

Alexander had big expectations for the coming season. "My object now is to win about 30 games for the Cubs and get them in to the next world's series," he had said on landing in New York. "I don't think my absence from the game has hurt my pitching arm for I have had a little light work abroad. The only real practice we had was after the armistice when we played a few games near Trier, Germany."[43]

The great right-hander had won thirty or more games in a season three times before, and hopes were high this year in Chicago. But Cubs fans didn't know the man who had returned. Despite outward appearances, Alexander was in bad shape, suffering from hearing loss from the loud guns, muscle damage to his right arm from pulling the firing lanyard, a minor shrapnel wound, and worst of all, shell shock. The pitcher was a "human wreck," according to biographer Jan Finkel.[44] Alexander's first start came at home May 9. Ray Fisher and the Cincinnati Reds beat him in a 1–0 heartbreaker.

"The big fellow wasn't quite up to his old time standard, but seemed to lack nothing except control," James Crusinberry wrote of Alexander in the *Chicago Tribune*. "He walked five batsmen, and it was one of those walks that was turned into the lone tally. He seemed to have the old curve ball working, and about 90 per cent of his old time speed. Another week of training and the great slab star should be right back in his form of ball and preceding years."[45]

But Alexander never regained his pitching form of 1917, and he struggled in 1919 before settling down to post a record of sixteen wins and eleven losses, albeit with a dazzling 1.72 earned run average. He approached thirty victories only once more in his career, winning twenty-seven in 1920. Battling alcoholism and epilepsy, "Ol' Pete" pitched in the Major Leagues until 1930.

"What the Cubs got when he came back from the war was a scarred, shell-shocked, half-deaf epileptic and alcoholic whose zest for life, without the inducement of liquor, was left somewhere on a muddy battlefield thousands of miles away," biographer John

C. Skipper has written.[46] "Many men survived the war, but they didn't recover from it," adds Finkel. "One of the many cruel coincidences of the war is that it destroyed the two greatest National League pitchers of the Deadball Era, if not of the twentieth century, Christy Mathewson and Grover Cleveland Alexander."[47]

The true emotional start of the 1919 major league season came late in May with the return of Hank Gowdy. The color sergeant arrived home April 25, reaching New York like so many others on the massive *Leviathan*. "The famous catcher and his genial smile loomed up conspicuously out of the sea of faces that limned the rails as the giant greyhound of the ocean was warped into her dock," Bill Macbeth wrote. "But Hank was in too big a hurry to get from khaki into sporting white or gray even to tarry for an interview."[48]

The catcher hurried to Grand Central Station to catch a train for Boston, planning to come to terms with the Braves as soon as possible. Nearly a month passed before he was under contract and in shape to play. The club designated May 24 at Braves Field as Hank Gowdy Day. "Hank is entitled to all the honor that can be heaped upon him," the *Boston Globe* declared on its front page.[49]

As with Alexander, Gowdy's first opponents were the Cincinnati Reds. Cheered by sixteen thousand fans, players from both clubs surrounded Gowdy on the field before the game. Boston's mayor made a short speech before presenting him $800 in Victory bonds, along with a gold watch, chain, and cigar cutter, all bought with funds contributed by fans. The Ohioan's reply was brief but heartfelt: "Holy cow, this is great."[50] His Braves teammates then gave him a traveling trunk and other gifts before trotting away to start the game.

"Former Sergeant 'Hank' Gowdy . . . hit the first ball pitched in the second inning to right field for a single. It was his first time at bat in a championship game since 1917."[51] His second time up, the catcher laid down a perfect sacrifice bunt. His return seemed to invigorate the seventh-place Braves, who went on to trim the Reds, 4–1. "They did it in such a way as to cause the every day brand of fan to emerge from the park in a daze and exclaim: 'How did those birds ever fall down into the subway?'"[52]

The *Boston Post* neatly summed it all up. "All the greater and lesser gods of baseball, weather, fortune and everything else that can make ideal a day of days for a deserving individual," sports-writer Ed McGrath wrote, "worked in entire accord to make Harry Gowdy's long-awaited formal welcome of yesterday the uttermost word in perfection.[53] Major League Baseball was back.

Epilogue

With the war over and the guns silent, Organized Baseball strove for what presidential hopeful Senator Warren G. Harding of Ohio (one of the game's great political supporters) would famously call a "return to normalcy." But what actually had changed for magnates and ballplayers? What had the World War meant for the Major and Minor Leagues?

Despite the valor of its warriors, professional baseball made no appreciable difference to the military conduct of the war. The numbers simply were too small—cumulatively, no more than one army regiment and a small ship's company. But Hank Gowdy, Grover Alexander, Leon Cadore, and other battle-hardened ballplayers at least had mitigated charges of slackerism aimed at the Major Leagues. While fewer fought in front-line units than critics might have preferred, ballplayers were fairly well represented within the American armed forces by the end of the war.

Contemporary newspaper accounts show about sixty current or former Major Leaguers serving in the American Expeditionary Forces in November 1918. Several others were in the navy with the fleet. To these numbers we can add the sportswriters and columnists also in the army, plus the managers or former players who went overseas as uniformed officials of the YMCA and the Knights of Columbus. Realizing the publicity value, and hoping to win back disgruntled fans, the Major Leagues waved the flag by releasing tabulations of their ballplayers' participation in the war. The two circuits used different formulas, each spinning the result to its own advantage.

The American League said shortly before the armistice that 264 ballplayers were under contract or reservation, an average of thirty-three men per club. Of these athletes, 144 (or 55 percent) were in the army, navy, or marines. The National League offered its own figures a month later, basing its calculation on active rosters of twenty men for each of its eight teams. Of the 160 National League players, 103 were serving in the military (64 percent). The league added that it had a total of 257 reserved players. "The facts probably are that baseball gave as great if not greater percentage of its employes [*sic*] than any other occupation," John Heydler said for the National League.[1]

The Major Leagues' figures seemed to compare favorably with those from the first Selective Service draft in June 1917, when registration totaled nearly 9.6 million men. "Experience to date has shown that 34 per cent, or slightly over one-third, of these men are eligible for service," the *Washington Herald* had reported. "The remaining two-thirds, because of dependency of families, industrial exemptions, and physical disability, are not eligible for present service."[2]

Altogether, the government registered 10.4 million men in the first and second drafts. The immense third draft in September 1918 came too late to have much effect. About 3 million men served in the U.S. armed forces during the war—roughly 30 percent of the useful draft pool, with enlistments before June 5, 1917, lowering that percentage somewhat.

The higher percentages claimed by the American and National leagues were contestable, however. The Major Leagues' tabulations included numerous ballplayers who had made a club in earlier seasons, but who hadn't played in 1917 or 1918. The figures also included prospects such as Mark Milligan, who might have been called up to a big club if they hadn't already entered the armed forces. Many men whose names appeared on an American or National League roster during the talent-drained war seasons played only briefly, and some never appeared again in the Majors. Hugh Fullerton particularly challenged the American League numbers. "Ban Johnson says 50 per cent of the American league players are in the service. His figures are wrong," the sportswriter wrote. "He probably means that the total number of players who belonged to American League clubs at various times are in the service. I have tried to secure a complete record of all major and minor league players (active) who went into the war, and it indicates that fewer than 20 per cent. of the major league players joined in active service, although undoubtedly many more were called in the final calls of the first draft and the first of the second draft."[3]

Nevertheless, many hundreds of American ballplayers clearly had entered the armed forces during the war. The Baseball and the Armed Forces Committee of the Society of the American Baseball Research (SABR) has identified 777 veterans of World War I, including players, umpires, scouts, and league officials. The list is eccentric and somewhat flawed. It has minor omissions, but includes such tangential figures as Dwight Eisenhower (who once reportedly played in the Minors) and Buster Keaton (who hired many Major Leaguers for his movies). It also mistakenly includes a few civilians such as Johnny Evers and Arlie Latham, who performed war-related work overseas, and adds several shipyard players as well. Nonetheless, the list is useful. Most of the listed men clearly were Major Leaguers in the seasons before, during, or after the war. The list also includes the names of fourteen African American players, including Dick "Cannonball" Redding and Hall of Famer Oscar Charleston, who played for independent teams before the first Negro Leagues were organized.[4]

Perhaps the simplest way of determining whether the Major Leagues' war effort compared favorably with that of the American male population as a whole is to consider only active ballplayers who entered the armed forces during the war, while omitting such men as Eddie Grant and Tillie Shafer, who had already retired. Of the 777 ballplayers on SABR's list, only 196 appeared in one or more games for a Major League club during the war. Using the American League's formula, based on reserved men (521 for the sixteen Major League teams), 196 represents nearly 38 percent of the players from both circuits. Using the National League's method, based on sixteen 20-man rosters (320 total), the figure is 61 percent. Either way, these percentages are lower than those originally claimed by the respective leagues.

The National League estimated, in addition, that more than one hundred of its players had found essential jobs in compliance with the work-or-fight order, "either during or just after the pennant season in ordnance, in nitrate and steel works, shipyards, aeroplane factories, or on farms."[5] The American League provided no corresponding number, but its total likely was similar.

Counting Minor League ballplayers who had donned khaki or blue during the World War is more difficult. No one assembled a roster or calculated a grand total. In what it acknowledged was an incomplete list, *Baseball Magazine* named 298 players from nine Minor League circuits who served in the armed forces during the war. The Southern Association alone claimed 53 men in service, including 11 of the 14 players on the Chattanooga Lookouts' roster—"which should forever silence the cry of slackers at Dixie major ball players."[6]

Secretary Farrell's earlier estimate of eight hundred Minor Leaguers in the armed forces was likely fairly accurate. By the armistice, the number certainly exceeded one thousand. The Minors' percentages, whatever they were, almost certainly matched or exceeded those of the Major Leagues. "The minor circuit players made a much better showing in France in 1918 than their more gifted comrades from the 'big time,'" said *Spalding's Guide*. "There were dozens of them in the army and some have paid the price of liberty with their lives. The great proportionate representation of minor leaguers in the American army last summer may be attributed to the fact that many small leagues had closed their gates early in the season."[7]

In addition to player enlistments and conscriptions, the Major Leagues significantly contributed to many civilian war efforts. Clubs and ballplayers helped to sell millions of dollars in Liberty Loan bonds, with the players themselves purchasing bonds worth more

than $250,000. Tris Speaker personally bought the first bond of the
second Liberty campaign from Secretary McAdoo in Cleveland in
October 1917; Christy Mathewson sold $100,000 in bonds in one
day. Led by Charles Comiskey, Major League clubs contributed
tens of thousands of dollars to the American Red Cross during the
two wartime seasons; players alone donated more than $14,000.
The Boston Braves and the other fifteen clubs opened their parks
for service games and other events, at which large crowds gener-
ously donated to soldiers' and sailors' recreation funds and various war-related charities. When he ended his Bat and Ball Fund in
Spring 1919, Clark Griffith had raised and spent nearly $150,000—
the equivalent of about $2.4 million a century later—on baseball
equipment for American troops at home, in the AEF, and as far
away as Jerusalem.[8]

Although too small to field a large body of men for military service overseas, the Major Leagues clearly had performed admira-
bly at home—if no more so than many other American businesses
and industries.

Complicated stories seldom have neat endings. Neither the country as a whole nor Major League baseball in particular ever really
returned to "normalcy" after the World War. The United States
went on to experience the lawless, failed experiment of Prohibi-
tion, the rise and boom of the Roaring Twenties, and the descent
into the hard times of the Great Depression.

Baseball returned not to glory but to the worst disgrace in its
history. The Black Sox scandal and corrupt World Series of 1919
permanently tarnished Joe Jackson's reputation and brought a life-
time ban from the sport for all eight implicated Chicago players.
"Shoeless Joe" might better have remained "Joe the Painter" at
the Harlan & Hollingsworth shipyard in Wilmington. The fall-
out also delivered Judge Kennesaw Mountain Landis, baseball's
first commissioner, a necessary and overdue change that further
reduced Ban Johnson's power and influence.

That Major League baseball managed to recover during the
1920s was due in no small part to the power game ushered in by

slugger Babe Ruth and to construction of Yankee Stadium, the magnificent House That Ruth Built. "Colonel Huston, a trained engineer, was on site almost every day, overseeing the sinking of the foundation, the pouring of the concrete, and the erection of the steel girders."[9] Huston sold his share of the club to Colonel Ruppert shortly after the great stadium opened in 1923.

Grantland Rice covered the heady days ahead in baseball, football, and other sports, and recounted them later in his autobiography. But like many old soldiers, the former artilleryman also discovered that his dreams sometimes took him to darker places. "My days were about to be caught up in the fantastic boom of business and sports, the Golden Twenties," Rice remembered. "But for years my dreams were of France and of those who made a crossing much bigger than those of us who made the long voyage home to the U.S.A."[10]

The world repeated the catastrophe one generation later. Former West Point baseball coach Harry "Moose" McCormick, shell shocked in the First World War, returned to duty during the Second. He was the only civilian director in the Army Air Forces, supervising physical training for the First Air Force at Mitchel Field, Long Island. Cincinnati Reds coach Hank Gowdy actually went back into uniform, as an army Special Services (athletic and recreational) officer attached to the Infantry School at Fort Benning, Georgia. McCormick was past sixty, Gowdy in his fifties.

"I advise all baseball players in service to play as much as possible while in uniform," Major Gowdy said in 1943. "It makes them top attractions in exhibition games for service men; meanwhile preventing them from thinking about losing their playing edge." He didn't know at the time whether the Major Leagues would continue playing throughout the war or end early as they had in 1918. "But I advise all baseball players in service to play as much as possible while in uniform. It makes them better soldiers now, and better players when the war is over."[11]

The old Braves catcher often worked in Georgia at Gowdy Field, the army ballpark dedicated in his honor in 1925. "I frankly tried to get the authorities to name the field . . . after Captain Grant, but was informed that the field must be named after an enlisted man," Major Gowdy said. "That's how it happens to be Hank Gowdy Field, an honor I'll treasure the rest of my days."[12] Captain Eddie Grant, whose bones lay interred in German-occupied France, would have approved.

NOTES

Introduction

1. Frederick G. Lieb, "Enright Believes 'Frat' Is Wrong," *New York Sun*, February 2, 1917.

2. "Spring Is with Us and the Baseball Gossip Trots Along," *Toronto World*, March 9, 1917.

1. Sergeants

1. "Baseball Again Is Booming Preparedness," *Washington Herald*, February 24, 1917.

2. W. O. M'Geehan, In All Fairness, *New York Tribune*, March 5, 1917.

3. Frederick G. Lieb, "Shaw's Circuit Hit First of Season," *New York Sun*, February 28, 1917.

4. Frederick G. Lieb, "Rain Halts Yanks' Work at Ball Park," *New York Sun*, March 3, 1917.

5. "Yanks Will Use Broomsticks When Guns Don't Appear," *Syracuse Journal*, February 27, 1917.

6. Frederick G. Lieb, "Huston's Regiment Begins Military Drill at Macon," *New York Sun*, March 7, 1917.

7. William B. Hanna, "Yankees Start Military Work," *New York Herald*, March 7, 1917.

8. "Yankees Enjoy First Military Drill at Macon," *New York World*, March 7, 1917.

9. "Yankees Enjoy."

10. Steinberg and Spatz, *The Colonel and Hug*, 49.

11. Lieb, "Enright Believes."

12. Steinberg and Spatz, *The Colonel and Hug*, 112.

13. Murdock, *Ban Johnson*, 119.

14. Bozeman Bulger, "Players Enthusiastic over Plan to Give Them Military Drills in Camp," *New York World*, February 10, 1917.

15. W. J. Macbeth, "Ball Players Will Train at 'Camps' as Grenade Throwers," *New York Tribune*, February 9, 1917. Macbeth also mentioned ex-pitcher Ed Ruelbach, formerly of the Cubs, Dodgers, Braves, and Brooklyn Tip-Tops, who had a plan to introduce hand grenade training at the Braves' spring camp in Florida.

16. "Ban Patriotic after Vacation at Dover Hall," *New York Tribune*, February 9, 1917. Although Huston is generally credited as the father of baseball's preparedness plan, the *Washington Post* claimed he had adapted a plan originated by Senators manager Clark Griffith in 1916 during America's border crisis with Mexican revolutionary Pancho Villa. An unnamed *Post* writer that summer overheard "a little confab on the subject between Manager Griffith and Capt. Huston. It was this fanning bee that probably led to Huston, with the aid of the United States government, putting thoroughly into effect Griffith's idea." "Griffith Conceived the Idea of Military Training for Ball Players," *Washington Post*, March 5, 1917.

17. W. J. Macbeth, "Capt. Huston Plans Military Training for Ball Players," *New York Tribune*, February 10, 1917.

18. Bulger, "Players Enthusiastic over Plan." *New York World*, February 10, 1917.

19. "Interest Centers on Yanks' Military Training," *Norwich Bulletin*, March 9, 1917.

20. "Huston's Military Plans for Players Adopted by League," *New York Tribune*, February 10, 1917.

21. "Six Enlist Here," *Racine Journal-News*, April 20, 1916.

22. Sports of All Sorts, *Chicago Day Book*, February 28, 1917.

23. "Get Your Seat for '17 Series!" *Chicago Tribune*, March 2, 1917.

24. Morris Miller, Sport Snap Shots, *Janesville Daily Gazette*, March 1, 1917.

25. "'Assemble' Order Brings Trouble," *Chicago Tribune*, March 11, 1917.

26. Edward T. Collins, "Eddie Collins Tells Benefits of Army Drill," *Chicago Tribune*, April 15, 1917.

27. Sports of All Sorts, *Warren Times*, March 19, 1917.

28. "Practice Grenade Throwing," *Racine Journal-News*, March 21, 1917.

29. W. S. Smiley, "White Sox Drill Sergeant Speaks for Military Training," *Sporting News*, April 12, 1917.

30. Bozeman Bulger, "Military Discipline Proving Wonderful Help to Players," *New York World*, March 15, 1917.

31. Smiley, "White Sox Drill Sergeant."

32. Collins, "Eddie Collins Tells Benefits."

33. "Military Drill Not Wanted by Tigers," *New York Sun*, March 21, 1917.

34. "Military Drills Not Harmful, Tuthill Says," *Brownsville Herald*, April 20, 1917.

35. "Lee Fohl Enters Positive Denial," *New London Day*, March 24, 1917.

36. "Neglect of Officials Caused Superbas to Miss Drilling," *Brooklyn Eagle*, March 21, 1917.

37. "Manager Robinson Not Raising the Dodgers to Soldiers," *New York World*, March 20, 1917.

38. "No Military Drill for Robby's Team," *New York Times*, March 20, 1917.

39. Thomas Rice, "Proper Spirit Is Displayed," *Brooklyn Eagle*, March 21, 1917. The columnist wrote under the byline "Rice."

40. "Ball Players and Military Training," *Janesville Daily Gazette*, March 30, 1917.

41. "Prize for Drill Is Offered," *Boston Post*, March 7, 1917.

42. "Military Training at Camps No Joke," *Sporting Life*, March 17, 1917.

43. Grantland Rice, "Yankees as Soldiers Captivate Inspector," *New York Tribune*, March 21, 1917.

44. Thomas Rice, "Proper Spirit Is Displayed."

45. "Mack Takes Military Training for His Players Seriously and Will Continue Drilling at Park," *Philadelphia Public Ledger*, April 4, 1917.

46. Frederick G. Lieb, "Yankees Begin Local Season with Red Sox," *New York Sun*, April 11, 1917.

2. Selective Service

1. Bozeman Bulger, "Major League Baseball, with Military Trimmings, Served Up to Fans To-Day," *New York World*, April 11, 1917.

2. Bozeman Bulger, "Red Sox Beat Yanks, but Latter Displayed Great Form in Drilling," *New York World*, April 12, 1917.

3. Grantland Rice, The Sportlight, *New York Tribune*, April 12, 1917.

4. "The Athletics Had the Breaks, but They Came on Walter Johnson's Curve Ball," *Philadelphia Public Ledger*, April 12, 1917.

5. "Wickland's Drive Wins Opener for Indians," *Huntington Press*, April 12, 1917.

6. I. E. Sanborn, "27,000 See Sox Drop Opener to Browns, 6–2," *Chicago Tribune*, April 20, 1917.

7. Smiley, "White Sox Drill Sergeant."

8. "Recruiting Station for Ebbets Field," *New York Sun*, April 12, 1917.

9. Many modern biographers view the White Sox owner as no worse than other magnates of the era. "The accepted wisdom that Comiskey was a notably tight-fisted team owner is erroneous, thoroughly refuted by actual player salary data now readily available." Lamb, *Black Sox in the Courtroom*, 7.

10. "Griffith's Plan Is to Help Soldiers in Camp," *Washington Herald*, April 22, 1917.

11. "Far Off Jolo the Latest to Respond to Bat and Ball Fund," *New York Herald*, December 16, 1917.

12. Denman Thompson, "Griffmen Find Batting Eye and Climb a Notch in Race," *Washington Star*, April 22, 1917.

13. "Base Ball Assured," *Washington Star*, April 8, 1917.

14. "Base Ball Assured."

15. Consider one Minor circuit as a case in point. The Ohio State League began in 1908 when four clubs broke away from the Ohio-Pennsylvania League to join two others in forming the new six-team circuit. The Class D league never comprised more than eight teams, yet it placed franchises in eighteen cities over nine seasons. The "Staters" endured fires, floods, scandals, controversies, recessions, occasional successes, and frequent failures. The circuit collapsed in 1916 with games still in progress, yet was fairly typical for a Minor League in the early twentieth century.

16. "Military Training Compulsory in A.A.," *Tulsa World*, April 11, 1917.

17. "Military Training," *San Antonio Light*, April 29, 1917.

18. "Foreign War Will Not Stop Game in Three-I," *Sporting News*, April 12, 1917.

19. "Virginia League Disbands," *Washington Star*, May 17, 1917.

20. "Interstate League Meeting Is Being Held at Bradford," *Warren Mirror*, May 3, 1917.

21. "Georgia-Alabama League Disbands for the Season," *Richmond Times-Dispatch*, May 24, 1917.

22. Bruce Copeland, "O'Hara Talks about Life in the Trenches," *Pittsburgh Press*, April 21, 1918.

23. "Former Giants Goes to Bat against the Kaiser," 51.

24. "Our Own Billy O'Hara Is Awarded the Military Cross," *Toronto World*, October 24, 1916.

25. J. B. Sheridan, "Learn the Underhand Throw in Baseball, If You Want to Be a Good Bomb Hurler," *Ogden Standard*, March 31, 1917.

26. "He's Bossing More Millionaires than Anyone Else in U.S.," *Bismarck Daily Tribune*, September 5, 1915.

27. "Former Giants Enlist in Army," *Binghamton Press*, May 4, 1917.

28. Grantland Rice, The Sportlight, *New York Tribune*, June 6, 1917.

29. Westbrook Pegler, Fair Enough, *Reading Eagle*, February 8, 1961.

30. Ed McGrath, "'Hank' Gowdy Joins Colors," *Boston Post*, June 2, 1917.

31. "'Hank' Gowdy First Big Leaguer to Enlist," *Columbus Citizen*, June 2, 1917.

32. "Gowdy Goes Home to Enlist in Army," *Boston Globe*, June 2, 1917.

33. "Shanks Holds Place in Ranks of Sluggers," *Washington Post*, June 6, 1917.

34. "Big Doings Booked at Shibe Park Today," *Philadelphia Public Ledger*, June 5, 1917.

35. "Sox Compress Year's Thrills in 6–3 Victory," *Chicago Tribune*, June 6, 1917.

36. W. O. McGeehan, "Rally in Ninth Wins for Yanks," *New York Tribune*, June 5, 1917.

37. McGeehan, "Rally in Ninth."

38. "Tener Protests Tax on Baseball," *Washington Times*, May 10, 1917.

39. "Fans Would Pay Tax; Magnates Satisfied," *Washington Times*, May 11, 1917.

40. "N.C. Base Ball League Disbands," *High Point Review*, June 6, 1917.

41. "Goes Out of Business," *Corsicana Semi-Weekly Light*, June 8, 1917.

42. "Minor Leagues Will Pull Through, Says Ed Barrow," *New York World*, June 1, 1917.

43. "Minor Leagues Will Pull Through."

44. "13 Minor Leagues Asked to Suspend Baseball Season," *Bisbee Review*, June 15, 1917.

45. "Aye, 'Twas a Mighty Hard Year on Baseball Magnates; Many Flivved," *Seattle Star*, October 6, 1917.

46. "Minor Players to Get Their Full Pay," *Washington Herald*, July 3, 1917.

47. "Northern League May Quit," *Oakland Tribune*, July 3, 1917.

48. "Dixie League Suspends, and Moultrie Won Pennant," *Thomasville Times Enterprise*, July 5, 1917.

49. Welly's Corner, *Harrisburg Telegraph*, July 9, 1917.

50. "New York State League Has Hard Luck Trying to Make Ends Meet," *El Paso Herald*, July 24, 1917.

51. "Tearney Blames War," *Arizona Republican*, Phoenix, July 9, 1917.

52. Edward Hill's Column, *Seattle Star*, July 16, 1917.

53. "N.W. Players Flocking to Ship League," *Tacoma Times*, July 28, 1917.

54. "C. A. Disbands for Season," *Daily Gate City*, August 9, 1917.

55. Foster, *Spalding's Official Base Ball Guide, 1918*, 6.

3. Buildup

1. Christy Mathewson, "What Will Draft Do to Baseball?" *Boston Globe*, July 1, 1917.

2. "To Hank Gowdy," *Pittsburgh Press*, June 29, 1917.

3. Ohl, "Buckeyes in the Rainbow," 32.

4. "Hank Gowdy Now Color Sergeant of Regiment," *Boston Globe*, July 30, 1917.

5. Cheseldine, *Ohio in the Rainbow*, 51.

6. "Baseball Again Is Booming Preparedness," *Washington Herald*, February 24, 1917.

7. "No Game, but Braves Line Up before a New Drill Master," *Boston Globe*, April 14, 1917.

8. "Best Ball Player of Army Drill Master of Red Sox," *Boston Post*, June 17, 1917.

9. Edward F. Martin, "Red Sox Buy Liberty Bonds and Drill Some," *Boston Globe*, June 8, 1917.

10. "Echoes of the Game," *Boston Globe*, July 4, 1917.

11. Paul H. Shannon, "Red Sox Duck Military Drill," *Boston Globe*, August 25, 1917.

12. "Barry and Lane Enroll as Yeomen," *Boston Globe*, July 29, 1917.

13. "Barry Now Yeoman in Naval Reserve," *Washington Times*, July 29, 1917.

14. "Johnson Urges Ball Players to Go to War," *Fort Wayne News*, July 28, 1917.

15. John Alcock, "Favor for Game at White House Cheers Majors," *Chicago Tribune*, August 4, 1917.

16. "Ebbets Says Service in War Is Sure to Ruin Many Good Ball Players," *Syracuse Journal*, August 2, 1917.

17. "Players Do Not Take Very Kindly to Ban Johnson's Plan to Do Away with the Coming World's Series," *Philadelphia Public Ledger*, July 31, 1917.

18. "Tener Changes Mind; He Agrees to Calling Off World's Series," *Philadelphia Public Ledger*, July 28, 1917.

19. "President Saves Ball Schedules to End of Season," *Washington Times*, August 3, 1917.

20. "President Saves Ball Schedules."

21. "Ebbets Says Service in War Is Sure."

22. Sport Chatter, *Bismarck Tribune*, August 6, 1917.

23. "Country Is First—Mack," *Seattle Star*, August 9, 1917.

24. Yockelson, *Forty-Seven Days*, 42.

25. Pershing, *My Experiences in the World War*, 1:30.

26. Sport Gossip, *Cedar Rapids Gazette*, August 27, 1917.

27. Denman Thompson, "Griffith's Team Put through Competitive Drill at Chicago," *Washington Star*, August 24, 1917.

28. Huhn, *The Sizzler*, 66.

29. "Big Ban Johnson Is Quite Liberal," *New London Day*, September 19, 1917.

30. T. L. Huston, "Cap Huston Issues Solemn Warning to All Baseball Folk," *New York World*, March 24, 1918.

31. "Browns Take Prize for Military Drill," *New York Sun*, August 28, 1917.

32. Lombard, "The Days at Plattsburg," 593.

33. Dayton Stoddart, "Eddie Grant of Harvard Working for Commission in the Army," *Ogden Standard*, July 14, 1917.

34. "Our Standard Bearer," *Grant Post News*, May 1940, 3.

35. Christy Mathewson, "Trouble Ahead for White Sox," *Boston Globe*, August 26, 1917.

36. "Regiments at Plattsburg to Be Sent Afield for Real Training in War Duty," *New York Herald*, July 15, 1917.

37. Adler, *History of the Seventy-Seventh Division*, 139.

38. Mathewson, "Trouble Ahead for White Sox."

39. Capt. Howard Y. Williams, foreword to Davies, *Twentieth Engineers, France*.

40. Christy Mathewson, "Matty Wants Chicago to Win," *Boston Globe*, September 2, 1917.

41. W. J. Macbeth, "Captain Huston Writes to Friends from France," *New York Tribune*, October 21, 1917.

42. Sport Gossip, *Cedar Rapids Gazette*, August 27, 1917.

43. "Selection for National Army Proceeds Slowly," *Philadelphia Public Ledger*, August 7, 1917.

44. "Here's What Three Ball Stars Would Like to Do If They Went to War," *Eau Claire Leader*, July 10, 1917.

45. Denman Thompson, "Griffith May Take Teams Abroad to Play in France," *Washington Star*, August 6, 1917.

46. "Pershing's Letter," *Honolulu Star-Bulletin*, October 26, 1917.

47. Denman Thompson, "Griffith Formulates Plan to Raise Another Big Fund," *Washington Star*, July 18, 1917.

48. Thompson, "Griffith May Take Teams Abroad to Play in France."

49. Denman Thompson, "League Pennant May Depend on Play of Griffith's Team," *Washington Star*, August 26, 1917.

50. Thompson, "League Pennant May Depend."

51. "Jim Scott Admitted to Presidio Camp," *Bakersfield Californian*, September 12, 1917.

52. "Scott Loses Big Money to Serve with U.S. Army," *Tacoma Times*, September 20, 1917.

53. "Gabby Street, War Hero, Visits Here," *Washington Star*, February 5, 1919.

54. "Gabby Street, War Hero, Visits Here."

55. "Walter Johnson Given Big Cut in Salary for Season," *Washington Herald*, January 13, 1918.

56. Louis Dougher, "Griff Presents Outfits to Drafted Contingent," *Washington Times*, September 22, 1917.

57. Louis Dougher, "Carrigan and Larry in Rumors about Yankees," *Washington Times*, September 23, 1917

58. Dougher, "Griff Presents."

59. Edward F. Marin, "Soldiers and Sailors Have Big Time at Double-header," *Boston Globe*, October 3, 1917.

60. "$30,000 Worth of Baseball Material Sent Abroad," *New York Herald*, December 16, 1917.

61. "Sammies to Get World Series News," *Berkeley Gazette*, October 4, 1917.

62. "Scotty Can't Even Watch Scoreboard," *Tacoma Times*, October 9, 1917.

63. Irwin S. Cobb, "Hank Gets Another Watch," *Pittsburgh Press*, October 11, 1917.

64. Damon Runyon, "Gowdy's Latest Accomplishment One of Most Spectacular in Baseball Game," *Kingston Freeman*, November 30, 1917.

65. "World's Series Notes," *Chicago Tribune*, October 14, 1917.

66. "Sox Beat Giants Again before 15,000 Soldiers of Rainbow Division," *New York World*, October 17, 1917.

67. "Cleveland Team to Play for Entertainment of Soldiers," *Sporting News*, October 18, 1917.

68. "Indians Defeats Soldiers 19 to 7," *Racine Journal-News*, November 1, 1917.

69. "Scott Does His Bit and Is Rewarded by Comiskey," *Philadelphia Public Ledger*, November 15, 1917.

4. Winter

1. Joe Vila, "Ban Johnson Says He Will Join the Army," *Pittsburgh Press*, October 10, 1917.

2. "Johnson Going to Trenches," *Milwaukee Journal*, October 17, 1917.

3. "Johnson May Enlist," *New York Sun*, October 11, 1917.

4. "Ban Johnson Volunteers," *New York Times*, October 23, 1917.

5. "Ban Johnson Will Not Go to France," *Washington Herald*, November 1, 1917.

6. "'Johnson Will Go When Yankees Reach Berlin,'" *New York Sun*, July 21, 1918.

7. "McCormick Writes League President," *Christian Science Monitor*, November 3, 1917.

8. "Four Boston Red Sox Now Naval Reserves," *Philadelphia Public Ledger*, November 20, 1917.

9. "A Pinch Hitter in Khaki," *Stars and Stripes*, February 8, 1918.

10. Pegler, Fair Enough, *Reading Eagle*, February 8, 1961.

11. Cheseldine, *Ohio in the Rainbow*, 87, 76.

12. "Cadore of Superbas Leads Draft Quota Off to Camp Upton," *Brooklyn Eagle*, October 8, 1917.

13. Sportsman, Live Tips and Topics, *Boston Globe*, August 28, 1917.

14. "Four Boston Red Sox."

15. "Three Brave Yeomen from Boston Town," *Sporting News*, December 13, 1917.

16. "Baseball Merger Rumored," *Philadelphia Public Ledger*, October 18, 1917.

17. Frederick G. Lieb, "New Quasi-Major League Assured," *New York Sun*, October 24, 1917.

18. "Sure of a Third Major League," *Ogden Standard*, November 6, 1917.

19. "War May Close New York League," *Washington Herald*, November 4, 1917.

20. "A. A. Scrap Which Threatened Split Is Now Adjusted," *Arizona Republican*, Phoenix, November 13, 1917.

21. "Johnson Shocks Fans with His Plan for Exempting Games' Stars," *New York World*, November 22, 1917.

22. Murdock, *Ban Johnson*, 123.

23. "Johnson vs. Griffith," *Washington Times*, November 22, 1917.

24. "Johnson Shocks Fans."

25. Frederick G. Lieb, "Ban Johnson Touched Off a Hornet's Nest with His Plea for the Wholesale Exemptions for Baseball Players," *New York Sun*, November 23, 1917. Tener privately wired to Pittsburgh owner Barney Dreyfuss: "If the president of the American League is quoted correctly he has put baseball in danger and seriously jeopardized the reputation and business interests of all concerned by offending every patriotic citizen and supporter of the game. The National League should be a unit in declining to ask for discrimination in favor

of its business or its players." Tener to Dreyfuss, telegram, November 22, 1917, Herrmann Papers, box 112, folder 26.

26. Lieb, "Ban Johnson Touched Off."

27. "Strike Three?" *Chicago Tribune*, November 22, 1917.

28. Dan Daniel, High Lights and Shadows in All Spheres of Sport, *New York Sun*, November 23, 1917.

29. Frederick G. Lieb, "Fans Continue to Criticize Johnson," *New York Sun*, November 24, 1917.

30. Lieb, "Ban Johnson Touched Off."

31. "Barrow Says Johnson Has Been Manhandled," *Washington Times*, November 26, 1917.

32. Lieb, "Ban Johnson Touched Off."

33. "Mack Defends Ban Johnson on Exemption Issue," *Syracuse Herald*, November 25, 1917.

34. Huston, "Cap Huston Issues."

35. George S. Robbins, "Crisis Reached in Games Says Robbins," *Sporting News*, November 29, 1917.

36. "National League Calls Upon Its Players to Join the Colors," *New York Times*, December 19, 1917.

37. "Johnson Shocks Fans."

38. "Barrow Resigns as League Head," *New York Sun*, December 13, 1917.

39. *The Reach Official American League Base Ball Guide for 1918*, 155.

40. "Minor Moguls Meet to Change Baseball Map; May Suspend Next Year," *Harrisburg Telegraph*, November 13, 1917.

41. High Lights and Shadows in All Spheres of Sport, without customary "Daniel" byline, *New York Sun*, November 17, 1917.

42. *The Reach Official American League Base Ball Guide for 1918*, 8.

43. Foster, *Spalding's Official Base Ball Guide, 1918*, 6.

44. Grantland Rice, Sportlight, *New York Tribune*, December 29, 1917.

45. *Cincinnati Enquirer*, quoted in *The Reach Official American League Base Ball Guide for 1918*, 10.

5. Spring

1. "A. L. Player Limit Abolished for 1918," *Washington Star*, January 20, 1918.

2. "Eddie Ainsmith, on a Visit Home, Tells of Henry's Going to A's," *Washington Times*, January 28, 1918.

3. "Spring Training Squads Reduced," *Ogden Standard*, January 21, 1918.

4. Frederick G. Lieb, "League Swamped with Ball Players," *New York Sun*, January 25, 1918.

5. "Central League Dies," *Daily Gate City*, March 16, 1918.

6. "Major League Service Flag Carries 76 Stars," *Chicago Eagle*, March 16, 1918. Less than two months later, according to Louis Heilbroner, publisher of

The Baseball Blue Book, the number had risen to 137. Press release, Herrmann Papers, box 113, folder 1.

7. "Scott's Work in Army Pleases Comiskey," *Albany Journal*, July 8, 1918.

8. J. B. Sheridan, "Professional Athletes Not in Best Odor for Patriotism," *Ogden Standard*, July 6, 1918.

9. "Cardinals' Ex-captain Qualifies as Marksman," *Boston Globe*, March 10, 1918.

10. "Wants to Fight," *Graham Guardian*, March 15, 1918.

11. "Dots Miller Back with Hard Luck Tale and a Grouch," *New York Tribune*, April 22, 1919. A comic tale circulated after the war about Miller's exchange with a general who questioned him about his incomplete mess kit:

"Do you know that you are shy a knife?" the general demanded.

"Never use one, sir."

"Don't you ever eat meat?"

"Yes, sir, but I never get a piece big enough to cut."

J. C. Kofoed, "Little Stories of the Stars," *Sporting News*, November 25, 1920.

12. "To Marvin Goodwin," Baseball By-Plays, *Sporting News*, December 27, 1917.

13. "Shafer Learning to Be an Aviator," *Pittsburgh Press*, August 13, 1918. Shafer actually made his "perfumed notes" remark following the 1912 season, then played one more year for John McGraw.

14. "Giants Toy with Aviators," *New York Times*, March 30, 1918.

15. "Crack Big League Battery Working for Uncle Sam," *Brooklyn Eagle*, January 11, 1918.

16. "Fred Toney Uses His Brains on the Ball Field Only—He Has Bases Full and Uncle Sam Up," *Philadelphia Public Ledger*, December 24, 1917.

17. "Pitcher Toney, Charged with Violating Draft Act, Is Arrested," *Albany Journal*, December 24, 1917.

18. "How about Fred Toney?" *Tacoma Times*, January 3, 1918.

19. Adler, *History of the Seventy-Seventh Division*, 23.

20. Yockelson, *Forty-Seven Days*, 258.

21. Rubin, *The Last of the Doughboys*, 72–73.

22. Joe Dooley, "Hank Gowdy Tells Dooley about World War," *New York World-Telegram*, August 3, 1937.

23. "Americans Hold Captured Trenches; Ten More Receive French War Cross," *New York World*, Friday, March 15, 1918.

24. "Hank Gowdy, Baseball's Hero, Bats .300 in France," *Sporting News*, February 28, 1918.

25. "No Military Training for Baseball Players," *New York Tribune*, March 13, 1918. Visiting French troops called the Blue Devils, however, caused a sensation when they marched into the Polo Grounds for a May 2 game between the Yankees and Athletics. "Then came the files of marching men in blue, guns lifted to a high position on their shoulders, slim, wicked looking bayonets flashing in the sunlight, swagger, confident men who had looked death in the face time and again and lived to tell of it, the elite of the defenders of France. Players and spectators

took off their hats to do them honor, the stadium rang with cheers as hearty as any that greeted a home run in a world series." "Wild Balls Fail to Daunt Blue Devils," *New York Sun*, May 3, 1918.

26. "'Veterans' at Camp Upton Are All New York City Boys, and All Eager for Action," *New York World*, March 4, 1918.

27. W. J. Macbeth, In All Fairness, *New York Tribune*, July 15, 1918.

28. Rice, *The Tumult and the Shouting*, 89–90.

29. "Rises Fast in His New Profession," *Sporting News*, December 20, 1917.

30. Rice, *The Tumult and the Shouting*, 93.

31. Louis Lee Arms, Facts and Fancies, *New York Tribune*, May 10, 1918.

32. T. L. Huston, "Cap Huston Issues Solemn Warning to All Baseball Folk," *New York World*, March 24, 1918.

33. Huston, "Cap Huston Issues."

34. Huston, "Cap Huston Issues."

35. Thomas Rice, "Huston's Warning Due to Christie," *Brooklyn Eagle*, March 24, 1918.

36. Dan Daniel, High Lights and Shadows in All Spheres of Sport, *New York Sun*, March 25, 1918.

37. W. J. Macbeth, In All Fairness, *New York Tribune*, March 25, 1918.

38. Dan Daniel, High Lights and Shadows in All Spheres of Sport, *New York Sun*, March 26, 1918.

39. "Insurrecto Attacks Prove Boomerangs," *Sporting News*, January 8, 1920.

40. Hugh S. Fullerton, "Baseball Season's Outlook as Fullerton Views It," *New York World*, April 15, 1918.

41. Louis Lee Arms, "4 Major League Clubs Will Quit, Says Official," *New York Tribune*, March 27, 1918. Giants president Harry Hempstead replied that no one on his staff had the authority to make statements "regarding the ability of any club in this league or any competitor as to whether they will last through the season or not. Every sign points to at least as good a year as last." Harry N. Hempstead, "Giants' President Predicts Good Baseball Year," *New York Tribune*, March 28, 1918.

42. "Syracuse Clubs Sends Contracts to Seventeen Players for 1918," *Syracuse Herald*, March 3, 1918.

43. W. J. Macbeth, "Buffalo and Binghamton in New League," *New York Tribune*, April 5, 1918.

44. "New International Circuit Completed," *New York Sun*, April 5, 1918.

45. "Says Minor Leagues Will Be Hit Hard," *Philadelphia Public Ledger*, April 8, 1918.

6. New Season

1. "Germans Hurled to Death by Thousands without Gain," *Boston Globe*, April 15, 1918.

2. Gilbert, *The First World War*, 404.

3. "It Was Good Headwork to Start the Season When the Teuton Push Was 'Flivving,'" *Philadelphia Public Ledger*, April 16, 1918.

4. Edward F. Martin, "A 7 to 1 Victory," *Boston Globe*, April 16, 1918.

5. Sportsman, Live Tips and Topics, *Boston Globe*, April 16, 1918.

6. Denman Thompson, "Huge Crowd Refutes Theory That Base Ball Here Is Dead," *Washington Star*, April 16, 1918.

7. "Liberty Bond Drive a Big Card at Season's Opening," *Washington Herald*, April 16, 1918.

8. John A. Dugan, "Yanks' Artillery Hammer Way through Griffs' Line," *Washington Herald*, April 16, 1918.

9. "Flyer Plunges to Death," *Silver Lake Record*, June 6, 1918.

10. Finkel, "Pete Alexander," SABR BioProject.

11. "Alex Surprised by Classification in List of Army Men," *La Crosse Tribune and Leader-Press*, January 18, 1918.

12. "Alex Must Serve in Army, Says Board," *Philadelphia Public Ledger*, April 17, 1918.

13. "Toney Is Charged with Evading Law," *Washington Star*, April 7, 1918.

14. "Toney Storming Cincinnati in Effort to Get into Play," *Philadelphia Public Ledger*, April 23, 1918.

15. Joe Vila, "May Save Baseball from Certain Death," *Philadelphia Inquirer*, July 25, 1918.

16. Hugh S. Fullerton, "Cubs' Sensational Work Due to Their Pitchers," *New York World*, May 6, 1918.

17. Charles A. Taylor, "Fred Toney's Out-Curves Baffle New York Batters," *New York Tribune*, May 17, 1918.

18. "Matty Gets Free Training for Reds," *New York Times*, February 25, 1918.

19. "Many Stars Refuse to Sign Contracts," *Stars and Stripes*, March 1, 1918.

20. "Soldiers in France Calling for Matty," *New York Times*, April 25, 1918.

21. "Come On, Matty," *Stars and Stripes*, May 10, 1918.

22. "Baseball Outfits for French Front," *New York Times*, March 16, 1918.

23. "144,000 Baseball Bats on Way Here for Army Recreation in France," *New York Telegram*, March 14, 1918.

24. "Soldiers in France Calling for Matty."

25. "Matty Has Not Refused," *New York Times*, May 5, 1918.

26. Fullerton, "Cubs' Sensational Work."

27. Thomas Rice, "Rickey and Mathewson Enter Chemical Warfare Service," *Brooklyn Eagle*, August 24, 1918.

28. "Matty's Call Is Cancelled," *Sporting News*, July 4, 1918.

29. J. G. Taylor Spink, Looping the Loop, *Sporting News*, May 21, 1942.

30. "Evers Prefers Going to France before Baseball," *Syracuse Journal*, June 6, 1918.

31. "Eastern Shipyards Signing Major and Minor Leagues," *Oakland Tribune*, May 19, 1918.

32. "Steel League Causes Worry to Magnates of the Majors," *El Paso Herald*, June 5, 1918.

33. "What If the Big Leagues Do Bust Up When We Have C. Schwab!" *Harrisburg Telegraph*, July 13, 1918.

34. Bat Wright, Sports of All Sorts, *Troy Times*, June 21, 1918.

35. Lewis Lee Arms, "Huggins Sounds Warning of 'Ship Building' Menace to Game," *New York Tribune*, May 15, 1918.

36. "Huggins Wants to Know about 'Shipbuilders,'" *New York Tribune*, May 16, 1918.

37. Lane, "A Rising Menace to the National Game," 372.

38. "Hurler Tesreau Has Jumped Giants Team," *Jamestown Journal*, July 26, 1918.

39. Bancroft to Herrmann, June 6, 1918, Herrmann Papers, box 113, folder 1. The Minor Leagues also objected to the industrial leagues' recruiting. "We have been annoyed constantly, ever since our season opened, by men representing the Steel League tampering with our players. They have taken 10 or 12," complained Thomas Hickey, president of the American Association. Quoted in letter, John A. Heydler to J. H. Ward, June 10, 1918, Herrmann Papers, box 113, folder 1.

40. Dan Daniel, High Lights and Shadows in All Spheres of Sport, *New York Sun*, June 26, 1918.

41. "Watching for Scout," *Montreal Gazette*, July 20, 1918.

42. Daniel, High Lights and Shadows, June 26, 1918.

43. "Joe Jackson Must Resign in Two Weeks," *Washington Times*, May 13, 1918.

44. James S. Carolan, "Joe Jackson Quits Sox to Help Build Ships," *Philadelphia Public Ledger*, May 14, 1918.

45. Louis A. Dougher, "Ban Johnson Opposes Players' Plan for Escaping Duty under Draft Law," *Washington Times*, May 17, 1918.

46. "Ban Johnson Opposes."

47. "Caught on the Fly," *Sporting News*, October 3, 1918.

48. Louis Lee Arms, Facts and Fancies, *New York Tribune*, May 19, 1918.

49. "Griffs Get Shipyard Jobs," *Washington Star*, August 21, 1918.

50. Louis A. Dougher, "Yankees Proud of Those Who Joined Colors; Don't Mention Rest," *Washington Times*, July 2, 1918.

51. George S. Robbins, "Desertions Rouse Old Roman's Anger," *Sporting News*, June 20, 1917.

52. "White Sox Lose Two More Players; Will Build Ships," *Albany Journal*, June 13, 1918.

53. J. B. Sheridan, "Professional Athletes Not in Best Odor for Patriotism," *Ogden Standard*, July 6, 1918.

54. Editorial, "Ship Yard Gates Closing," *Sporting News*, July 18, 1918.

55. Baseball By-plays, *Sporting News*, August 22, 1918.

56. Thomas S. Rice, "Class Will Ascend Like Cream to Top," *Sporting News*, June 27, 1918.

57. "Shipyard Players Do Not Camouflage," *Sporting News*, August 8, 1918.

58. "Shipyard Players on Same Footing as Other Workers," *New York Tribune*, August 15, 1918.

59. Vila, "May Save Baseball from Certain Death."

60. Louis Dougher, "Uncle Sam Gets Monroe after His Leaping," *Washington Times*, July 25, 1918.

61. "Steel Leaguers Not Slackers," *Harrisburg Telegraph*, May 31, 1918.

62. "More Defense for Jackson," *Sporting News*, May 30, 1918.

63. Frederick G. Lieb, "Baseball Back on Its Former Plane," *New York Sun*, April 20, 1919.

64. Quoted in "There Would Be Many," *Kokomo Tribune*, July 8, 1918.

7. Work or Fight

1. "'Work or Fight,' Choice Given Men within Draft Age," *Washington Star*, May 23, 1918.

2. "'Work or Fight,' Choice Given." A bucket shop was a type of stock brokerage operated from a drugstore, hotel, or cafe—essentially, a betting shop, where often the supposed trades were never made.

3. "Every Man of Draft Age Must Work or Fight by July, Declares Provost Marshal," *New York World*, May 23, 1918.

4. "Crowder Mandate Strikes at Leagues," *New York Sun*, May 24, 1918.

5. "What Officials Say about New Crowder Order," *New York Tribune*, May 24, 1918.

6. "Base Ball Men Are Aroused by the Proposal to Compel Players to Work or Fight," *Washington Star*, May 23, 1918.

7. "Virginia League Off to Its '18 Campaign," *Washington Times*, May 23, 1918.

8. Louis Lee Arms, "Professional Sports Hard Hit by Command to Work or Fight," *New York Tribune*, May 24, 1918.

9. W. W. Flannery, "Blue Ridge Gives Up Ghost," *Sporting News*, June 20, 1918.

10. "Blue Ridge to Quit," *Washington Star*, June 13, 1918.

11. "More Trouble for Majors," *El Paso Herald*, July 6, 1918.

12. "Army Baseball Killed the Southern League," *Bridgeport Times*, July 6, 1918.

13. Daniel, High Lights and Shadows, June 26, 1918.

14. G. W. Krick, *Fort Worth Record*, quoted in Scribbled by Scribes, *Sporting News*, July 18, 1918.

15. "Season Is Failure," *Salem Capital Journal*, July 3, 1918

16. Wants No 'Liberty League,'" *Topeka State Journal*, July 8, 1918.

17. "Coast League Baseball Quits Until after War; Last Game Tomorrow," *Ogden Standard*, July 13, 1918.

18. W. D. B., "Darmody's Distress Causes Coast to Quit," *Sporting News*, July 18, 1918.

19. "Coast League Baseball Quits."

20. "More Than 800 Baseball Players from Minor League Clubs Answer Call

to Colors; Flaherty Listed," *Rochester Democrat and Chronicle*, July 12, 1918. Louis Heilbroner reported 423 known Minor League players in the service on May 10, 1918. Devising a formula based on Major League statistics alone, and factoring in the Minor Leagues that had folded or suspended operations, he calculated "not less than 1,100 professional ball players with the Colors." Press release, Herrmann Papers, box 113, folder 1.

21. "Crowder's Message to Men of 21," *New York Tribune*, June 5, 1918.

22. "Notice to All Major League Clubs," National Commission, July 2, 1918. Herrmann Papers, box 113, folder 1.

23. "Status of Hornsby Credit to League," *Washington Herald*, July 26, 1918.

24. "Parnham May Be Center of Baseball's Important Case in 'Work or Fight' Rule," *Toledo News-Bee*, July 5, 1917.

25. Denman Thompson, "Ruling on Ainsmith's Appeal to End Work or Fight Doubt," *Washington Star*, July 12, 1918.

26. Smythe, *Pershing*, 6.

27. Denman Thompson, "Holds Base Ball to Be Essential," *Washington Star*, July 14, 1918.

28. Dougher, "Uncle Sam Gets Monroe."

29. Dan Daniel, High Lights and Shadows in All Spheres of Sport, *New York Sun*, July 25, 1918.

30. Charles A. Taylor, "Cubs Increase Lead at Giants' Expense," *New York Tribune*, August 2, 1918.

31. "Giants Get One Hit from Vaughn Hippo," *New York Times*, August 2, 1918.

32. Denman Thompson, "Ball Players and Magnates Entitled to Know Their Fate," *Washington Star*, July 17, 1918.

33. "Statement of Secretary Baker Ruling Base Ball Non-essential," *Washington Star*, July 20, 1918.

34. "Base Ball Ruled a Non-essential," *Washington Star*, July 19, 1918.

35. Denman Thompson, "Continuation of Base Ball Is Up to League Directors," *Washington Star*, July 20, 1918.

36. Dan Daniel, High Lights and Shadows in All Spheres of Sport, *New York Sun*, July 22, 1918.

37. Herrmann to Crowder, June 15, 1918, Herrmann Papers, box 112, folder 31.

38. W. J. Macbeth, "Baseball Dealt a Heavy Blow by Ruling of Secretary Baker," *New York Tribune*, July 20, 1918.

39. Frederick G. Lieb, "Big Leagues May Soon Be a Memory," *New York Sun*, July 20, 1918.

40. "Will Let President Decide Whether Parks Shall Close," *Washington Star*, July 20, 1918.

41. Thompson, "Continuation of Base Ball."

42. "Cleveland's Owner First to Comply with Baker's Work Fight Order; Will Close Up Park To-Morrow," *New York World*, July 20, 1918. Boston owner Harry Frazee suggested an early shutdown for everyone. "If the president confirms Sec-

retary Baker's order of today I urgently suggest that we close our season after playing one hundred games and the winners in each league play nine games to decide world's championship," he wired Garry Herrmann. Frazee to Herrmann, telegram, July 20, 1918, Herrmann Papers, box 113, folder 1.

43. "Parks Must Close If Players in Draft Quit, Says Tener," *New York Tribune*, July 20, 1918.

44. "Keep On, Says Ebbets," *Boston Post*, July 20, 1918.

45. Rice, *The Tumult and the Shouting*, 93.

46. "Stars and Stripes Is Hauled Down with This Issue," *Stars and Stripes*, June 13, 1919.

47. Grantland Rice, Setting the Pace, *New York Sun*, September 3, 1943. Hank Gowdy offered another version, which involved Captain Guy T. Viskniskki, the army paper's editor and general manager: "He was disappointed with baseball's showing in the war and said he planned to discontinue publishing news of baseball activity in the United States on that account. . . . I suggested to Capt. Vishiniski [*sic*] that even though he thought baseball hadn't contributed the number of men he desired, the fact remained that there were a good many of us in service in France and that his plan to discontinue running baseball news would be a discrimination against us." J. G. Taylor Spink, Looping the Loop, *Sporting News*, May 21, 1942.

48. "Editorial Staff Consists Wholly of Enlisted Men," *Stars and Stripes*, February 7, 1919.

49. "The Sporting Page Goes Out," *Stars and Stripes*, July 26, 1918.

50. "League Winds Up Today," *Richmond Times-Dispatch*, July 20, 1918.

51. "Eastern League to Wind Up Tomorrow," *Boston Globe*, July 20, 1918.

52. "Majors Will Benefit," *Topeka State Journal*, July 13, 1918.

53. "A. A. Magnates Meet," *Washington Star*, July 21, 1918.

54. "American Association Men to Hunt War Jobs," *Boston Globe*, July 20, 1918.

55. Louis Lee Arms, "Major Leagues May Play Out Schedules," *New York Tribune*, July 22, 1918.

56. "Tom M'Carthy after Major League Stars," *Washington Herald*, August 6, 1918.

57. "Tom M'Carthy after Major League Stars." Many ballplayers agreed with the argument, but turned instead to the industrial leagues. Various unnamed "prominent players" wrote to Bethlehem's Harlan yard in Wilmington asking for work. "Many of the players believe that the 'big leagues' will not continue throughout the season, basing their opinions upon the Work or Fight Measure," a company official reported. Letter, John L. Collyer to H. E. Lewis, June 12, 1918, Herrmann Papers, box 113, folder 1.

58. Sid C. Keener, "Walter Johnson Silent about Northern Offer," *Washington Times*, July 26, 1918.

59. "Magnates Will Obtain Status," *Washington Herald*, July 26, 1918.

60. "Baseball to Continue till September 1," *Washington Herald*, July 27, 1918.

61. "Baseball Reprieve Granted by Baker," *New York Times*, July 27, 1918

62. Louis A. Dougher, "Baseball Due to Strike Rocks as Two Leagues Fight about Series," *Washington Times*, August 1, 1918.

63. "Owners Overrule Johnson Closing Plan," *Chicago Sunday Tribune*, August 4, 1918.

64. "Owners Overrule."

65. "McGraw Hands Out Praise to President Ban Johnson," *Washington Star*, August 7, 1918.

66. "Big Leagues Vote to Start World's Series Sept. 4," *New York Sun*, August 4, 1918.

67. "Baker Formally Gives Sanction to Big Series," *New York Tribune*, August 24, 1918.

68. "Baseball to Continue till September 1."

69. "John K. Tener Resigns as President of the National Baseball League," *New York Tribune*, August 7, 1918.

8. Calibers

1. J. B. Sheridan, "Professional Athletes Not in Best Odor for Patriotism," *Ogden Standard*, July 6, 1918.

2. "Could Gather Strong Team of 'Has Beens,'" *El Paso Herald*, July 16, 1918.

3. Dan Daniel, High Lights and Shadows in All Spheres of Sport, *New York Sun*, May 28, 1918.

4. Frederick G. Lieb, "Lineups These Days Seen Like a Joke," *Sporting News*, August 15, 1918.

5. Frederick G. Lieb, quoted by Dink Carroll, Playing the Field, *Montreal Gazette*, May 23, 1942.

6. "Sea Going Red Sox Prepare for Action," *Stars and Stripes*, March 8, 1918.

7. Hugh S. Fullerton, "Cubs' Sensational Work Due to Their Pitchers," *New York World*, March 8, 1918.

8. Harry Frazee letter of January 23, 1918, "Correspondence concerning Red Sox Players at the Boston Navy Yard, 12/1917–02/1918," National Archives, www.archives.gov.

9. "Not Enlisted for Baseball," *Sporting News*, May 2, 1918.

10. "Jack Barry's Baseball Team Is Disbanded," *New York Tribune*, August 4, 1918.

11. "BANG!" *Utica Herald-Dispatch*, August 7, 1918.

12. Sport Penpoints, *Waterloo Courier*, July 17, 1918.

13. "Great Lakes Win Naval Baseball Title," *Waterloo Courier*, August 6, 1918.

14. "Recognizing Rank and Experience," *Sporting News*, September 26, 1918.

15. Sports item, no headline, *Oakland Tribune*, May 12, 1918.

16. "Would Go 2,000 Miles for Title," *Kokomo Tribune*, October 7, 1918.

17. "Would Go 2,000 Miles for Title."

18. Chubb, *Regimental History*, 11.

19. "Still One of the Big Guns," *Sporting News*, May 9, 1918.

20. "Still One of the Big Guns."

21. Foster, *Spalding's Official Base Ball Guide, 1918*, 221.

22. "Dodgers Down Cubs Again as Pfeffer Twirls," *New York Tribune*, July 20, 1918.

23. John V. Lawrence, *New York Mail*, quoted in "Ignored Navy Team to Play for Yanks," *Chicago Eagle*, September 7, 1918.

24. "Shawkey Was There When the German Fleet 'Kicked In,'" *Albany Journal*, December 19, 1918.

25. "Maranville Hailed as Real Warrior," *Sporting News*, July 18, 1918.

26. Baseball By-Plays, *Sporting News*, July 18, 1918.

27. "Dodgers to Honor Cadore," *New York Times*, June 8, 1918.

28. Bruce Copeland, "Polo Grounds Meet Proves Athletics' Help to Soldiers and Sailors," *New York World*, May 27, 1918.

29. "Former Yankee on Mound for Fort Slocum," *New York Tribune*, May 27, 1918.

30. Copeland, "Polo Grounds Meet."

31. "U.S. Soldiers Play Baseball in Paris," *Philadelphia Public Ledger*, April 12, 1918.

32. "Baseball League Blossoms Out in Paris," *Stars and Stripes*, April 12, 1918.

33. "Touraine Circuit Is Real Big League," *Stars and Stripes*, July 19, 1918.

34. "St. Sulpice Has Crack Colored Baseball Nine," *Stars and Stripes*, April 25, 1919

35. "Bats and Gloves Being Made Here," *Stars and Stripes*, June 21, 1918.

36. "Baseball Propaganda," *Times* (London), August 30, 1918.

37. Raiguel, "The Fourth of July That Rang Round the World," 119.

38. "The Ball Game," *Times* (London), July 5, 1918.

39. "A Great Anglo-American Occasion: The Historic Baseball Match Attended by the King and Queen," *Illustrated London News*, July 13, 1918.

9. World Series

1. Grantland Rice, The Sportlight, *New York Sun*, April 20, 1919.

2. Frederick G. Lieb, "Baker's Approval Saves Big Series," *New York Sun*, August 24, 1918.

3. "Yankees Win Final Game to Stay in First Division," *New York Times*, September 3, 1918.

4. "Adios, Local Baseball!" *New York Sun*, September 4, 1918.

5. Denman Thompson, "Base Ball Season Receives Fine Send-off on Last Day," *Washington Star*, September 3, 1918.

6. John A. Dugan, "'Base Ball, Adieu!' Says Washington," *Washington Herald*, September 3, 1918.

7. "Toronto Takes Flag," *Washington Times*, September 1, 1918.

8. Editorial, *Toronto Daily Mail*, August 14, 1918; reprinted in "A Canadian Viewpoint," *Washington Star*, August 29, 1918.

9. "Baseball Superstar Casts His Lot with Devil Hounds," *Washington Herald*, August 19, 1918.

10. "Tough on the Browns," *Washington Star*, September 2, 1918.

11. W. J. Macbeth, "Players Save Baseball from Getting Black Eye by Placing Wishes of the Fans above Principle," *New York Tribune*, September 11, 1918.

12. "No Baseball in Cleveland," *Chicago Eagle*, September 7, 1918.

13. "Close Ebbets Field," *Washington Star*, August 8, 1918.

14. "Park Storage Plans Indicate Absence of Baseball in 1919," *El Paso Herald*, August 21, 1918.

15. "Farewell to Ebbets Field as Uncle Sam Takes It for Cold Storage Plant," *Chicago Eagle*, September 14, 1918.

16. James Crusinberry, "White Sox Backstop Quickly Finds 'Essential' Work," *Chicago Tribune*, September 15, 1918.

17. "Hendricks Going Across," *New York Times*, November 5, 1918.

18. "Boston Owner against Plans," *Rock Island Argus*, August 25, 1918.

19. "Arrangements for World Series Are Somewhat Changed," *Arizona Republican*, August 25, 1918.

20. W. J. Macbeth, "Chicago Fans Rally to Baseball Classic," *New York Tribune*, September 4, 1918.

21. "Register Sept. 12," *Rockingham Post-Dispatch*, September 5, 1918.

22. Hugh S. Fullerton, "Near Capacity Crowd Indicated for Series Opening," *New York World*, September 3, 1918.

23. "World's Baseball Series Opens This Afternoon," *Maysville Public Ledger*, September 4, 1918.

24. "Service Men 'Over There' Sure of 'Series' News," *New York Tribune*, September 3, 1918.

25. Macbeth, "Chicago Fans Rally."

26. W. J. Macbeth, "Baseball Stage Ready, with Poor Setting," *New York Tribune*, September 3, 1918.

27. I. E. Sanborn, "Red Sox Player Hurt; Rain Gives Him Time for Repair," *Chicago Tribune*, September 5, 1918.

28. James Crusinberry, "Clan of Scribes Hears the Call from Over There," *Chicago Tribune*, September 5, 1918.

29. Charles J. Doyle, "Young Pirate Star Killed in Service," *Pittsburgh Gazette Times*, September 5, 1918.

30. "First Gold Star," *Pittsburgh Gazette Times*, September 5, 1918.

31. "He Died for You," *Anniston Star*, September 7, 1918. Lt. Arthur Joquel, a flying instructor, former Minor League catcher, and St. Louis Browns prospect, was killed November 2 in another air crash, at Barron Field, Texas. "Another Gold Star in Baseball's Flag," *Sporting News*, November 14, 1918.

32. James Crusinberry, "All Primed to Yell but Precise Hurling Gives Fans No Chance," *Chicago Tribune*, September 6, 1918.

33. "Boston Takes First World Series Contest in Brilliant Fashion," *Fairmont West Virginian*, September 6, 1918.

34. James Crusinberry, "Cubs Even World's Title Series by Beating Red Sox, 3 to 1," *Chicago Tribune*, September 7, 1918.

35. "World's Series Receipts," *Chicago Tribune*, September 8, 1918.

36. "Players to Protest to Commission on Reduction of Purse," *Chicago Tribune*, September 9, 1918.

37. "Players in World Series Uneasy over Meagre Receipts," *New York Times*, September 9, 1918.

38. Edward F. Martin, "Players Seek More Cash," *Boston Globe*, September 9, 1918.

39. I. E. Sanborn, "Tripling Ruth Makes Good; Red Sox Win Frantic Game," *Chicago Tribune*, September 10, 1918.

40. Stout, *The Selling of the Babe*, 7. Accounts of the incident varied greatly. One front-page article described Ruth's injury this way: "An iodine-painted finger on his pitching wing, which was bruised during some sugarhouse fun with [Boston pitcher] W. W. Kinney, bothered him constantly, causing the ball to shine and sail." Edward F. Martin, "Sox Win on Wild Chuck to Merkle," *Boston Globe*, September 10.

41. Macbeth, "Players Save Baseball."

42. Macbeth, "Players Save Baseball."

43. Robert Maxwell, "Fifth Game Nearly Was Shortest World Series Engagement on Record," *Philadelphia Public Ledger*, September 11, 1918.

44. "Jangle over Money Retards Game Hour; Means Series' Knell," *Chicago Tribune*, September 11, 1918.

45. Macbeth, "Players Save Baseball."

46. Macbeth, "Players Save Baseball."

47. "Harry Hooper Saved Situation," *Boston Post*, September 11, 1918.

48. "Wrangling Players Do Their Bit for Wounded," *Washington Times*, September 11, 1918.

49. "'For the Good of Baseball,'" *Stars and Stripes*, September 20, 1918.

50. "Jangle over Money."

51. Macbeth, "Players Save Baseball."

52. Editorial, "A Second Guess on the Strike," *Sporting News*, September 19, 1918.

53. "Jangle over Money."

54. I. E. Sanborn, "Cubs Grab Victory under Shadow of Dollar Sign, 3 to 0," *Chicago Tribune*, September 11, 1918.

55. "Red Sox Beat Cubs 2 to 1 and Put World's Series of 1918 to Their Credit," *New York Times*, September 12, 1918.

56. "World's Series Notes," *Chicago Tribune*, September 12, 1918.

57. "Fans Glad Teams Will Go to Work," *Chicago Tribune*, September 12, 1918.

58. "Club Owners Agree to Try to Increase Purse for Players," *Chicago Tribune*, September 12, 1918.

59. "Red Sox Players Each Draw $1,108," *Chicago Tribune*, September 13, 1918.

60. "Cub Boss Sends Thanks to Sox," *Chicago Tribune*, September 15, 1918.

61. Sportsman, Live Tips and Topics, *Boston Globe*, September 13, 1918.

62. "Frazee Complains," *Washington Times*, September 20, 1918.

63. One article had cited the percentage of farmers within Organized Baseball as an argument for exempting ballplayers from the work-or-fight order. "Large numbers of them are farmers who devote half their time to that business and direct the managements of their farms while playing ball." "Parnham May Be Center of Baseball's Important Case in 'Work or Fight' Rule," *Toledo News-Bee*, July 5, 1917.

64. "'Cap.' Huston Says Suspension Will Be a Help to Baseball," *Brooklyn Eagle*, October 22, 1918.

10. Strain of Battle

1. Edgar Wolfe as "Jim Nasium," "Harlan Team Is Ship Yard Champ," *Philadelphia Inquirer*, August 29, 1918.

2. "Jackson's Homers Defeat Standards," *New York Sun*, September 15, 1918.

3. "Game for Service Title," *New York Times*, August 25, 1918.

4. "Army Nine Tamed by Jeff Pfeffer," *New York Times*, September 15, 1918.

5. "Fourth District Wins," *Richmond Times-Dispatch*, September 6, 1918.

6. Caught on the Fly, *Sporting News*, October 3, 1918.

7. George Y. Henger, "Great Lake Team Disbanded," *Sporting News*, October 17, 1918.

8. Pershing, *My Experiences in the World War*, 2:327.

9. Harry Chapman, formerly a catcher with the Cubs, Reds, Browns, and St. Louis Terriers, died of pneumonia following influenza October 21 at a sanitarium in Missouri. A farmer, Chapman had entered the hospital for an operation to relieve an old baseball injury, not a war wound as is sometimes stated. "War's End Clears Way for Settling Game's Problems," *Sporting News*, November 14, 1918.

10. "'Cap.' Huston Says Suspension Will Be a Help to Baseball," *Brooklyn Eagle*, October 22, 1918.

11. Lawrence Perry, From the Field of Sport, *New York Post*, July 15, 1918. Gowdy later recalled that Douglas MacArthur, then a colonel in the Rainbow Division, had ignored his advice to carry a mask in a frequently gassed forest.

12. "Lank Hank Gowdy Grins as of Yore," *Stars and Stripes*, August 23, 1918.

13. "Boston Red Sox Give Toast to Hank Gowdy," *Philadelphia Public Ledger*, April 15, 1918.

14. "Same Old Johnny Evers Home from France," *Albany Journal*, December 17, 1918. Gowdy had also chatted with Capt. T. L. Huston and Lt. Moose McCormick that spring when they drove over to visit him at regimental head-

quarters. Gowdy would later meet Col. Bozeman Bulger in Coblenz, Germany, after the armistice.

15. "Soldiers 'Sore' on Big Leagues," *Philadelphia Public Ledger*, August 14, 1918.

16. Dan Daniel, High Lights and Shadows in All Spheres of Sport, *New York Sun*, August 14, 1918.

17. "Soldiers 'Sore' on Big Leagues."

18. W. J. Macbeth, Dusting 'em Off, *New York Tribune*, November 7, 1918.

19. Hugh S. Fullerton, "Baseball Fighters Recite Experiences of Great Conflict," *Atlanta Constitution*, May 6, 1919.

20. Harold C. Burr, "It Wasn't Cricket, but McCormick's Work at Wicket Fitted Him for Career as Game's Greatest Pinch-Hitter," *Sporting News*, May 27, 1943.

21. J. B. Sheridan, "Big Players Have Saved Baseball from Slackerdom," *Ogden Standard*, November 10, 1918.

22. Pershing, *My Experiences in the World War*, 2:90.

23. "Hugh Miller, Baseball's Best Bet as War Hero, Writes," *Sporting News*, December 12, 1918.

24. *Congressional Medal of Honor, the Distinguished Service Cross, and the Distinguished Service Medal*, 375.

25. "Hail Hugh Miller, Hero with Marines," *Sporting News*, June 27, 1918.

26. "Hugh Miller, Baseball's Best Bet."

27. Yockelson, *Forty-Seven Days*, 136–37.

28. "Negro Soldiers Are Praised for Their Work at Front," *Grand Forks Herald*, February 8, 1919.

29. "Cadore, Dodger Hero, Returns from France," *Corning Leader*, February 27, 1919.

30. George B. Underwood, "Gowdy Will Be among First and Alexander among Last Big Leaguers to Return, Says Lt. Cadore," *New York Sun*, February 15, 1919.

31. Underwood, "Gowdy Will Be among First."

32. Henry P. Edwards, "Big Days When Ball Players Come Home," *Sporting News*, November 14, 1918.

33. "Brownie Burke Reaches Home after Long Service," *Billings Gazette*, July 27, 1919.

34. "M'Adoo's Nephew Severely Wounded," *New York Times*, September 27, 1918.

35. "Capt. Bull, Crescent Man, Near Death as Shell Rips Coat," *Brooklyn Eagle*, November 29, 1918.

36. "Same Old Johnny Evers."

37. Baseball By-Plays, *Sporting News*, December 26, 1918.

38. "No Bomb-Proof Jobs for Cobb and Matty," *Boston Globe*, September 9, 1918.

39. Louis Lee Arms, "Chemical Warfare Service Should Appeal to Fandom," *New York Tribune*, September 8, 1918.

40. Louis Lee Arms, Facts and Fancies, *New York Tribune*, October 10, 1918.

41. Louis A. Dougher, Looking 'em Over, *Washington Times*, October 18, 1918.

42. Sisler, "Why I Enlisted in the Army," 265.

43. "Matty in French Hospital," *Brooklyn Eagle*, October 22, 1918.

44. Cobb and Stump, *My Life in Baseball*, 189–90.

45. Pershing, *My Experiences in the World War*, 2:294.

46. Gilbert, *The First World War*, 470.

47. "Lieut. Col. Huston Back from France," *New York Times*, January 3, 1919.

48. Harry T. Brundage, "Gabby Street, a Fighter All of His Life, Spurns Title of Miracle Man, but Career Shows He Deserves It," *Sporting News*, October 2, 1930. Although a sergeant when discharged, Street was listed as a corporal in the regimental history.

49. "Gabby Street, War Hero, Visits Here," *Washington Star*, February 5, 1919.

50. Coyne, "Ultimate Sacrifice," 78.

51. Adler, *History of the Seventy-Seventh Division*, 8.

52. Adler, *History of the Seventy-Seventh Division*, 73.

53. Adler, *History of the Seventy-Seventh Division*, 75.

54. Damon Runyon, "Grant's Grave Few Yards from Where He Fell," *Syracuse Herald*, October 23, 1918, reprinted from *New York American*.

55. Woollcott, *The Command Is Forward*, 134–35; "Baseball Loses Big League Star in Greater Game," *Stars and Stripes*, October 25, 1918.

56. "Army Chaplain Writes of Eddie Grant's Last Charge; Buried in Cemetery Prepared by Germans," *Rochester Democrat and Chronicle*, January 4, 1919.

57. Coyne, "Ultimate Sacrifice," 80.

58. "Baseball's First Gold Star Eddie Grant's Bit for U.S.," *Utica Tribune*, October 27, 1918.

59. "Williams Pitcher Killed," *New York Times*, December 29, 1918.

60. "This Soldier Had Pneumonia," *Lockport Union-Sun and Journal*, November 29, 1918.

61. "Inseparable in Life Were 'Leo' and 'Matt,'" *Lockport Union-Sun and Journal*, December 11, 1918.

62. "Comrades Fell around Him," *Lockport Union-Sun and Journal*, November 29, 1918.

63. "Inseparable in Life."

64. "Corporal Leo Dolan Buried by Cataract City Man in France," *Lockport Union-Sun and Journal*, December 18, 1918.

65. "Professional Baseball's Roll of Honor," 36.

66. "Tom Quinlan Is Out of Hospital," *Warren Chronicle*, January 20, 1919.

67. Jack Veiock, "Jack Hendricks Is Back from France," *Utica Herald-Dispatch*, December 21, 1918.

68. "Tom Quinlan Is Out of Hospital."

69. Yockelson, *Forty-Seven Days*, 320.

11. Armistice

1. Maranville, *Run, Rabbit, Run*, 41.

2. Rice, *The Tumult and the Shouting*, 95.

3. "Matty May Not Return to Reds," *New York Times*, January 10, 1919.

4. Junius B. Wood, "Players Anxious to Get Back Home," *Washington Star*, March 2, 1919.

5. "Baseball Battery Last to Shoot," *Sporting News*, December 26, 1918.

6. "After firing every day at targets unknown to them, the gunners were allowed to pick targets of their own, and the last rounds of the regiment were in most cases fired by the Chiefs of Section." Chubb, *Regimental History*, 47.

7. Thomas S. Rice, "Mitchell Has Hopes of Early Reporting," *Brooklyn Eagle*, February 5, 1919.

8. "Send Greetings through Post," *Boston Post*, December 25, 1918.

9. "Send Greetings through Post."

10. "Giants and Pirates Sure of Baseball," *Washington Herald*, November 22, 1918.

11. "Baseball or Not, That Is the Issue," *Sporting News*, November 7, 1918.

12. Hugh S. Fullerton, "Reconstruction Period in Baseball Promises to Be Extremely Lively," *New York World*, November 20, 1918.

13. "Baseball Sure to Be Back in Spring," *New York Times*, December 5, 1918.

14. "National League to Discuss Plans for Resumption," *Schenectady Gazette*, December 6, 1918.

15. "Rickey Willing to Serve Country; Anxious to Return to St. Louis," *New Castle News*, December 14, 1918.

16. "Lieut. Col. Huston Back from France," *New York Times*, January 3, 1919.

17. "Nation Assured Good Baseball," *Lockport Union-Sun and Journal*, December 11, 1918.

18. "An Answer to Those Who Cry 'Slacker' at Players," *Sporting News*, November 7, 1918.

19. Robert Edgren, "Ballplayers in Shipyards Haven't Any 'Snap Jobs,'" *New York World*, November 16, 1918.

20. "Major Kolnitz Former Player Defends Jackson," *New Castle News*, February 6, 1919.

21. Bob Pigue, The Sporting Spotlight, *Memphis News Scimitar*, January 16, 1919.

22. "Times and Spirits Change," *Sporting News*, January 2, 1919.

23. J. L. Ray, "'I Am Lacking in Brains,' Says Pitcher Fred Toney," *Pittsburgh Press*, April 10, 1919.

24. Frederick G. Lieb, "Brooklyn Slides into League Lead," *New York Sun*, May 5, 1919.

25. Frederick G. Lieb, "Benny Kauff Signs Up with the Giants," *New York Sun*, January 4, 1919. Shawkey's second wife, Marie "Tiger Lady" Lakjer, had shot her wealthy first husband in the head and successfully claimed self-defense. The pitcher enlisted after she refused to support his application for deferment. The couple divorced in June 1918 while the pitcher was on active duty. Shawkey's

nickname after the war was "Sailor Bob." See Rice, "Bob Shawkey," SABR Bio-Project, sabr.org/bioproject.

26. Lieb, "Benny Kauff Signs Up."

27. "Christy Mathewson May Return to Scenes of Former Triumphs as Assistant to McGraw," *New York Times*, February 18, 1919.

28. "Matty to Be Next Leader of Giants," *New York Times*, March 8, 1919.

29. Rice, *The Tumult and the Shouting*, 96–97.

30. Rice, *The Tumult and the Shouting*, 97.

31. "Cleveland Player Badly Hurt When Truck Turns Over," *Stars and Stripes*, April 25, 1919.

32. Charles J. Doyle, "Joe Harris Is Spectator at Polo Grounds," *Pittsburgh Gazette Times*, May 27, 1919.

33. "Will Alex Be as Effective as in Past?" *Pittsburgh Press*, January 5, 1919.

34. "Minor League Outlook Bright, Says Farrell," *New York Sun*, April 27, 1919.

35. *Reach Guide 1920*, 261.

36. "Cadore and Pfeffer Win Two for Uncle Wilbert," *New York Tribune*, April 20, 1919.

37. Ed McGrath, "Braves Are Beaten by the Dodgers in Both Contests, Stallings' Tribe Miscues," *Boston Post*, April 20, 1919. Five other returned servicemen appeared in the doubleheader: Lew Malone and Ernie Kreuger of Brooklyn and Ray Powell, Dana Fillingim, and Joe Kelly of Boston.

38. James C. O'Leary, "Braves Beaten, 5–2, in the Opening Game," *Boston Globe*, April 19, 1919.

39. McGrath, "Braves Are Beaten."

40. "Cadore and Pfeffer Win Two."

41. "Lieut. Joe Jenkins and Sergt. Aleck Meet Up in the Loop," *Chicago Tribune*, April 23, 1919.

42. James Crusinberry, "One Hot Rally in Frigid Air Means Victory for Cubs, 5–1," *Chicago Tribune*, April 25, 1919.

43. Roy Grove, "Grover Cleveland Alexander's Ambition, Now That He's a Cit Again, Is to Win 30 Games," *Bismarck Tribune*, April 23, 1919.

44. Finkel, "Pete Alexander."

45. James Crusinberry, "Alexander Shows He's Great as Ever, but Reds Beat Him," *Chicago Tribune*, May 10, 1919.

46. Skipper, *Wicked Curve*, 77.

47. Finkel, "Pete Alexander."

48. W. J. Macbeth, "Star Catcher of the Braves Home Again," *New York Tribune*, April 26, 1919.

49. "Hank Gowdy's Day," *Boston Globe*, May 24, 1919.

50. "'Holy Cow,' Shouts 'Hammering Hank,'" *Washington Times*, May 25, 1919.

51. "Gowdy Back in Game; Helps Trim Reds, 4 to 1," *New York Tribune*, May 25, 1919.

52. Ed McGrath, "Braves Celebrate Gowdy Day by Victory before Bumper Crowd of Fans," *Boston Post*, May 25, 1919.

53. "Braves Celebrate Gowdy Day."

Epilogue

1. "National League Gave More Than Half Its Men to War," *New York Tribune*, December 2, 1918.

2. "Class 1 Draftees Sufficient to Match Kaiser's Increment," *Washington Herald*, May 22, 1918.

3. Hugh Fullerton, "Reconstruction Period in Baseball Promises to Be Extremely Lively," *New York World*, November 20, 1918.

4. Many African American ballplayers, including Jess Hubbard, have yet to be added to SABR's list of World War I veterans. The powerful Twenty-Fourth Infantry team, for example, gained the notice of New York newspapers while training for France at Camp Upton. Redding, a future Negro Leagues star, won twenty consecutive games for the New York Lincoln Stars in 1915. Others in the lineup had played for a dozen African American teams, including the Lincoln Giants, Chicago American Giants, and Brooklyn Royal Giants. "They are the best colored players in the business," an army officer said. "Buffaloes Organize Fast Baseball Nine," *Brooklyn Eagle*, May 23, 1918.

5. "National League Gave More." The Remington Arms Union Metallic Cartridge Company had contacted the Cincinnati Reds, and perhaps other clubs, to inform players that Remington was hiring in Bridgeport, Connecticut. The employment manager made no mention of a company baseball team. Letter, Hermann Papers, box 113, folder 3.

6. "Service of Uncle Sam," *Chattanooga News*, January 17, 1919.

7. "Prominent Players in France," *Spalding's Official Base Ball Guide 1919*, 229.

8. "Complete outfits for four teams were shipped from Washington today by the Clark Griffith ball and bat fund at the request of the Zionist organization of America. The outfits will be delivered to the Jewish legion for service in Palestine, composed of Jews from this country serving with the British army, who are below or above the draft age or are politically disqualified for service with the American Forces." *Spartanburg Herald*, August 14, 1918.

9. Steinberg and Spatz, *The Colonel and Hug*, 198.

10. Rice, *The Tumult and the Shouting*, 97.

11. Jack Cuddy, "Keep Playing Ball Is Advice of 'Sergeant,'" *Uniontown Standard*, August 26, 1943.

12. J. G. Taylor Spink, Looping the Loop, *Sporting News*, May 21, 1942.

BIBLIOGRAPHY

Addison, James Thayer. *The Story of the First Gas Regiment*. Boston: Houghton Mifflin, 1919.

Adler, J. O., ed. *History of the Seventy-Seventh Division, August 25th, 1917, November 11th, 1918*. New York: W. H. Crawford, 1919.

Alexander, Charles. *Rogers Hornsby: A Biography*. New York: Henry Holt, 1995.

Bacon, William. *History of the Fifty-Fifth Field Artillery Brigade, 1917, 1918, 1919*. Memphis: Benson Printing, 1920.

"Baseball News from the Military Camps." *Baseball Magazine*, March 1918.

Berger, Ralph. "Arlie Latham." SABR BioProject, sabr.org/bioproject.

———. "Moose McCormick." SABR BioProject, sabr.org/bioproject.

Carey, Charles. "Walter Johnson." SABR BioProject, sabr.org/bioproject.

Cheseldine, R. M. *Ohio in the Rainbow: Official Story of the 166th Infantry, 42nd Division in the World War*. Columbus: F. J. Heer Printing, 1924.

Chetwynd, Josh. *Baseball in Europe: A Country by Country History*. Jefferson NC: McFarland, 2008.

Chubb, Walston. *Regimental History, 342nd Field Artillery, 89th Division*. New York: Regimental Historian, 1921.

Cobb, Ty, with Al Stump. *My Life in Baseball: The True Record*. Garden City: Doubleday, 1961. Reprint, Lincoln: University of Nebraska Press, 1993.

Congressional Medal of Honor, the Distinguished Service Cross, and the Distinguished Service Medal. Washington: War Department, Office of the Adjutant-General, 1920.

Correspondence concerning Red Sox Players at the Boston Navy Yard, 12/1917–02/1918. RG 181, National Archives (www.archives.gov).

Costello, Rory. "Tom Burr." SABR BioProject, sabr.org/bioproject.

Coyne, Kevin. "Ultimate Sacrifice." *Smithsonian*, October 2004.

Davies, Alfred H., ed. *Twentieth Engineers, France, 1917–1918–1919*. Portland: Twentieth Engineers Publishing Association, [1920?].

Dickson, Paul, and Skip McAfee, eds. *The Dickson Baseball Dictionary*. New York: W. W. Norton, 2009.

Faber, Charles F. "Jack Quinn." SABR BioProject, sabr.org/bioproject.

Finkel, Jan. "Hippo Vaughn." SABR BioProject, sabr.org/bioproject.

———. "Pete Alexander." SABR BioProject, sabr.org/bioproject.

"Former Giants Goes to Bat against the Kaiser." *American Magazine*, January 1919.

Foster, John B., ed. *Spalding's Official Base Ball Guide*. New York: American Sports, 1918.

Gilbert, Martin. *The First World War: A Complete History*. New York: Henry Holt, 1994.

Ginsburg, Daniel. "John Tener." SABR BioProject, sabr.org/bioproject.

Goldfarb, Irv. "Charles Comiskey." SABR BioProject, sabr.org/bioproject.

Herrmann, August. August "Garry" Herrmann Papers, 1877–1938. BA MSS 12, National Baseball Library and Archives, Cooperstown NY.

Hornbaker, Tim. *Turning the Black Sox White: The Misunderstood Legacy of Charles A. Comiskey*. New York: Sports Publishing, 2014.

Huhn, Rick. *The Sizzler: George Sisler, Baseball's Forgotten Great*. Columbia: University of Missouri Press, 2004.

Kavanagh, Jack. *Ol' Pete: The Grover Cleveland Alexander Story*. South Bend IN: Diamond Communications, 1996.

Kofoed, J. C. "Why Athletics Are So Essential in an Army Training Camp." *Baseball Magazine*, July 1918.

Lamb, William F. *Black Sox in the Courtroom: The Grand Jury, Criminal Trial, and Civil Litigation*. Jefferson NC: McFarland, 2013.

Lammers, Craig. "Fred Thomas." SABR BioProject, sabr.org/bioproject.

Lane, F. C. "Baseball's Bit in the World War." *Baseball Magazine*, March 1918.

———. "A Rising Menace to the National Game." *Baseball Magazine*, August 1918.

Lanigan, Ernest J. *Baseball Cyclopedia*. New York: Baseball Magazine, 1922. Reprint, Jefferson NC: McFarland, 2005.

Leeke, Jim. "Art Rico." SABR BioProject, sabr.org/bioproject.

———. *Ballplayers in the Great War: Newspaper Accounts of Major Leaguers in World War I Military Service*. Jefferson NC: McFarland, 2013.

———. "The Delaware River Shipbuilding League, 1918." *National Pastime* 43 (2013).

———. "Ed Lafitte." SABR BioProject, sabr.org/bioproject.

———. "Ernie Shore." SABR BioProject, sabr.org/bioproject.

———. "Hugh Fuller." SABR BioProject, sabr.org/bioproject.

———. "Mike McNally." SABR BioProject, sabr.org/bioproject.

———. *Nine Innings for the King: The Day Wartime London Stopped for Baseball, July 4, 1918*. Jefferson NC: McFarland, 2015.

———. "Royal Match: The Army-Navy Service Game, July 4, 1918." *nine: A Journal of Baseball History & Culture* 20, no. 2 (Spring 2012): 15–26.

Lesch, R. J. "Jeff Tesreau." SABR BioProject, sabr.org/bioproject.

Lombard, Morris. "The Days at Plattsburg." *National Magazine*, July 1917, 589–95.

Macht, Norman. "Jack Barry." SABR BioProject, sabr.org/bioproject.

Maranville, Walter. *Run, Rabbit, Run: The Hilarious and Mostly True Tales of Rabbit Maranville*. Phoenix: SABR, 2012.

"Marine Corps Sports News." *Recruiters' Bulletin*, USMC, April 1919.

Marshall, Brian. "Fred Toney." SABR BioProject, sabr.org/bioproject.

McKenna, Brian. "Bethlehem Steel League." SABR BioProject, sabr.org/bioproject.

———. "Tillie Shafer." SABR BioProject, sabr.org/bioproject.

McMains, Carol, and Frank Ceresi. "Hank Gowdy." SABR BioProject, sabr.org/bioproject.

Murdock, Eugene C. *Ban Johnson: Czar of Baseball*. Westport: Greenwood, 1982.

———. *Baseball Players and Their Times: Oral Histories of the Game, 1920–1940*. Westport CT: Meckler, 1991.

Newspaper Cuttings: Scrapbook [1918–24]: Baseball in England. National Baseball Library and Archives, Cooperstown NY.

Ohl, John K. "Buckeyes in the Rainbow: The 166th Infantry Regiment in World War I." *Timeline*, October–December 2004.

"Our Standard Bearer: Capt. Edward L. Grant." *Grant Post News*, May 1940.

Pershing, John J. *My Experiences in the World War*. 2 vols. New York: Frederick A. Stokes, 1931.

"Professional Baseball's Roll of Honor: Players of the Major and the Leading Minor Circuits Who Entered Some Branch of Uncle Sam's Military Service." *Baseball Magazine*, May 1919.

Raiguel, George Earle. "The Fourth of July That Rang Round the World: The Greatest Baseball Game Ever Played." *Ladies' Home Journal*, July 1919.

Reports of the Department of Commerce, 1918. Washington: Government Printing Office, 1919.

Reppy, Alison. *Rainbow Memories: Character Sketches and History of the First Battalion 166th Infantry 42nd Division American Expeditionary Force*. New York: Carey Printing, 1919.

Rice, Grantland. *The Tumult and the Shouting: My Life in Sports*. New York: A. S. Barnes, 1954.

Rice, Stephen V. "Bob Shawkey." SABR BioProject, sabr.org/bioproject.

Richter, Francis C., ed. *The Reach Official American League Base Ball Guide*. Philadelphia: A. J. Reach, 1918, 1919.

Rubin, Richard. *The Last of the Doughboys: The Forgotten Generation and Their Forgotten World War*. Boston: Houghton Mifflin Harcourt, 2013.

Sammons, Jeffrey T., and John H. Morrow Jr. *Harlem's Rattlers and the Great War: The Undaunted 369th Regiment and the African American Quest for Equality*. Lawrence: University Press of Kansas, 2014.

Sandoval, Jim. "Dick Kinsella." SABR BioProject, sabr.org/bioproject.

Santry, Joe, and Cindy Thomson. "Ban Johnson." SABR BioProject, sabr.org/bioproject.

Simon, Tom. "Eddie Grant." SABR BioProject, sabr.org/bioproject.

Sisler, George. "Why I Enlisted in the Army." *Baseball Magazine*, March 1919.

Sixteenth Engineers Veterans Association and John T. Jans. *History of the Sixteenth Engineers (Railway), American Expeditionary Forces, 1917–1919*. Detroit: La Salle Press, 1939.

Skipper, John C. *Wicked Curve: The Life and Troubled Times of Grover Cleveland Alexander*. Jefferson NC: McFarland, 2006.

Smythe, Donald. *Pershing: General of the Armies*. Bloomington: Indiana University Press, 1986.

"The Star-Spangled Banner." Baseball-reference.com.

Steinberg, Steve, and Lyle Spatz. *The Colonel and Hug: The Partnership That Transformed the New York Yankees*. Lincoln: University of Nebraska Press, 2015.

Stevens, John D. "Hero of the AEF: Hank Gowdy." *Timeline*, March–April 1996.

Stout, Glenn. *The Selling of the Babe: The Deal That Changed Baseball and Created a Legend*. New York: Thomas Dunne Books, 2016.

Tan, Cecilia, and Bill Nowlin. *The 50 Greatest Red Sox Games*. Hoboken: John Wiley & Sons, 2006.

Tener, John K. "Hank Gowdy, the Man Who Blazed the Trail." *Baseball Magazine*, March 1918.

"Then and Now." *American Legion Monthly* 55, no. 2 (October 1927).

Thomas, Henry W. *Walter Johnson: Baseball's Big Train*. Lincoln: University of Nebraska Press, 1998.

Vaccaro, Frank. "Herb Pennock." SABR BioProject, sabr.org/bioproject.

Weatherby, Charlie. "Bill Killefer." SABR BioProject, sabr.org/bioproject.

Westcott, Rich. "Whitey Witt." SABR BioProject, sabr.org/bioproject.

Woollcott, Alexander. *The Command Is Forward: Tales of the A.E.F. Battlefields as They Appeared in* The Stars and Stripes. New York: Century Company, 1919.

"World War I Veterans." Baseball-reference.com.

Yockelson, Mitchell. *Forty-Seven Days: How Pershing's Warriors Came of Age to Defeat the German Army in World War I*. New York: NAL Caliber, 2016.

INDEX